Before
Pearl Harbor
Making the Pacific War

ISBN: 1-4392-1045-4
EAN-13: 9781439210451
Visit www.booksurge.com to order additional copies.

Before Pearl Harbor

Making the Pacific War

Robert Ditterich

CONTENTS

This book is dedicated to the memory of

Rev. E. Keith Ditterich, B.A., B.D., Dip. Ed., M.B.E.

a third generation Australian *Child of the British Empire*
who, if he were alive, might feel uncomfortable with
some of the conclusions drawn in this book but would be pleased
with the search represented by them.

Hold Fast That Which Is Good

CONTEXT

UNDER ME, ONE HUNDRED
CAPTAINS BEAT THEIR CHESTS... BROKEN
GROUND THEIR MEMORY [1]

Rabaul. January 23, 1942.

AS IT HAD done throughout China, Indochina, and the Pacific, the Imperial Japanese war machine made real the ideas elaborated by the militarists at home on the islands of Japan. The abstraction of a 'Greater Asia' was being smudged across the atlas where nineteenth-century European concepts of dominion had remained unchallenged for generations.

The awesome steel expression of this idea rumbled along the coast of New Britain in the form of an armada manned by battle-hardened men whose confidence was matched by the pride of its achievements. Their path had been prepared by waves of air strikes toppling the guns at Praed Point and killing the first of over 1,000 Australians who would die as a consequence of the

---

[1] R. Ditterich, 2006.

defense of this peripheral outpost of Australian Administration. More than 3,000 Japanese soldiers died in the subsequent battle to secure the beaches of this beautiful volcanic island adjacent to New Guinea, north of Australia.

What were they doing there? Why had the 1,400 Australian soldiers of the 2/22 Battalion faced an invasion force numbering over 15,000? Why were Australian allies from World War I invading Australian Mandated Territory? What had unleashed this brutality, at such human cost, over the vast area of the Pacific? Why had the world retreated once again into carnage?

This book began as a personal search for particular answers to these questions and those implied in the title, but with the search came the astonishing realization that these issues are hardly discussed in Australia, nor are they a significant part of the Australian public awareness.

It is probably fair to say that many Australians think of Europe when they think of the war, even though their own family experience may have been of war in Southeast Asia or northern Australia. Australians had traditionally seen themselves as shadows of the real world (an island off the coast of France), but as society changed in the years since the War, Australia's real position in relation to Asia has become more obvious and significant.

The garrison forces stationed in a precarious, sacrificial arc to the north of Australia, from Singapore, Ambon, and Timor to New Guinea and New Britain, consisted mostly of men who enlisted in the belief that they would be fighting alongside the British forces in the European War.

The bulk of Australian Infantry was already serving in the northern hemisphere. We can explain this sense of the 'real' war being in North Africa, the Middle East, and Europe in the predominant attitude of the time, that Australia was a British nation, separated only by geography.

The British Empire was a global phenomenon; in fact, it was widely regarded as a positive, creative one in Australia. Nevertheless, Australia's real war was a separate, very local one, which began in China during the 1930s and through which America gained enormous influence and power throughout the vast area of the Pacific Ocean.

With the passing of many of those who survived World War II, a new interest has been kindled amongst subsequent generations in the events of the war. There is a real need amongst descendents of these generations to re-examine the wartime challenges through new eyes, their parents and grandparents having passed away.

Some of us need to 'connect the dots' concerning the family experience simply because painful events and memories were never openly spoken about. Others of us sense that the very empathy we have for the experience makes a more objective understanding of the war very difficult, or even impossible.

We've grown up with the comfort of some home truths about the war. We've put the lid on our family tragedies and come to terms with them. The fact that family members may have been killed, wounded, or damaged makes us very sensitive to any analysis of the events that may challenge the conventional view of the war, but it is very important that we open ourselves to a deeper understanding of these things, particularly in the way that they relate to current issues. World events continue to throw at us the same old challenges to freedom, responsibility, and tolerance, and a new level of difficulty has also arisen in the government and self-determination of parts of the post-colonial world.

The pace and uncertainty of modern materialism make us receptive to stories that help define us or give our culture some sense of meaning. Stories of courage and sacrifice are worth telling, and some of those emerging now have been suppressed for decades by the silent suffering of grieving families.

Every year we see the solemn rekindling of respect for the actions of our soldiers from a growing number of young people who make pilgrimages to Gallipoli and Kokoda. Despite the passing of time, these places have grown in significance, becoming powerful symbols in the Australian national story. There is a poignant beauty in this, but there are also dangers in nurturing romantic and triumphal feelings about these places and events, especially if we allow them to feed into a tendency or need to see the wars in simple terms of good winning over evil.

War stories highlight the inspiration and heroism in the struggles of ordinary people facing extraordinary challenges. The facts, the actions, and battles tell us about the horrors as well as the capacities of people to become better, or worse, under awful pressure. However, these are not the only lessons to be learned from war.

The context and the causes of these struggles are often passed over superficially in the media, and there is a danger that our search for meaning and value can become self-congratulatory, blinding us to an uncomfortable possibility: Our people may have offered their lives for causes that were much more complex than they had been portrayed. They fought the good fight, but was it a 'good' war?

This is an incredibly challenging question. It is especially so for people whose remembrance of the war is still charged with emotion. It goes to the very heart of the meaning that we have attached to our family losses. It is only possible to address this question if a clear separation can be made in our minds between the causes of the war and the conduct of it.

One of the aims of this book is to compare the orthodox view of some of these events with various 'positional' views by historians. Inevitably, in one book this will be somewhat superficial, but it is very interesting to explore the difference between versions of events.

Most information is disseminated to advance the case for a particular point of view. That is arguing 'from a position,' and it will represent the worldview or bias of the writer or the people represented by the writer. An 'orthodox view' is often representative of those in control. For instance, the orthodox view of Apartheid in South Africa was that it was designed to allow for 'separate development.' Mandella's view would have emphasized oppression more than separateness.

Even in an extreme case, a differing view may be a difference of emphasis more than of fact. Marxist historians often adopted a position that examined events through a theory of economics, and these often portrayed events as inevitable economic stages in the evolution of history.

The passing of the 20th Century and the end of the Cold War has led to the discrediting of many of these analyses, but it is important to see that one doesn't need to be a Marxist to find insight or value in a Marxist historical point of view, if only because it provides another perspective or makes sense of a sequence of events.

Sometimes, after considering all the available information, we may need to adopt a position on an event, but this is quite different from beginning with a position and finding the facts that demonstrate the truth of it. Much of the information that we have been exposed to since the war with Japan has its roots in the rhetoric of the time. This information needs to be seen for what is was.

In the 1950s, the simple answer to the schoolboy question, "What caused the war with Japan?" was, "It was caused by the Japanese attack on Pearl Harbor." This is disturbingly simplistic, and it is worrying that many Australians and Americans have never been challenged to look beyond it.

The question becomes very murky when the issues are examined. The more we peel back the layers for a deeper understanding, the more gray the issues become, and the more it seems that the West was involved in setting the scene and providing some motivating forces for the conflict.

The research for this book began with an attempt to understand the reasons underlying the Japanese attack on America but ended exploring the factors that led the US and Japan to go to war with each other, involving others as well. You can see that the first question contains some assumptions. Those were relics of the author's childhood and education.

Post-war generations in Australia were led to believe that a peaceful, morally good West was invaded by a militarist, morally corrupt Japan, and many people will always want to see it that way. But it just wasn't that simple. This realization needn't be threatening. We don't have to excuse or put aside the horrors and atrocities of the Pacific War to admit that its causes were more complex than we were led to believe.

This process can be a very healing experience. Finding the truth about the forces at work in the creation of war allows us to build an empathy with individuals who were former enemies. They responded to the environment around them, the information available to them, and the call of their country just as our people did.

Only by personalizing the issues can we go beyond the blame and the rhetoric of wartime politics. Reading the names of individuals who grappled with the problems in Japanese society allows us to identify with them in our common struggle to live decent lives: To live them with viable governments, in the hope that they can protect us from the baser human instincts, but still allowing us the hope of achieving our potential.

The events of the 1930s clearly illustrate conditions under which nations, for all sorts of complicated reasons, sometimes cause other nations to behave badly.

We are dealing with more than a simple chronology of events. There are issues arising out of the Japanese emergence into the modern world, factors within America and within

China, issues concerning European colonization of Asia, the future of the British Empire, as well as issues of nationhood and the rights of self-determination for peoples. And the most difficult issue of all, race.

The book begins with a brief outline of the sequence of events and issues that affected Japan's emergence from almost total isolation, into the 'modern' 19th Century. While this commences well before the period of the war, the Japanese experience is so unique and so poorly understood in the West that it was felt that to omit this background would make the pre-war events more difficult to understand. This is particularly so because the difficulties faced by Japanese negotiators and diplomats trying to represent the foreign policy of their nation during the 1930s had their roots in the very structures upon which the modern Japanese state was based. There was also a cumulative effect in the Japanese relationship with the West, which provides the historical context for the 1941 negotiations.

Internal issues and themes that can add to our understanding of Japanese society as it developed are given particular attention. These take the form of essays within the narrative roughly in sequence, but because themes evolve over time, there is some overlap and out-of-sequence elaboration.

The final chapters examine the international situation, its issues, and the negotiations that ultimately converged into war.

Like many Australians, my family was deeply affected by the war, and current tensions across the world lead me to think that the issues of racism and colonialism, which I believe were inherent in the causes of World War II, are unraveling further. The West appears to have learned little, if the subsequent sixty years are any guide. As a moral or political force, Western governments will not be taken seriously in the Third World unless the implications of their colonial adventures are recognized, confronted, and addressed.

Western technological leadership became quite exploitative, and the maintenance of its dominance has inevitably created a great deal of resentment. It did not seem necessary to occupy the moral 'high ground' while the power balance was so disproportionately in the West's favor. Western leaders should be asking on behalf of their people, how would we like to be treated in a world in which the power may, and probably will, be arranged differently?

What were the legacies of the 'white man' in Asia? And since the Japanese were the first to challenge this between 1905 and 1945, what lessons can be learned from the Japanese experience before the war? Their experience has never been more relevant to the world than it is now.

This book attempts to answer the questions associated with the beginnings, roots, and meanings of the war with Japan, partly from an Australian perspective.

America has provided the majority of post-war film and media images and stories of the war, and the point of view seems unerringly Western. Even the best popular, blockbuster views are often as dehumanizing as the worst propaganda.

All violence is failure at some level. World violence is world failure. One of the chief factors in this failure is the popular ignorance that allows even quite 'liberal' governments to harness a fear of 'the other' in motivating people for the purposes of aggression and power or internal repression.

A paradox in my hesitant view of the world is that in it, two cornerstones of conflict are by nature almost opposite. *Certainty* and *ignorance* are two of the cornerstones, and in order to be possessed of the former, one needs to be under the influence of the latter. The other two cornerstones are *greed* and *control*. This book will illustrate that the industrial and economic agendas on both sides of the Pacific Ocean created the governments that were necessary for the pursuit of the imperialistic goals that caused the war.

We will see that the three major protagonists went to war for economic control of people, resources, and land that were external to their own territory. Japan was not alone in this.

In the battles for regional control, Australia was a small player of no great account to Britain, America, or Japan, but important in the sense that, in enemy hands, it could create significant difficulties of supply. Australia was therefore of some strategic value. It was also useful and potentially useful for the supply of food, soldiers, and a range of essential raw materials, but none of the major players needed to own or occupy Australia to control the use of these.

Many Australians have always assumed that the Japanese were invading them, but the attacks that occurred cannot be fully understood in such simple terms. There were certainly groups within Japan who had such plans, but Japanese intentions during the first four and a half decades of the Twentieth Century can never be represented simply, for reasons that become obvious in the text of this book.

Australia had a brief moment on the world stage at the 1919 Peace Conference, when its Prime Minister used the opportunity to give voice to Australia's insecurity concerning its hold on a territory adjacent to Asia, by almost single-handedly defeating a Japanese proposal for the racial equality of nations. This caused a massive loss of face for the moderates in Japan.

In this, Australia was a contributor to the escalations that followed. Of course, there were powerful elements of fanatical racism in Japan at the time, but Western arrogance only added strength to their cause in the hatred of what they saw as 'white Barbarians.'

The point is that hypocrisy does not make an effective weapon against irrationality, and Australia missed its small opportunity to be part of a meaningful change in world politics. The Australian Prime minister was not the only leader representing an insecure and fearful electorate, and it is difficult to know how judgmental to be in observing these events.

Australians need to feel that their dead were given for a worthwhile reason and that they had a value. In this, they are no different from those of the other combatant nations. Australia had no territorial or strategic goals beyond defensive and somewhat idealistic, supportive ones, and a more robust truth about these things should be helpful in healing those of us who still harbor darkness.

Many Australian men enlisted willingly to defend the British Empire, but while Britain was preoccupied with Germany and the balance of power in Europe, the old Empire was strategically indefensible against the Japanese. This allowed America's challenge to become its prize. Australia had no choice but to defend the old order. There was a desperate fear that a very angry enemy would consume Australia, but when the new order came, it was neither Japanese nor British.

Japan and Australia had enjoyed a mutually advantageous trading relationship right up to the declaration of war, and on various diplomatic and commercial levels, the two nations were in accord.

The Pacific War had its roots in a power struggle rehearsed since the 1920s by Japan and America, and was part of the inevitable emergence of the Asian peoples from their domination by Western Imperial powers. That emergence need not have occurred violently.

Amidst the pessimism and gloom of the dark days of 1942, Australia felt very alone and very vulnerable. America seemed to provide the only sources of additional equipment, know-how, manpower, and hope, as the euphoric Imperial Japanese war machine spun out cyclonically from the Asian mainland through the arc of colonial islands.

The United States delivered help in so many ways that Britain no longer could. Any old Digger will tell you that, without America, Australia would have 'been sunk.' That assertion rings true emotionally, but it is not as straightforward as it sounds.

The question arising from it is whether we would have had a Pacific war at all, if the American Administration had acted differently between 1931 and 1941.

If China was the anvil upon which the Japanese sword was forged, America in particular was the stone against which it was sharpened.

I make no claim to be a scholar of Japan and defer utterly to those who have studied these issues as a specialty. Presenting an eclectic mix of viewpoints is an attempt to fly the flag for pluralism.

1

JAPAN CONFRONTED

JAPAN CHOSE TO DO BATTLE with itself, to allow a safe engagement with the world. Between the self-imposed 'restoration' and the opportunistic pre-emptive attack on Pearl Harbor, Japan muscled onto the modern stage because the architects of change saw no sensible alternative. The frameworks they created allowed the first real challenge to the European exploitation of Asia, but the challenge became entangled in the European war, and this needn't have occurred.

This tragic eventuality had as much to do with Western needs of, and responses to, Japanese modernity and militancy as it did with Japanese impatience and diplomatic failure. To understand the Pacific War one needs to understand something of the Japanese struggle to modernize from within and also their difficulty in engaging with the colonizers of Asia.

The threat of American force in 19th-Century Japan represented a huge technological gulf that had developed between Japan and the West during Japan's time of self-imposed isolation. It wasn't an implied threat from a speech reported in the papers or even a diplomatic message.

It was the uninvited and unwelcome presence of black, steel-hulled steam frigates, armored harbingers that reduced a proud, reluctant Japan to the status of semi-colony. Commodore Perry was declined entry to the port, but he refused to leave. He wished to present a letter professing friendship, from the President of the United States of America, Millard Fillmore.

The Americans wanted the benefits of trade and they fancied having bases from which they could counter European monopolization of Asian trade routes. Their determination to have friendship was emphatic. Perry threatened the use of force if his request was denied. The Japanese government accepted Perry's proposal of friendship to avoid bombardment.

Twenty years later, the Japanese acted in a similar way towards Korea. They had learned to acquire friends by force, too. This reach across the water was a bold first step in the acquisition of a Western-style empire. Within ninety years, Japan would be defending an empire that stretched across the Pacific and down through Asia and included former British, Dutch, American, and Australian colonies and territories.

It is arguable that Japanese imperial expansion was a lesson learned, not an inherent inclination. As the Western powers baulked at her expansive actions, the Japanese had to learn another lesson, that global power was based upon colossal hypocrisy. This is not to excuse invasion or colonization but to suggest that the responsibility for Japanese aggression belongs not just with Japan alone. How that aggression was expressed is another issue and is the stuff of another kind of book. With regard to the methods of war and of governance used in expansion, we have no difficulty in condemning brutality wherever it is perpetuated. We do not need to endorse or support war crimes to appreciate the conditions under which the war evolved.

We will examine the reasons for Japanese expansion, and to judge them fairly, we need to apply the same standards to the

Japanese as are used to judge Western expansion. Modernity demands materials and markets. Japan did not expand into an empty Asia, any more than the European powers did.

Western imperialism provided the context in which Japanese modernization occurred, creating a range of responses within Japanese society. Contact with the West required a total re-examination of national self-image to imagine itself capable of being something other than a colony and still become 'modern.' As an intellectual process, this produced a range of philosophical responses, and some of these were adjusted and adopted by militarist elements. However, there was a fundamental difference between the imperialistic exploitation of China's weakness enjoyed by many powers, including Japan in the 19th Century, and the situation engineered by the Japanese military forces in Manchuria during 1931. The world had tried to move on, but there was a perception in Asia that it only did so when it suited Western interests.

There is a very defensive quality in the Japanese response to the context into which they 'emerged,' and in this they have something in common with Britain, which showed on numerous occasions that it was prepared to go to war to maintain an acceptable balance of power in Europe. This of course is no coincidence. Japan always recognized similarities in the two situations; both Britain and Japan were small islands stoically adjacent to large, sometimes-unstable continents. Most people in the West, though, have never really been asked to consider the possibility that a 'Johnny-come-lately' power could be subject to the same fears and insecurities that tested and molded Britain over centuries.

The growth of the West and the sudden technological imbalance in its favor is complex, and it is not intended to be dismissive of it here. Certainly, those colonized were not altogether without benefit. The British in particular brought a powerful, practical idealism parallel to their economic engorgement, although it often did so at the cost of local culture, language, and values.

If in a balanced rear view, we allow for expansionist tendencies of the time and the power vacuums existing in decaying and feudal countries, then that can apply to all expansion, not just that of the West.

The appearance of the American Commodore and his refusal to be ignored must have shaken the Japanese worldview that had been contentedly isolationist for more than two centuries. They must have felt suddenly very vulnerable as Western powers advanced into their locale, carving up and laying claim to bits of China and Southeast Asia.

The ancient regime in China had failed to survive the self-serving intrusions from the West. The once grand empire had become a series of frontiers for opportunists and warlords, as well as a hotbed of discontent and resentment. Modern economies wanted commerce and trade and raw materials, and to facilitate this, China was impregnated with legations and settlements from competing powers, and no Chinese government could control any of this. Most of Asia was unable to resist Western power and technology.

In Japan, though, the Westerners found something different. Perhaps the Japanese sense of identity was so cohesive, based as it was on an incredibly homogenous national story, that their response to the threat helped to define them. Or perhaps it was just that they had a history of paternalistic, disciplined government and consequent national unity within clear island boundaries. Whatever it was, this country was not to become a colonial possession of America or Europe.

A line of defense was needed. Japan saw Korea's independence from the West as fundamental to Japanese security. In a leap of nationalist logic, it therefore became important to modernize Korea. The Sea of Japan is very narrow between Japan and Korea.

Meiji period writings often used clichés about Western powers as 'ravenous wolves' and similar imagery that portray the outside world as a force that cannot be ignored. 'Modernity' and 'progress' were and are paradigms that assume superiority, and to interface with them from any other position is to accept inferiority.

To save face, the Japanese needed to be able to find a position that allowed them to see their progress as unique to them and yet part of a universal worldview in which they were not inferior. This will be discussed further in the context of Japanese moderate voices and philosophy.

In the 1850s, Japan was subject to the sort of very unequal treaties that were also imposed on other nations for the purposes of European economic growth. Treaty Ports, fixed tariffs, and 'most-favored nation' clauses applied to Persia, Turkey, Siam (Thailand), and China, among others. Japanese nationalists railed against these as insulting infringements of national sovereignty and the revision or abolition of these treaties, which took until 1911, was the most pressing and explosive issue in domestic politics.[2]

Late 19th-Century imperialism provided a threatening setting, and we have seen how Japanese expansion at that time had a defensive and reactive quality, which attempted to pre-empt European control of areas essential to Japanese strength and stability. China and Korea were seen as defenseless and inept, and they tempted Western aggression by acting as a sort of power vacuum, 'sucking' Western influence in.

The 'Social Darwinist' ideas prevalent at the time suggested that 'biological'—that is racial—differences determined the political capacities of various peoples. The conclusions from this assumption were many and varied, as this was never a definitive theory. However, one common conclusion relevant

---

[2] Myers, Ramon H, & Peattie Mark M. (ed), *The Japanese Colonial Empire, 1895–1945*, Princeton University Press. NJ, P 62

to the development of nations was that races should evolve separately, according to their inherent capacities to modernize. In addition, 'superior races' had a moral right or responsibility to guide the destiny of 'lesser' peoples.

Many scholars seem able to accept that, during the last years of the Meiji period, most articulate Japanese were prepared to accept the argument that Darwinian selection and competition in the international order made imperialist expansion the natural path for a healthy population that needed to have some control of its destiny and survival. Since 1868, Japan had been in a struggle to gain equity with the West, but many wanted more than equity in their own region. The need for expansion fit the pattern of world events, and the Japanese assumed that their efforts would be accepted and respected, once their strength was understood.

In 1881, a well-known Japanese essayist, Fukuzawa Yukishi, explained this need by likening Korea to a wooden house. This is paraphrased by historian Oka Yoshitake:

> "Suppose we have a stone house. If there are wooden buildings in the neighborhood, we must still worry about fires. In fire prevention, we have to think about the whole neighborhood, and not only our house. If there is an emergency, we give aid, of course. But it is a serious matter to enter a neighbor's house on an ordinary day and demand that he reconstruct it in stone, like ours. The neighbor will do as he pleases and may or may not build a new house. In an unusual case, we might have to force our way in and build this house ourselves, not for the sake of the neighbor but to stop the fire from spreading. The way in which Western countries are now expanding their influence in Asia is analogous to the spreading of fire. Neighboring Korea and China, which have no equal in foolishness, are

like wooden houses unable to survive a fire. So Japan must 'give them military protection' and 'be their cultural inspiration,' not for their sake but for ours. If necessary, 'we must threaten to use force if they don't make progress' and allow no opposition."[3]

This 'fable' is indicative of the thinking being consumed at the time, even if the process of the thinking seems indefensible to modern readers. This kind of interventionist view does have a familiar echo in recent world politics, despite the quaintness of the analogy.

The steady advance of Western influence and the occupation of Asia increasingly alarmed the ruling class of Japan. The powerful sense of independence, which came from centuries of isolation, was deeply and profoundly threatened. A role model for national defense was found in that situation enjoyed by the island states of Great Britain. Both are small Island nations situated off a large continental mass, yet Britain was strong and wealthy with many dependencies as a result of being able to navigate the seas to Asia.

Imperialism

The expansive drive that was such a prominent feature of all modernizing states at the end of the 19th Century applied equally to Japan. There were very few critical voices even in the West since the moral justification for expansion was the promise of bringing civilization and Christianity to 'backward' races.

It is difficult to find any examples in the English writings of the time that use the word 'imperialism' in a pejorative way. In fact, the mood in Britain near the turn of the century can be seen as triumphant with comparisons often made

---

[3] Mayo, Marlene J. (ed.) *The Emergence of Imperial Japan*, Lexington: Heath, 1970

to the greatness of Rome. This was generally expressed in conjunction with a belief in the responsibility to 'take up the task of civilization.'

In a similar way, support was given to the US decision to annex The Philippines in 1899—the export of scripture went parallel to the import of sugar.[4] It was not until the Boer War that the first voices of alarm were raised at the rampant power of imperialism.

Even in Australia as late as the 1950s, the British Empire was seen widely as representative of all that was fair, decent, and (by the standards of the day) inclusive, although those of Irish, European, or Aboriginal ancestry were often justified in having a different view. Imperialism was understood to be natural and inevitable, and in any case, good for everyone. A 21st-Century observer would find imperialistic attitudes incredibly patronizing and humiliating.

The founder of the modern Japanese Army, Yamagata Aritomo, has often been quoted from the memos he wrote to colleagues in the late 1880s. In summary, his vision was that Japanese problems were caused by Russia and England as they each advanced toward Japan. He defined Japanese sovereignty in terms of 'home islands' and a 'line of advantage' that included the Korean peninsula.[5]

So the seeds of modern Japanese expansion date well back in the 19th Century, and future alliances and conflicts were already being considered as a natural consequence of modernization as well as defense against the West. Ironically, in the sort of contradiction the Japanese seemed to be master of, this involved having the best fleet of any navy in the Far

---

[4] Myers, Ramon H, & Peattie Mark M. (ed), *The Japanese Colonial Empire, 1895–1945.* Princeton, NJ: Princeton University Press, 1984, P 64

[5] Jansen M. Japanese *Imperialism; Late Meiji Perspectives* in Myers, Ramon H. and Mark M. Peattie (ed), *The Japanese Colonial Empire, 1895–1945.* Princeton, NJ: Princeton University Press, 1984, P 67.

East, but these six modern battleships were engineered, built, and armed in British shipyards.

Acquisitions in the 19th Century proved Japan's growing industrial and economic capacity but also demonstrated the lack of equality with the West. The cession of Liaotung to Japan by China in 1895 was controversial in its revocation after warnings delivered by Germany, France, and Russia in the 'Triple Intervention.' This can be seen as evidence that, although Japan could wield considerable influence locally, it could still only do so by Western rules, and at their pleasure. The domestic effect of this was to justify new sacrifices for military expansion at the cost of domestic comfort and progress. Expansion became a popular goal despite its cost because of the desperate need for prestige and national pride. Sacrifice for national destiny became entrenched. Any voices opposed to this became progressively silenced, or at best, censored.

Religious groups were increasingly powerless as voices of restraint. Shinto had been appropriated by the state, as the expression of the cult of the divine ruler. Buddhism had suffered from Shinto prejudice early in the Meiji period and was not a vigorous force. Christianity had some early converts amongst those who saw it as a positive part of the fashion of modernism, but it too had suffered by the 1890s and was attacked as unpatriotic and pro-foreign.

The Optimism of Individuals

The interface of cultures was not all negative or defensive. The Japanese engagement with the West also involved a significant degree of fascination on both sides. The opening up of Japan created a fascination for Japanese culture in Europe and America involving the absorption of Japanese motifs and visual paradigms that radically transformed Western painting, poetry, and architecture. Similarly, Western ideas and fashions gained favor among many sections of the Japanese community.

We have set out to understand the causes of war between the Allies and Japan and, as we move forward, the story will by necessity serve to emphasize points of difference, disagreement, and contrast between peoples. It is therefore important to acknowledge at the outset that there were many points of commonality and many thousands of people on both sides, whose experiences and expectations of life were shared and mutually respected.

Many writers, intellectuals, diplomats, artists, and business people from both sides of the Pacific partook of an international cultural feast during the new decades of the twentieth century in confident disbelief that it could ever come to war.

While a survey of this cultural interchange is beyond the scope of this book, it is worth a very brief look at the work of one person who represented this optimism and goodwill, but whose efforts were undermined by circumstance.

Nitobe Inazo was a figure whose life and career followed with joy the opening up of Japan, just as his failure and death paralleled the rise of militarism in the Japanese Empire. Educated in Tokyo, the United States, and Germany, he played a significant role in Japan and Taiwan in modernizing agriculture and adapting Western methods to Japanese problems. While in America as a student he made many contacts including the young Woodrow Wilson. He later spent time writing in California, marrying an American woman.

He taught as professor of political science, first at Kyoto and then Tokyo universities, becoming professor of colonial policy at Tokyo in 1913. His lecture notes when collected and published amounted to almost 15,000 pages in twenty-four volumes. His educational involvements also incorporated a spread of other institutions until he was named Undersecretary of the League of Nations in Geneva in the period immediately after the war.

This was a phenomenal achievement, and it has never been surpassed as the highest international post held by a Japanese. His eloquence and generosity of spirit were enjoyed widely, and this gave him the confidence to found the International Committee for Intellectual Co-operation, which in the later United Nations was to evolve into UNESCO.

Nitobe did see a major role for Japan in the economic leadership of Asia, but he was clear about the way this should unfold. He wrote, "if we treat the peoples of these areas harshly; if we are unfair to the whites in commercial rivalry; if in competing with Chinese labor, we treat the Chinese badly; if in a word we neglect humanitarianism, then our great mission will have little success."

This is a more humanitarian viewpoint than many being expressed in the West at the time and represents the difficulty in forming an assessment of the Japanese as a people based solely on the actions of its army. Public opinion and intellectual thought will always form a continuum through a spectrum of positions representing fear and greed at one extreme, and idealism and inclusive compassion at the other. In pre-war Japan, pragmatic forces, motivated by fear, ignorance, propaganda, greed, and hubris, distorted and therefore subverted idealistic principles, but sometimes they did so simply because they were responding to hypocrisy.

Nitobe retired in 1927 but remained very busy in Japan. The activities of the Japanese Army in Manchuria during 1931 had a profound effect on him in two ways. First, he was appalled at the potential of the army to unravel decades of work in international politics. Second, the government of the day used him to advocate and justify the Japanese position on the creation of Manchukuo to the international community. He was sent on a punishing tour of lectures and meetings in the United States during 1932 and died the following year, having failed to achieve a most difficult task.

He had been unsuccessful as a bridge across the divide of Japanese modernization. The achievement of the first of Japan's international aims, the development of viable self-defense, unfolded to be incompatible with its diplomatic engagement with the international community.

Nitobe's emergence as an international thinker and spokesman was devalued by events within the League of Nations. The failure of the Japanese proposal for the racial equality of nations diminished the stature of Nitobe's position and the organization he represented in the very critical gaze of the nationalists in Japan.

During his tour in America in 1932, thinking he was talking 'off the record' he was quoted as saying that Japan faced two great threats, international communism and the Japanese Army, adding that, of the two, the army posed the greater threat. Within days of the publication of these comments, "army assassins murdered a number of Nitobe's close friends and colleagues in positions of high authority who had been known for their moderate views."[6]

When the League officially reprimanded Japan for its actions in Manchuria, Japan left the League. This amounted to the scuttling by the army of all Nitobe's efforts, leaving Japan unrepresented and dangerously exposed. A substantial part of Japan's educated population supported the ideals for which Nitobe had stood. Their loss of influence and representation would ultimately bring an enormous cost.

---

[6] Howes John F. *Japan's New Internationalism and the Legacy of Nitobe Inazo: Sixty Years later,* Occasional Paper #5, Lecture presented for the Annual Dorothy and David Lam Lecture Series, Oct 21 1993 P11.

2

A PLACE IN THE WORLD

JAPAN'S RELATIONSHIP WITH Britain in the early 20th
Century was not altogether a comfortable one, but it suited
the purposes of both countries. Japan basked in the glory
of being good enough to be an ally of the greatest naval power
on earth. British thinkers, on the other hand, had become
aware that they were soon to be overtaken as an industrial
power by Germany and the US and that Britain would lose the
dominance maintained since 1815.

With Japan as an ally, Russia could be controlled with a
reduced British presence, enabling them to concentrate more
ships in the Mediterranean. The Boer War in Africa had shown
that the British were over extended in sea power. Industrial
rivals were building newer navies, which could render much
of the fleet obsolete.

The Anglo-Japanese alliance was made official in October
1902. The events that followed are worth a brief examination,
because Japanese action against Russia contained many
elements of behavior that would be repeated later in the
century.

Russia had been involved with other European nations in putting down the Boxer Rebellion in China, and on that pretext, Russian troops had entered Manchuria, creating a buffer for the Trans Siberian Railway to Vladivostok, dangerously close to Japanese interests in Korea. After Russia refused to withdraw its troops, Japan attacked Russian forces in a hugely costly battle, and one undertaken without any declaration of war. It would repeat this precedent more than once.

With a smaller budget and fewer troops, Japan used surprise, speed, and decisive action to maintain its control of Korea. The Japanese foreign Office 'forgot' to inform her ally of the attack. Following this, the Russian Fleet was defeated by Japan at the naval battle of Tsushima.

Although American and Japanese interests in the Pacific began to intensify in parallel, relations between them were essentially friendly until the Japanese crushed the Russian fleet at the battle of Tsushima in 1905. At this point, Japan could no longer be regarded as benign or backward. Relations were tested further as a growing number of Japanese 'aliens' moved to Hawaii and California. The American response was "alarmist, racist, and vehement," reaching a climax in the discrimination episodes of 1906–07 in California[7], which surrounded ill feeling towards Japanese laborers on one side and racist and discriminatory behavior on the other, culminating in strikes and the widespread importation of Philippine labor in preference to Japanese.

The shock of these incidents was felt in Japan as national humiliation. Having gained respect and prestige through naval prowess, its confidence was shaken. In both nations, the press took up the issues, rousing popular sentiment. Also in both nations, popular novels were set to the imaginary scenario of an American-Japanese conflict in the Pacific. In America, it

[7] Peattie, Mark R. *Nanyo: The Rise and Fall of the Japanese in Micronesia, 1885–1945* Honolulu, HI: University of Hawaii Press, 1988, P35

was *The Valour of Ignorance,* written by Homer Lea that caught the public imagination, while, in Japan, it was *The Next Battle* (*Tsugi no issa*) by Mizano Hironori[8] that allowed the Japanese pride to be restored in fiction, at least.

A Stone Thrown into the Pond

Although both governments went to some length to calm the situation, both recognized that each was a potential threat and began strategic planning for a hypothetical war.

This is stunning. In the first decade of the new century, Japan and America began to practice and plan for the naval war with each other, which would actually occur thirty years later. Yet within a few years, Japan would be an ally of Britain and later the US, in World War I.

This was not yet a totalitarian or fascist Japan planning a war on America. The two countries were imagining a conflict over power, security, and control in the Pacific. That this should occur strengthens the argument that the causes of the Pacific War pre-existed Japanese totalitarian and militaristic government.

As people and as peoples, our imaginings are often self-fulfilling. Our future actions frequently fit our previous planning, and people often behave in accordance with their treatment. If you are treated as a potential enemy, you will tend to see yourself in that light.

Planning in staff colleges on both sides of the Pacific operated on two common assumptions. The first was that the Japanese would strike at the Philippines at the outset of a war. The second was that the US would have to move west across the Pacific to relieve the small garrison there. For the Americans, time and distance were the limiting factors. For Japan, superior American strength numerically was the point of concern.

---

[8] Ibid P36

Maneuvers were carried out by Japan with the US fleet as the hypothetical enemy in the waters off Kyushu in 1908.

A thorough study was undertaken of potential actions against a westward moving fleet in 1910 and it was concluded that "Japan's best hope of victory lay in a strategy of attrition, whereby the size of the American fleet would be reduced by continuing flanking attacks by light Japanese forces until, at some point, probably in the Western Pacific, an eventually superior Japanese fleet could challenge it in the final encounter."[9]

The Japanese military had a gift and a passion for gathering information. As it turned out in 1941, the opportunity offered at Hawaii made this scenario redundant, but probably only so because of this planning, and the Japanese grasp of its costs and flaws.

In German hands, the islands of Micronesia were not particularly important in strategic terms. It was their potential role as 'satellites' for both sides of a bi-polar dual that increased the importance of them as possessions. For America, Guam was initially useful as a conveniently situated coal supply station to supply coal-powered ships. It has only recently gained prominence again as it is built up as a major US outpost with China in its sights.

For Japan, these islands formed part of the long held romantic dream that was responsible for its development as a naval power. Since the Meiji period, interest in the Pacific, from the equator upwards, waxed and waned as the nation sought a convincing picture of itself in the wider world. There was trade and adventure to consider, as well as resources. There was also strategic advantage and national prestige.

In the national consciousness, thinking coalesced towards two essentially opposite options. Interests to the north and on the continent represented one, while the other was the

---

[9] Ibid P36

romantic appeal of resources, opportunity, and trade in the South Seas.

Public debate on this polarity of possibility included lectures, military and political commentary, and wide interest in the media. Success against Russia had brought national pride and security to the north. This line of potential expansion was called *hokushin*, or expansion north. South expansion was called *nanshin*.

Takekoshi Yosaburo, a Diet member and journalist, was emphatic that Japan's future interest lay in the equatorial regions because of economic, strategic, and security concerns. His goal was to have Japan's navy increased along with the merchant marine and the extension of trade routes.

This southward strategy came to be identified as a naval one, and this put it at odds with the army, which strongly favored *hokushin*, northward expansion. Each had a lot to gain from the debate, and each had its own hypothetical enemy in its scenario of growth. The army had its sights on Russia, and the navy focused on America.

From 1910, Japanese interests had developed in Malaya, the Philippines, and the Netherlands East Indies, but it operated at the pleasure of their respective colonial governments. The rumblings of the European War soon presented an unexpected opportunity.

Was it the possibility of advancing both strategies together that caused Japan to become allied to Britain in World War I, or was it an echo of the Anglo-Japanese alliance of 1902 in which Japan had been very helpful in isolating Russia? Certainly, the Japanese navy had been inspired by their British connection, and it had many Anglophile elements within it. The culture, the discipline, and even the equipment were based upon a British set of prototypes.

In either case, their challenge was to gain advantage in China on the continent and German possessions in the Pacific without going so far as to antagonize their British allies.

For its part, Britain had more than a few reservations about the dangers of a further active alliance with Japan, but the German East Asia Squadron under Admiral von Spee was a powerful adversary in the region, and Britain put aside her concerns about Japanese ambitions. The Japanese acted quickly to neutralize later changes of heart by the British and set about a very creative period in 'having its cake, and eating it too.' Japan needed to be careful.

The Importance of Micronesia

The humiliation of the 'Triple Intervention' was still fresh after twenty years. The Japanese treaty with China at the conclusion of the first Sino-Japanese War, involving the ceding of the Liaodong Peninsula to Japan, had been undermined by the combined intervention of Russia, Germany, and France in 1895. Britain failed to support Japan while Russia was quick to replace Japan on the Peninsula.

Even then, Japanese militarists learned that force was the effective language of diplomacy, an echo of the 19th Century implicit, if unspoken, notion that 'might is right.' Japan had been forced to give up what it had gained by force, and worse, saw its prize appropriated by a more powerful nation.

Several strong voices in the Navy Ministry and the Foreign Ministry felt that it was not worth risking the relationship with Britain to gain a South Seas foothold. Against these moderates were assembled a powerful arrangement of nationalist groups, individuals, and commercial interests who were aggressive in canvassing Japanese sovereignty in Micronesia.

Ultimately, the 'hawks' won the day, and it seems the most telling argument came from Naval General Staff who argued that bases in Micronesia represented an essential strategic advantage in any future conflict with the United States.

While the Japanese First South Seas Squadron campaigned against largely-undefended German-controlled islands, another squadron had been requested by the British to chaperone Australian and New Zealand troop contingents on their journey north to support the British Army. Many 'Diggers' saw both sides of the Japanese in their experiences of two World Wars.

The Japanese claimed a great many small islands, some with significant potential as bases, and they set about the task of ensuring that they would remain under Japanese control. At the same time, Australia was moving against German possessions in its turn, and to avoid a possible accidental clash between them, the British suggested that the equator should be the operational dividing line between British (Australian) and Japanese forces.

The outcome of Japanese flag-raising was, as predicted by the moderates, an angry rebuke by the British at what they considered "to be the rank opportunism and the furtive and devious manner by which Japan had acquired its spoils of war."[10] They were also unhappy with Japan's refusal to commit men, ships, or material to the war where this contribution would have been helpful. Between 1915 and 1917, the Japanese cynically declined to respond to requests for help, while Britain, France, and Germany, and all their allies and dominions, threw hundreds of thousands of men into the bottomless pit of entrenched warfare.

Japan continued to press for support in its claim for permanent control of the former German colonies, but it was not until early 1917 that the best opportunity arose. Britain requested anti-submarine support in the Mediterranean. This was given and was seen as potential leverage to Japan's claims.

[10] Ibid P44

Britain finally agreed to support Japan in this. When the US entered the war in 1917, it had not been officially informed of the agreement and the strategic implications of the changes of control. The American military viewed with some considerable alarm the extra reach that Japan had been given through the manipulation of these events.

After 1914, very little pressure seems to have been exerted for the Japanese Empire to expand physically. The gain of the islands formerly under German control was more of a windfall than it was a colonial project, albeit one that was fought hard for, in diplomatic terms. The island redistribution, which also included Australia's mandate over the former German colony of New Guinea, meant that Australian and Japanese interests were only 285 miles apart. Japan was mandated control over Mariana, Caroline, and Marshall Islands. The island of Truc and its sheltered lagoon later played a major role in the conquests of 1942. Guam remained in US hands.

The possession of the islands in general, and Truc in particular, was the result of a major shift in global events. It could not have happened without enormous determination and skill by the Japanese and major assistance from Britain. With this help, Japan had built a modern navy, trained it, and used it successfully in two wars, thereby establishing itself not only as a regional power but also as a naval power; and that was at a time when naval power was more important to national security and prestige than were the other branches of armed forces. Naval power took the flag, the language, and the national agenda wherever it went. It was mobile, formidable, and powerfully symbolic.

There does seem to have been a genuine interest in developing the existing colonies more effectively. "We do not need more colonies than we already have," declared Takekoshi Yosaburo in 1912; "anyone who attempts to acquire more would act contrary to sound imperial policy and for his own private venture. Japan's imperial policy today calls for the development of Korea and Manchuria, as well as Formosa, and Japan's colonial policy should not be otherwise than to fulfill her responsibility to those lands." [11]

This voice of restraint was soon overtaken by the events described above, but it is given here to represent the inclination of some in Japan simply to manage better what they had. Takekoshi talks of responsibility to, not rights from, those colonies.

The Beginning of the Inter-war Period

In 1917, the Russian Revolution threatened to bring significant change to the situation in Manchuria. Tsarist Russia had been a traditional enemy in one sense, but it was also an important supporter of the notion of 'spheres of influence' in China. The new regime in Russia would be opposed to imperialism and could become a political 'loose cannon' on the Amur frontier. The Bolsheviks seemed for a while to be more immediately threatening to Japanese trade and influence in the unstable region than any other power. China was engaged in its own particularly bloody civil war, and Korea was far from stable. Communism had an appeal that was able to cross borders and infiltrate workforces.

Following the war, Japanese manufacturing and industry were experiencing a slump that led to a wave of strikes, a significant movement towards unionism, and the organization of labor. These factors led to a re-examination of the Treaty Port system, which was operating to carve up foreign access to Chinese markets. The war had also acted to reduce the influence of France and Germany in the Treaty Port system. They, like Russia, had supported the alternative idea of 'spheres

---

[11] Takekoshi Yosaburo. *Japan's Colonial Policy, in Japan to America*, P98 cited in Myers, Ramon H., and Peattie Mark M. (ed), *The Japanese Colonial Empire, 1895–1945*. Princeton, NJ: Princeton University Press, 1984, P 91.

of influence' but their participation in China was weakened by the costs of the war to their economies. This left Britain and the United States as major competitors with Japan for influence in China.

As the interwar period played itself out, circumstances could have brought Japan and the United States closer in their common distrust and fear of Communism, but other factors were to have the opposite effect.

The United States emerged from the war a stronger country, both militarily and economically. The US also entered the post-war era with a determination to put its own stamp on the international scene. China and the Pacific formed a significant point of focus in this desire for influence and control, which would inevitably be achieved at the expense of Japanese interests.

Events in Siberia and Russia became very complex, involving disastrous multi-national attempts to support 'moderate' anti-Bolshevik forces. At one point, US, Japanese, and Czech forces were all operating against the Bolsheviks, but co-operation was fraught with difficulties and suspicions from all sides, and ultimately, the Japanese were accused of interfering by all concerned. At one point, Japan had seventy-thousand troops there, but reports were that the various Russian groups involved were as likely to fire on each other as on the Bolsheviks. The Japanese experience made more urgent their perceived need to strengthen anti-Soviet resistance within China, and particularly within Manchuria.

The American Secretary of State at the time was Robert Lansing, who was of the opinion that the task of nurturing the Chinese economy should fall to the United States. He feared that American technical and financial expertise would be unable to do this because of Japanese hegemony there. He therefore focused his policy towards preventing Japan from securing exclusive rights, except in Manchuria, where Japan was already dominant.

In 1917, Japan and the United States sought limits on each other's behavior with regard to China. The Americans wanted a clear statement that the Japanese intentions were not to develop a monopoly there, while the Japanese for their part wanted American recognition of the gains Japan had made in China. Through the representations of Ishii Kikujiro, Japan expressed the desire to co-operate with America in developing China's resources, but in doing so, Japan would insist on protecting its 'special interests' in that country.

> "Internal disturbances in, or a collapse of, China would have no direct consequences for other countries, but were of vital concern to Japan. [because] if Japan cannot see sound administration for the defense and general safety of China, she cannot feel secure in her own defense. This is why Japan deems it a natural obligation, without prejudice to China's independence, to counsel that country in administrative reform and assist by supplying instructors."[12]

At this point, we come to a divergence in perceived American interests, expressed on one hand by the Secretary of State and on the other by the President. The former was primarily concerned with the continued security and progress of American interests in China while the latter had his vision focused on a more global level.

In 1917, despite his vision of US dominance, the Secretary was prepared to accommodate Japan on the issue of Manchuria to secure wider agreement, but he was limited in this by Wilson's adherence to 'high moral principle' in regard to the policy of the Open Door. The result of his discussions with

---

[12] Kajima, *Diplomacy* III, 310–11 cited in Ibid P164. Beasley is a most worthwhile text on Japanese imperialism, going into these issues in some depth.

Ishii was therefore what has been described as a dangerously vague joint statement on the 7th of November. It affirmed, "territorial propinquity creates special interests between countries." And it acknowledged that Japan had such interests in China, "particularly in the part to which her possessions are contiguous."[13]

At Versailles, the carve-up of territories previously controlled by those defeated in the war created a great deal of tension. The Japanese made a claim for the German rights in Shantung. On this issue, Lansing was keen to further American interests by opposing Japan and supporting the Chinese, but Wilson felt that Japanese support was necessary in the creation of the League of Nations. A compromise was therefore agreed to, through which Japan would ultimately hand back Shantung but retain the economic privileges previously gained by Germany. To an extent, the compromise only served to strain Chinese relations with both Japan and America.

Economic investment in China obviously involved growth and development, there, but also profit for the investors. Secretary of State Lansing was very enthusiastic about ensuring the continued provision of American investment funds as an alternative to the Japanese. He therefore advocated America's re-joining the international banking consortium, his country having withdrawn from it in 1913.

This banking initiative had goals somewhat different from those of Japanese investors. Japan was primarily interested in rail and mining ventures and in securing raw materials for its growing manufacturing industry. Initially, Japan was also somewhat limited in its ability to raise capital for consortium-type investment and was therefore at a disadvantage in that

---

[13] Beasley W. G. *Japanese Imperialism, 1894–1945.* Oxford: Clarendon Press, 1987, P164.

regard. Japan's reliance on China for raw materials set it significantly apart from its Western competitors.

All of the foreign investors needed access, security, and control for their investments. The consortium of bankers secured these through interest payments directly from Chinese revenue. In other words, the Chinese tax structure became subject to foreign intervention and supervision. On the other hand, Japanese enterprise was generally more direct, using local and expatriate labor. The differing nature of this investment created a basic tension between Japanese and Western interests in the last years of the Treaty Port system.

Despite misgivings expressed by the American President, and within his stated limitations, talks took place in 1917 and 1918 for an agreement with French and British banks. In the belief that membership would make Japan susceptible to restraining pressure, it was invited to join the following year.

This attempt to control Japanese imperialism fell very short of American State Department expectations. American bankers sought stability and safety for their investments and were reluctant to support ventures on the unstable mainland of China that didn't involve partnership with Japan. They might not have approved of Japanese success, but the fact was, things got done and done securely when the Japanese were involved. This enabled Japan to force the exclusion of its interests in Manchuria and Inner Mongolia from the consortium's control.

If Japan felt significant pressure on its Chinese ventures from America, the situation was made considerably worse by the formal notification in 1921 that the renewal of Japan's long alliance with Britain would not be automatic. Britain had adopted this position but not without misgivings.

Canada and Australia stood against the alliance, and their position was supported by the United States Far East Department under Victor Wellesley. He preferred a tripartite arrangement including America, which would be capable of reigning in Japan's foreign policy. This view prevailed despite nagging British doubts, particularly with regard to the usefulness of the alliance in naval terms and a restraining force on German and Russian interference in the area.

The news that the alliance with Britain might be put aside, and that further negotiations would be absorbed into the package of issues to be discussed in the much larger forum of a Pacific Conference, caused public dismay in Japan and anger in the Japanese cabinet.

In his major work on Japanese Imperialism, W. G. Beasley wrote that the move "looked remarkably like an Anglo-American conspiracy to isolate Japan; or in the more emotive words of Lieutenant-General Tanaka Kunishige, one of the Japanese delegates, 'an attempt to oppress the non-Anglo-Saxon races, especially the colored races, by the two English-speaking countries, Britain and the United States.'" [14] Certainly, the change from membership of a dominant alliance of two, to junior partner in a proposed alliance of three, was felt as a very public humiliation.

The timing and presentation of these events created a very defensive mood in Japan in the preparation for the conference beginning in Washington in December 1921. What transpired should be understood in that light and will be expanded in Chapters 5 and 6.

By the end of World War I, Japan had a modest colonial empire and, had the government been content with that, our view of Japan's achievements might have been very different. Some of the events that unfolded in the conferences and treaties following the war saw Japan pressing its needs and rising to the world stage with a new confidence, but once more, despite some gains, it was left feeling humiliated and excluded from

---

[14] Beasley, W. G. *Japanese Imperialism, 1894–1945*. Oxford: Clarendon Press, 1987 P167.

the 'inner sanctum' of power. Japan was about to confront a new Western idealism, in which they spoke in expansive terms of idealistic principles but would not apply them in any way that would threaten the status quo.

As the new century unfolded and while Japan attempted to interact positively with the international community, the tension in Japan intensified between security needs, the management of rapid change at home, and the expectations of its trading and treaty partners abroad. The Japanese response to the international crises leading up to and including the Depression was determined by the interplay of these things. The following chapters attempt to explore Japan's inner workings.

3

MANAGING CHANGE: STRUCTURAL AND SYSTEMIC

MANY OF THE factors that made Japan vulnerable to domination by militarism were inherent in the conception of the political system that was established in the Meiji period. In fact, these were the very things that were adopted to ensure security and safety in an unstable situation. The superimposition of a modern state onto a pre-industrial and agrarian society posed many challenges in the creation of a constitution but also in educating and training the population to adapt to change. It was recognized very early in the process that in a turbulent world and a particularly turbulent region, a compliant and organized society was essential.

In the minds of the architects of the Meiji restoration, the social project demanded the sort of mobilization that would be required for war. Planners could not rely upon a large and comfortable middle class to provide stable social ballast. The kinds of change necessary would entail a radical reorganization of social systems and re-structuring the economy. The motivations for this came as much from a fear of internal unrest, even revolution, as it did from fear of foreign domination.

Japan's internal context provides the focus for this chapter. This includes structural factors such as those in the design of the constitution that created tensions within the chain of command. It also includes systemic measures adopted in an effort to absorb modernity while also producing a disciplined population, such as the conscription of vast numbers of men into military service. This program alone had a huge on-going impact on the responsiveness of the population and the power of the armed forces. We will see that the success of conscription and its allied systems compounded and magnified the fundamental flaws inherent in the constitution.

When the Meiji regime toppled the Bakufu—the Tokugawa family's personal regime that had governed in Japan for two-hundred and fifty years—it set in place what has come to be thought of as a revolution 'from above,' which had the aim of restoring the more ancient relationship between the Emperor and his subjects.

This was done in the firm belief that it was the 'true' relationship that revealed the authentic Japanese story and culture. The Kyoto Imperial Court claimed to be the legitimate government of Japan. This is possibly a unique phenomenon in that modernity was met, not by perceiving the Japanese experience in terms of the imposed values of the world, but by re-imagining those values according to an even more ancient political structure than any that were current.

One of the most important thinkers of the Meiji period, Inoue Kowashi had the ear of many of the most powerful men at the time. His influence extended from education to social organization, and his personal experiences in Europe enabled him to publish vast amounts of his observations and translations.

Two of the most formative were his translations of French texts in 1875, which contained the articles of the Prussian and Belgian constitutions, to which he added personal observations. Inoue had compared the Imperial Prussian model to the French democratic constitution and concluded that the Prussian one was superior, since it achieved a harmony between the interests of the monarch and its citizens and was better able to maintain order.[15] His observations were considered as a first in a series of stages in the creation of an appropriate constitution for Japan.

In January 1868, the court issued an Imperial edict declaring a restoration of state administrative power to the emperor. He was to be the focus of sovereignty, but significant differences existed as to the systems that should be placed in support of him.

The allocation of real power was the element most in dispute. Public participation was considered, but the regime soon settled on government by oligarchy. Two major movements opposed this. One of these stood for direct rule by the emperor (*tenno shinsei undo*). The other advanced the cause of freedom and civil rights (*jiyu minken undo*).

Further, the final construction of the constitution contained some very subtle allusions to Japanese tradition, on one hand, and Western concepts of the distribution of powers, on the other. Although these two elements are only slightly different, they represent a fundamental contradiction that created future tensions.

The constitution created two possible conceptions of the emperor. This dichotomy was one of the factors that enabled the demise of the party system in the late 1930s. How this could be possible is a compelling, if convoluted, story. In trying to express the complexity of this, the author acknowledges in

---

[15] Khan, Yoshimitsu. *Inoue Kowashi and the Dual Images of the Emperor of Japan,* Pacific Affairs vol 71, issue 2, University of British Columbia. Gale Group,1998 P217.

particular the work of Yoshimitsu Khan, who was at the time of writing, an assistant Professor of Japanese and East Asian Studies at Union College, Schenectady, New York.

Writing about Inoue Kowashi and his centrality in the design of the constitution, Yoshimitsu provides an insight into the synthesis of ancient Japanese thinking with modern Western constitutional practice. There are two main articles of the Imperial Constitution that relate to the role of the Emperor:

Article I. The Empire of Japan shall be reigned over and governed by a line of Emperors unbroken for ages eternal.

Article IV. The Emperor is the head of the Empire, combining in himself the rights of sovereignty, and [he] exercises them, according to the provisions of the present constitution.[16]

These combine to address several issues that concerned Inoue, who provided examples from foreign constitutions as references to his drafts. Yoshimitsu explains:

> "Article I, Inoue felt, was too important to compare with foreign references and did not enumerate any at all. His view was that there were absolutely no examples in foreign constitutions comparable to Article I, which stipulates the uniqueness of Japan's *kokutai* (national polity). Inoue was very uncomfortable defining the Emperor simply in legal terms, since a constitutional ideology, by its nature, was derived from modern (i.e., Western) concepts, not based in Japanese history, language, culture or sentiments."[17]

Article I is related to the will of the Imperial ancestors, and its position in the constitution establishes the 'moral' strength

---

[16] English translation adapted from Ito Hirobumi. *Commentaries on the Constitution of Japan* Baron Ito Miyoji trans. Tokyo Daigaku, 1906. Cited in ibid P219.

[17] Ibid P219

of the Japanese tradition. It is therefore a value statement, whereas Article IV is value neutral, but in it the Emperor is placed within the frameworks of both the constitution and the political system, and it is therefore a different conception of *kokutai*.

This is the essence of the troublesome interplay of ideas of governance. To Western eyes it may seem very subtle, but it may be seen for example as representing both sides of a coin. Constitutional scholars often tended to treat the kokutai as a legal and political concept, but this was not Inoue's intention, according to Yoshimitsu,

> "...one interpretation of the Imperial system is to view the emperor as an absolute monarch possessing unlimited authority and power. Another is that the emperor is a constitutional monarch who has limited authority and power under the constitution. The dual roles were intended to tell the people that the emperor could mobilize their energy for any national cause, yet Western-influenced Imperial subjects could perceive, if they wished, constitutional limits on that authority."[18]

The need to create a constitution for a new, modern state could be assumed to bring with it the twin advantages of being able to model it on suitable examples and doing so without baggage from centuries of historical dilemmas. Yet the constitutional structure, or rather the failure to reconcile two opposing elements of it in modern Japan, was clearly at the heart of the governance issues that almost guaranteed Japan's failure to create a peaceful state.

---

[18] Ibid P220

Training and Governing the Military

"It is said that in times of civil disorder, arms are placed to the right and letters to the left; in peace, letters are put to the right and arms to the left." (Proverb)

The conduct of the Franco-Prussian War (1870–71) influenced the interrelationship of the various agencies of power in Japan. The French were defeated in the war by a more militaristic Prussian State. In modernizing, the Meiji leaders were emphatic in their desire to 'back a winner' in adopting a model suited to their needs.

Their frame of reference for this was that, if national interests were served, it would also serve the needs of the people. The starting position is the national interest. Had they adopted the French model, it would have necessitated quite a different paradigm, in which the needs of the people would be the primary concern, with a consequential benefit to the national interest.

In the Meiji constitution, the emperor is granted "sole right of supreme command" of the armed services. "He would be greatly assisted by the chief of the general staff of the army and the chief of the naval staff. The Cabinet was not to serve the emperor by giving him advice in matters concerning such affairs of state."[19] This was understood to be consistent with practice since the first Emperor, who personally led his troops to battle.

It also suited various factions of the time who were concerned that the Meiji restructuring might be undone by 'subversive elements' in particular, and in maintaining public order in general.

Japan's visible success over China and Russia on either side of the turn-of-the-century enormously enhanced the reputation of the military. On a practical level, for example,

---

[19] Ibid P220

the cabinet of 1898-1900 was made up of ten members, and half of those were army or navy officers. They were able to use their position to force through the Diet a large and expensive program of expenditure on armaments. In terms of long-term influence on the culture of the country, however, the most profound effect was from the development of their system of conscription and on-going military association.

Conscription

Even though conscription was an idea imported from the West, it became one of the most powerful forces in shaping the country. With one simple decision, unparalleled control to mold the lives and attitudes of the people was given to the state.

In the early stages of the Meiji era, Masujiro Omura campaigned for the abandonment of the feudal army and the adoption of compulsory military service based on the French model. In 1872, the government stripped the Samurai class of its exclusive military profession, and in their place a national standing army was designed, based upon conscription in several forms. We will see that for the designers of modern Japan, military service was not just for the purpose of being prepared for war. It was in itself a tool for the readjustment of the national ethos.

Every male citizen from all ranks and classes was to serve Japan as a conscript. This comprised three years of active service, followed by two years in the first reserve and another two years in the second reserve.

A minimum of seven years of each young man's life was to be spent in some form of military discipline and training, and by the 1930s, this was also preceded by military training for the nation's youth. Initially, there were fears that the sons of peasants and laborers would make poor soldiers, but this was soon shown to be far from the truth. Poverty and lack of education created soldiers receptive to simple messages of national purpose and self-sacrifice. They could be made brutal by being trained brutally.

Using the earliest elements of the new standing army, the Satsuma rebellion of 1877 was suppressed, and a strong tradition of modern military method was established, perhaps in that confrontation.

The new army had a profound impact on society. The conscription system preserved military traditions by drawing upon the Samurai ethos in a modern format, and in doing so, it provided a level of internal security that allowed the orderly development of the political and economic experiments of Meiji modernization.

This stability attracted foreign capital, speeding industrial progress. Strength at home allowed the new forces to become expeditionary in the pursuit of imperialistic aims in Korea and in China. Most importantly, though, compulsory service became part of the complete educational process that the state adopted to create a disciplined population. Lessons of national greatness, patriotism, obedience, self-sacrifice, and loyalty to the Emperor began in school and continued through adolescence and into young adulthood.

Even the service of men in the reserves provided an on-going influence on them by their former commanders, and all of these things were preventative factors in the spread of subversive ideas. When recruits had finally done their time, they returned to society as frugal, disciplined, and obedient citizens, and part of a life-long network of military contacts.

Modernization and Rural Poverty as Factors in Conservatism

The large agrarian population had perhaps the least to gain from modernization. Without wishing to romanticize the lifestyle, there was stability in the social structure and comfort in local self-sufficiency, which compensated to some extent for the truly arduous labor attached to small-scale farming.

The industrial revolution threatened to undermine the structure and dominance of the rural agrarian sector. More than ninety percent of agrarian families possessed holdings of less than seven acres and, of that astounding statistic, fifty per cent were holdings of less than 1.2 acres.[20]

In 1928, 5.5 million farm families were either tenants or only part owners of their farms. Although the rural landowners had considerable political clout, tenants farmed nearly half of all cultivated land. This group was most challenged psychologically by modernity.

The first concerns were felt, as the traditional local economies became increasingly dependant on capitalist world markets. By the Taisho era, subsidiary income from handcraft industries had been reduced by the need to change production to fit in with national production values and urban fiscal controls.

During the 1920s, the agrarian economy struggled to cover production costs, as the price of products collapsed. Debt, poverty, and loss of hope led to rural unrest, while urban interests were challenging the landowners for political supremacy, as power became more centralized at the expense of rural elites.

Exploring the personal and cultural issues of the rural populations, Robert Scalapino wrote:

> "Having given up a goodly measure of his economic security, the farmer still struggled to avoid losing that traditional way of life and set of values which had provided him with psychological security. He did not want to give up reverence for his ancestors who had

---

[20] Peattie M. *Japanese Attitudes Towards Colonialism*, P125 in Myers, Ramon H. & Peattie M. (ed) 1984. *The Japanese Colonial Empire, 1895–1945*, Princeton, NJ: Princeton University Press.

worked the soil before him, the superstitions which
had simplified life's mysteries, or the native faith in
superiors and the acceptance at face value of their moral
maxims."[21]

The most obvious expression of these tensions was in
tenant disputes with landowners, and both groups were being
squeezed by outside pressures. By the 1920s, many tenant
unions were raising the issue of land redistribution, and this
can be seen as the basis for the tentative beginnings of left-
wing ideas in the Japanese countryside.

This was a movement that would never evolve beyond a
very basic level. The people remained inherently conservative
under their class-caste heritage. The power of paternalism was
such that peasant organizations could never rally sufficiently
against their masters when, by such a large measure, the enemy
was seen to be in foreign ideas, democracy, and modernity.

In addition, universal suffrage enabled rural landowners
to accommodate the needs of the tenants sufficiently to prevent
too many explosions of frustration. The anti-foreign and anti-
urban tendencies made it much easier to channel feelings of
dissatisfaction in the direction of ultra-nationalism instead of
socialism.

The urban working class was in part more inclined to
sympathize with the process of modernization, and perhaps
also, leftist polemics. Displaced from traditional localities,
culture, and social structures, urban workers thus transplanted
were more open to new affiliations. Working against this,
however, was the labor surplus caused by the large drift of
workers from rural to urban centers in search of employment.
This involved two factors. First, the new workers brought with

---

[21] Scalapino R. *Democracy and the Party Movement in Pre-war Japan: The
Failure of the First Attempt*, Berkeley: University of California Press, 1953,
P309.

them traditional values, and second, the labor surplus devalued the workers and reduced their bargaining power.

Beyond these factors, however, a unique Japanese form of paternalism created a labor-management relationship consistent with workers' apparent needs, and strong enough to marginalize, at least partially, the union movement. Scalapino maintained that "employers conditioned by the paternalistic nature of business-government relations, as well as by the dominant values of their heritage, assumed the parental role to an extent sufficient to give the classical virtues of harmony, loyalty, and obedience some appeal, in spite of generally bad labor conditions."[22]

The system had costs in terms of efficiency, but also compensations in stability, only possible because management showed a capacity to nurture their workers and make some effort to earn their loyalty. The result was that, by 1929, the union movement could only claim six percent of the total workforce despite pressures that, in other countries, had led to a significantly unionized workforce.

In most countries, the left was constituted from the labor movement and intellectual socialism. The former sprang from the needs of ordinary people in combining to bargain collectively, while the latter was born of idealism. We know that deeply nationalistic and militaristic governments are often anti-intellectual if only because it is difficult to support racism or national aggression within an intellectual framework. They are by their nature pragmatic and self-serving.

In some situations, though, the labor movement, being grounded in local and down-to-earth issues, is inclined to adopt nationalist ideals. This happened for instance in Australia when the union movement feared the effects of imported cheap labor and took a national position on racial issues, where the

---

[22] Ibid P314

Australian socialists had always taken an international one, rejecting the White Australia Policy.

As a young socialist, then trade union leader, then Labor Party candidate and, ultimately, Prime Minister of Australia, John Curtin straddled both positions over time, somewhat uncomfortably.

What of the intellectual left in Japan? We have seen elements that could have become a labor movement channeled instead into ultra nationalism, and we will see that the potential leaders of that movement could never overcome the anti-intellectual forces at work in Japan.

The Japanese experience of modernism deviated from Western models in the concept and role of the individual, as placed in society. This also applied to the evolving Japanese left, which had to develop in the absence of a background of individualism. Outwardly, such a situation may seem to lend itself well to concepts such as collective bargaining, but in practice the result was an ambiguity and fusion between radical left and radical right. An early example of this was a party called *Toyo Jiyuto* or Oriental Liberal Party, which began with socialist inclinations expressed in support for the poor, combining this with extreme nationalism, predictive in its nature of the later national socialist movement. This example illustrates the way in which Japanese social movements could be subsumed by anti-democratic tendencies by appealing to national values and Confucianism.

One of the legacies of the widespread military influence was a prevalence of violence on both extremes of the radical movements. Anarchists plotted the assassination of the Meiji Emperor, while at the other political extreme militarists and ultranationalists carried out many assassinations, some of which have been referred to within this book. The prevalence of violence on both sides may be another expression of the traditional view in which the value of the group overrides that of the individual.

Systemic Conservatism in the Control of Education

The 'left' in Japan played a larger role in the evolution of militarism and totalitarianism than those within it must ever have realized. It performed the essential function of providing a definition of the parameters of plurality, giving force and form to the 'right.' The extreme left never became a real force in Japanese politics, but it provided a target for extremism and an excuse for a formidable series of restrictive and censorial laws.

The more moderate left provided meaning in political competition, potentially giving the lower economic classes a political voice, but ultimately it did so, not from the votes of the poor, but from the intellectual classes who spoke on their behalf.

The huge, rural laboring class and the urban poor should have provided the popular base for the growth of the left in representational government, but these groups remained disengaged. In part this was due to political immaturity, in part to the culture of deference, and in part to the influence of military associations and conscription.

Political immaturity in this context refers to low levels of individualism, personal responsibility, and self-confidence. This is obviously a Western perspective, and it is given within the qualification that we are analyzing an attempt to Westernize the Japanese political system by means of Western concepts of individual suffrage. The working people existed on a daily basis within a very traditional system of obedience and loyalty to landlords and local elites.

The role of the Japanese education system is interesting in its contribution to the evolving participatory government. By 1896, the House of Peers had decided that moral education should be controlled by the state and, just after the turn of the century, primary textbooks were mostly prepared by the

Education Department. These books emphasized traditional ethics, Shintoism, and Japanese history written "in an extremely mythical and chauvinistic manner."[23] A professor from Waseda University wrote in 1908, "The present system of education makes for the perpetuation of an Oriental type of despotic government, it is no preparation at all for the adoption of constitutionalism of a Western type."[24]

This voice demonstrates that liberal values had gained a hold in intellectual circles as much as it explains why they didn't affect the masses of working people.

In 1921, Tanaka Sannai, a member of the House of Peers, demanded a longer period of compulsory education that should include citizenship training, and he said to Premier Hara:

> "The Meiji education has been too anti-political. In framing an educational policy adapted for present day Japanese, it is not enough to aim at the cultivation of the spirit of obedience, but it must at the same time try to instill the spirit of independence…The evils attending elections of various kinds arise from the fact that the Normal School {secondary} education in this country has completely neglected imparting political knowledge to students. Lack of political knowledge among the nation may be productive of evil results in the event of universal suffrage being introduced."[25]

To this, Hara was not very receptive, claiming that foreign ideas weren't always suitable. Tanaka's observations are unbelievably prescient and acute, and yet even now there are those who believe democracy can simply be planted into a culture without thorough preparation of the ground.

---

[23] Scalapino, Ibid P297

[24] Ibid P297

[25] Tanaka Sennai 1921 cited in Ibid P298

At about the same time that universal male suffrage was introduced, various 'Peace Preservation Laws' were enacted, as if giving freedoms with one hand and withdrawing them with the other. The 'peace laws' were primarily aimed at curtailing communist and anarchist elements but could be used against anyone seeking to bring about social or economic change, as well as restricting the threatening effect of suffrage by providing a mechanism for muzzling unsuitable voices.

As the new century progressed, more moderate liberal forces began to strengthen in universities and schools. A high point in the development of the moderate left was the contribution of Minobe Tatsukichi, whose ideas appealed to intellectuals, bureaucracy, and business groups alike. In July 1911, Minobe presented a series of lectures to secondary school teachers, which explored the Japanese Constitution and the interpretation of the power structures within it. His gentle attempt to simplify the very core of the distribution of power in the constitution could have set Japan on a very different path.

The Emperor as Organ Theory

At the heart of Minobe's lectures was a strange-sounding theory containing a very complex set of arguments concerning the exact role of the emperor. The 'Emperor as Organ Theory' represented the reverberations of Inoue's determination to define the role of the emperor with two separate meanings. A conflict started among several university professors who were trying to contribute to the debate to define political paths through what had become a difficult political period.

In essence, as political parties were subsumed by military influence, Minobe Tatsukichi put forward the proposition that the state could be likened to a type of governing 'person' and that the emperor was an organ of the state, that his role had limitations, as suggested by Article IV—which (as we saw) stipulated that his role was exercised "according to the provisions of the present constitution." In other words, the emperor played a limited role within the state but had no authority over or above it.

The opposing view, promoted by Uesugi Shinkishi, was that the emperor had unlimited authority as granted in Article I of the constitution, which appealed to the historical and uniquely Japanese relationship between emperor and people. There are no prizes for guessing which view the Army held, with its unique access to the Emperor.

Although Minobe had been widely criticized, he had contributed to a profound academic shift in general feelings against authoritarianism, and the development of political science, with a consequential openness to liberal and democratic thinking. Yoshino took up the baton, becoming an energetic writer, lecturer, and political enthusiast, and in the eyes of many at the time, he became the great symbol of the moderate left.

In the context of the various 'incidents' of the time, outlined elsewhere here, the push to reject Minobe's interpretation was part of a larger campaign to discredit liberalist scholars. The result was the banning of certain publications and forced resignations of several Privy Councilors and other office bearers. The professor had been an honored member of the Peers and had made a long-term contribution to the Civil Service Examinations Board, and he tried without success to defend his long-held position. He was forced to resign his peerage, his professorship emeritus, and all other honors.

Under pressure from the militarists, the Okada administration issued a powerful statement of condemnation for ideas "which run counter to the sacred constitution and do a great harm to its true conception…"[26] The government then began a program of indoctrination on the Constitution for the benefit of one-hundred and fifty university professors.

---

[26] Government statement, Oct 22 1935

What Minobe had unsuccessfully attempted to achieve was a crucial element in the Japanese passion to find the philosophical basis for their state and to accomplish this without merely creating a pastiche of the Western models. Specifically, he saw the need to synthesize the romantic, mythological, and tribal elements that gave the Japanese a sense of being a 'people' with the rational, classical, and liberal philosophical elements necessary for a progressive state.

The ultranationalists and many in the army saw the mythical and romantic elements as the true expression of the people and the constitution, while the bureaucracy and the intellectuals tended towards the liberal and rational.

Despite Minobe's humiliation, Hajime Tanabe and others in the Kyoto school of philosophy revisited this issue and others throughout the 1930s. They advocated a 'third way' often since misinterpreted as fascist in Japanese Studies literature, but which was in fact was quite central to the intellectual resistance to the actions of Major General Tojo, by significant elements including senior members of the Japanese Navy.

The maintenance of this philosophical search was a consequence of a proud, sophisticated culture surviving and emerging from a tectonic collision with a worldview in which it was assumed that to be real and capable of rational intercourse with the world, one needed to embrace certain liberal and rational values. How then was it possible to hold on to one's traditional values, become real in the world, *and* overcome authoritarianism?

Casting forward from Minobe in this way we will have a clearer grasp of the events of the 1930s when we get there. The noted scholar and writer David Williams juxtaposes the two thinkers in the following way.

"Minobe as a legal thinker sought to make the law speak Japanese, that is to make two distinct modes of being, thinking and feeling, work in tandem…In a parallel project, Tanabe sought to make the Greco-Roman philosophy of the rational state speak Japanese, thus to overcome the dynamic tension between state and nation/people in order to realize an effective Japanese amalgam of the nation/state (*minzoku-kokka*), or national-popular state."

Despite the power of fear and conservatism, there are further examples of liberality that were fought for, and even died for. This is perhaps more remarkable than the success of conscription. Movements against militarism existed right through the periods leading up to World War II, but they were fragmented, diverse, and less visible than the militarist ones. An example is appropriate at this point, despite the fact that it takes us forward to the 1920s.

Waseda University students offered organized resistance in 1923 when faced with compulsory military training. The university had a fine academic tradition, priding itself on the number of its ex-students who had served in the Diet. Several of the student societies combined to hold meetings protesting the introduction of military instruction, and it seems they met with success. The peace movement at Waseda quickly associated itself with progressive and socialistic movements in other colleges. Professor Sazuko Yoshino sponsored this movement at the Imperial University of Tokyo, which led to the formation of the Intercollegiate Association for the Study of Social Science. This tendency to embrace a left-wing agenda ultimately brought the movement into direct confrontation with those reactionary forces that campaigned against 'dangerous thoughts.' As the post-war period unfolded, the limits of acceptable liberalism were stretched and re-set as idealists attempted what the romantics feared most.

The Japanese ruling oligarchy had learned some very graphic lessons in observing the conduct of World War I. They saw just how far Western governments were prepared to go to fight for an acceptable balance of power in Europe. They observed the European ruling class condoning a massive tribal war, burying a whole generation of men and boys under acres of bloodstained mud, in wasteful and obscene battles.

They would have noted that hundreds of thousands of lives could be focused on a single geographic line for years with no clear result, except massive carnage. What Europe took from all this was a sense of disgust and futility.

The lesson for the militarists in Japan was quite different. They learned that to be able to compete in that kind of contest, they would have to produce a population that was willing and capable of paying the full price. If Britain and Germany were the gods of progress, and if they were prepared to slaughter their own so readily, then each Japanese soldier would need to be made in that god's image. The capacity for national brutality would need to be personalized.

They also learned that the disruption of German fuel supplies ultimately broke the impasse.

4

DEALING WITH INTERNAL TURMOIL:
DEMOCRACY, CORRUPTION,
MEDIA, AND INDUSTRY

T HE TAISHO PERIOD (1912–1926) is seen as a time of
attempted liberalization, and some call it a period of
democracy. To the extent that perhaps more people were
able to participate in the political process, this is true, as signs of
a public life emerged with the establishment of political parties.
A later chapter will assert that the flirtation with democracy
was a causal factor in the transition to totalitarianism. Before
that, though, the nature of the period needs some unraveling.

Democratic possibilities at the time allowed heightened
debate concerning the nature of representation, but an
eventual consequence of the growth of public debate and the
highlighting of corruption in the media was a tightening of
governmental controls. In addition, capitalist ventures and
industrial successes undermined traditional power structures
and allegiances, threatening the old elites. The nature of
Japanese capitalism was changing rapidly, as were the location

and loyalties of the workforce. Admitting the possibility of the questioning voice allowed everything to be questioned. The answers when they came were native, traditional, conservative, and reactionary.

Prior to 1912, non-democratic groups controlled most institutions. The institution of the Emperor oversaw two houses of parliament as well as the military leadership. The 'Old Guard' had managed to establish Japan as a force to be reckoned with but seemed unable to relinquish power or allow those with progressive or creative views a hearing. Many felt that Japan could never evolve into a world power without a more dynamic public life and that would have to include debate, dissent, and discourse.

In the absence of a strong or inspirational Emperor, the Taisho period saw the birth of political parties with a view to these developments and for the application of some restraint on the oligarchs and the traditional power-brokers. If the aim of the parties was to bring progress and representation to government, their attempt was ultimately self-destructive.

Elder statesmen representing a closed and elite club ran the old cabinets, but the parties that replaced them brought confusion and chaos in their enthusiasm to discredit each other. Public bribery and vilification only served to discredit the political process in the eyes of the public.

'Pork barreling,' undisclosed conflicts of interest, and other forms of corrupt behavior are not unique to any country or any political system, but all of these were endemic in Japan at this time. Almost as damaging as the real corruption were the incessant accusations and innuendo published in the press, as party loyalists attempted to score political points.

The fallout from corruption and perceived corruption is reflected in the killing of Yasada Zenjiro, the head of one of the 'big four' *zaibatsu*, and the wealthiest man in Japan. A protestor disgruntled about inequality and corruption killed him. This was very unsettling for the rich and the powerful, who were not accustomed to feeling exposed and vulnerable.

The development of party politics aggravated long-standing tensions between the military and more liberal political thinkers. In engaging with the West, Japanese thinkers had been exposed to the anti-war movements of the time. They gave voice to the revulsion at the colossal human waste resulting from European competition for colonial wealth and imperial strength.

Japan was involved in disarmament, if unhappily, and was intellectually engaged in the changing values abroad in international relations. In addition to tensions within the political system, the concept of an autonomous military was also re-examined.

One of the shocks of World War I, from the Japanese point of view, was that her military role model, Germany, had suffered a humiliating and total defeat. Despite the fact that Japan had been allied with Britain, and its navy was inspired by the British one, its constitutional model was German for reasons of perceived strength and military integrity.

This was not the only irony that would confront the Japanese during the first full century of engagement with the world. Strictly speaking, Japan would have felt more vindicated in the choice of constitutional system if its own wartime enemy had succeeded. Germany's loss had implications for democratic tendencies within Japan, which were quick to unfold. The Japanese military attributed the German loss to disunity between government politics and the armed forces within Germany.

This suggested the need for a structure that would enable the military and the political arms of government to become more united. Some people felt the solution to be in bringing civilians into official roles within the military forces. The result ultimately was the opposite, as powerful vested interests, not just of military people but also of those in industry, stood to lose power and wealth from a limitation of the autonomy of the army.

Media Independence. Managing and Enabling Unrest

Restraint of the Media was a core method of social control from the Meiji period onward. In 1868, publishers of pro-Shogun (anti-restoration) bulletins and papers were gaoled, and the publications were banned. One of the early laws passed by the new government was the Newspaper Publishing Ordinance, which enshrined the publisher's responsibility for the content of their papers. Although there was no pre-publication censorship, the meaning was clear. Anti-restoration articles would be published at a cost. This set a long-term pattern for self-censorship, which remained a very effective control on press freedom.

Despite this, the government was not seen to be overly restrictive during the early part of the period. It looked to the printed media to help disseminate information and to educate the general public. The need to modernize and to raise public awareness outweighed the dangers in the potential for dissent. In that context, self-censorship 'with consequences' looks very smart as policy.

The new government oversaw a period of great civil turmoil. As many as thirty riots a year threatened the peace, and we can conclude that the population contained passionate and activist elements, but these weren't in evidence in the newspapers. By 1873, the original ordinance was extended by three articles designed to discourage further any editorial opinion not in keeping with government expectations.

Following a revolt of conservative Samurai, tighter restrictions were enacted in law with a new Press Ordinance of 1883 that effectively enabled fines and imprisonment for any criticism of the state at all. Later that year, a new libel law was enacted and, in 1876, the Home Affairs Ministry was granted the power to enforce a press ban in response to any threat to national security. Unbelievably, liberal opinion was still expressed by brave or short-sighted editors who, by 1887, were faced with the Peace Preservation Law on top of the further forty-two provisions of the 1883 ordinance.[27] The last forty years of the 19th Century saw laws enacted that were like a boa constrictor on press freedom and expressions of liberal idealism. Tighter, ever tighter.

The Meiji constitution contained three articles aimed directly at the control of free speech in the press. Article 8 granted that extraordinary ordinances could override any other laws. Article 29, in contrast, granted the citizens that they "shall within the confines of the law, enjoy liberty of speech, writing, publication, assembly and association." Inviting generations of problems, however, the article made no attempt to define 'the confines of the law.'

The 'freedoms' enshrined in these articles allowed the suspension of almost five-hundred publications between 1892 and 1895. However, while the number of publications decreased, the capacity of newspapers to reach a wide audience increased, due to technical improvements in printing.

The war with China in 1895 and the war with Russia in 1905 gave rise to public criticism of militarism resulting in the closing of many Tokyo newspapers. Already, at this point in time, signs had emerged that the militarist agenda inherent in the 'restoration' should be protected from public criticism.

In the opening of a new century, the way forward was fairly clear to those in power. Every corner of Japanese society would be exposed to carefully planned restrictions, repressions, and

---

[27] For a good summary of the laws see *Japan Press, Media, TV, Radio, Newspapers* at www.pressreference.com/Gu-Ku/Japan.html

education, to create a nation that would be capable of achieving the goals inherent in the Meiji national vision.

The Media and Popular Sentiment

In the period roughly spanning 1912–1918, the press played a particularly active role in urban protest movements, and they became champions of anti-cabinet sentiment in the push for party government. This tendency was not universal, though, as some press elements supported military and more conservative ones. It has been argued that these positions were based more on commercial populism than on principle.[28]

Between 1910–1920, the press supported massive rallies and covered many riots in sordid detail, contributing to the felling of three cabinets and impacting government policy.[29] In 1913, the press supported two parties in bringing down the Katsura cabinet over military interference. This occurred despite a huge raft of legislation to control publication of anti-government agendas. A similar thing, referred to as the Siemens scandal, happened the following year over scandals concerning the navy.

In the context of numerous rallies and general discontent, the news that the Siemens Company of Germany had made secret payments to several senior naval officers in exchange for major naval contracts, caused a major national uproar. Demands were made for impeachment of the cabinet, and a public gathering, numbering about 40,000, began days of violence and over 400 arrests. All this eventually led to the resignation of Yamamoto as well as the rejection of planned naval expansion.

Riots and demonstrations in 1918, across hundreds of cities and rural centers, went on for weeks. The major issue

---

[28] Huffman, James L. *Creating a Public: People and Press in Meiji Japan.* Honolulu: University of Hawaii Press, 1997, P360.

[29] Ibid P364

emerging from them was the popular push for universal male suffrage. The possibility of women being allowed to vote hadn't even been seriously considered, and yet these demonstrations actually began as an evening meeting of fishermen's wives in a coastal village, protesting the high cost of rice.

By the time the protests had spread, 100,000 troops had been dispatched, resulting in nearly 25,000 arrests and over 8,000 prosecutions, with consequential death and damage to property. This was civil disobedience on a colossal scale, and it placed in some perspective the legislative attempts by government to control dissent. Here was the explosive interplay between the rights and needs of the population and the fear of lawlessness and descent into chaos, a fear shared by government, military, and many ordinary people as well.

This was a political vacuum in which the vast majority would welcome any strong champion, capable of standing up with a clearly stated vision of a safe and prosperous future. It is a situation not unlike that which occurred in Germany and Italy of the 1930s but as we will see, the response in Japan was quite different.

In the media, one newspaper emerged as a particular champion of the liberal movements. *The Osaka Asahi Shimbun* (*Morning Sun*) gave mass exposure to the people's rights movement, but after the riots of 1918, press restrictions were implemented on top of martial law. The press coverage of these events differed from that of earlier riots in that accounts were more "reactive than proactive and even less unified" according to Huffman.[30] Despite coverage that was more circumspect than some had been earlier, the Prime Minister's response was vehement and decisive.

On August 14, Home Minister Mizano Kentaro banned news coverage, stipulating that only the Home Ministry's daily summaries could be published. In itself, this was the cause of

---

[30] Ibid P366

more rallies and discontent, particularly amongst reporters and supporters of a free press.

Predictably, it also led to calls to overthrow the cabinet. The response to this issue was particularly provocative by the *Asahi Shimbun*. In the August 26th issue, an *Asahi* reporter wrote in colorful terms which, amongst other things, alluded to an ancient Chinese peasant revolt, also noting "the people suffer in misery; hungry sparrows weep in empty storehouses."

After unprecedented censorship, *The Asahi Shimbun* published blank spaces where censored articles would have been. Their defiance was not able to withstand a threat of closure. In response to accusations of transgressions, including one of inspiring treason, an apology was published in an attempt to remain in business. The fulsome apology, along with several management resignations, saved the paper. *Asahi* was not universally supported through this, as several pro-government papers ran with the sales opportunity brought about by the humiliation of their competitor.

This effectively killed any mass coverage of the movements for universal suffrage and constitutional representative government. Other papers also suffered when, having drawn a line in the sand, the government made clear its intentions. It simply became impossible for media publications to become partisan opponents of the government, particularly after the assassination of Prime Minister Hara by a right-wing activist in 1921.

This murder had apparently been carried out because Hara "had not led a crusade to punish government officials involved in bribery cases,"[31] although the real motivation may have been more reactionary. If there is irony in this, it is that the Hara government was mildly reformist, but the outcome

---

[31] Mitchell, Richard H. *Political Bribery in Japan*. University of Hawaii Press, 1996, P44.

was repressive on the media and on the liberal movement in general.

The contribution of Hara Takashi as Prime Minister deserves a little elaboration at this point. He was born into a high-ranking Samurai family and was a university graduate, embarking on a career in journalism. All of these factors made him powerfully suitable to become the first Prime Minister to achieve power through party politics.

He was very well connected, but these connections sometimes appeared too close. In his leadership role, he was faced with extraordinary difficulties domestically and abroad. At home, his population was becoming disillusioned with what appeared to be a slow march towards reform. He also faced the formation of organized labor and local exposure to communism and socialism.

In 1925, the Diet finally approved 'universal' male suffrage, but with certain restrictions. Males had to be over twenty-five years old and had to be resident in their electoral district for at least one year and not be in receipt of relief support. Despite these restrictions, the voter base was increased from about three million to twelve and a half million voters.

Interestingly, during the same year, some very comprehensive legislation was passed to make the electoral system more fair and equitable. These attempted to curb vote buying and aggressive vote canvassing, and controls were placed on electoral literature. Heavier penalties were also introduced to curb bribery. Some modern observers view these outwardly egalitarian restrictions as an attempt to keep the new voters who were by definition from the lower classes, from taking an active role in the political process. The motivation for this was said to be fear of socialism.[32]

---

[32] Ibid P45

Despite these reforms, the election that followed was widely regarded as the most corrupt since 1915[33] as political power brokers used 'influence money' to hold factions together in their push for power.

Whereas self-censorship began as the method of choice for controlling print media, film censorship was much more pervasive. All films intended for public viewing were pre-screened by the Home Ministry. Bureaucratic control was implemented with typical thoroughness, and the Home Ministry men were motivated with a "highly paternalistic attitude, an underlying belief that officials were not merely a political elite but a moral elite qualified to oversee every aspect of social life."[34]

Even more restrictive, though, were the controls on radio that was only allowed as a state/private enterprise. The monolithic radio organization that operated across Japan was called Nihon Housou Kyoukai (Japanese Broadcasting Corporation). This organization was very centralized in the hands of former officials of the Communication Ministry.

By the end of the Taisho period, newspapers had become large and very profitable enterprises serving a very different market from that served by the early Meiji press. Whereas once they had served a learned minority, they now served the masses. Advertisements had become bigger and more dominant. Cartoons, sketches, and sensational headlines made the papers much more like their Western counterparts.

The classical writing styles used by educated people were pushed aside in favor of simplified *kanji* and the speech patterns of common folk. Advertisements for common goods, travel schemes, medicines, and books of all kinds occupied a large percentage of the page area.

---

[33] Ibid P45

[34] Kasza, Gregory. *The State and the Mass Media in Japan 1918–1945.* University of California Press, 1993.

In parallel to this, there was an increasing professionalism among reporters. By the 1920s, entrance examinations were given to selected applicants from the country's best universities. The new breed of reporters became more assertive and more aggressive in sensationalizing a possible story, in a very competitive atmosphere. Populist taste also demanded coverage of intrigue, murders, and morality tales. Throughout this time, the market penetration of newspapers grew enormously. The press was able to reach many more people with news, and with that came an increased ability to inflame, incite, and to bring emotion to debates and issues that might otherwise have been considered in more reflective ways. What a huge responsibility even small freedoms are, when the political system is still defining itself, and power structures within the country are still competing for dominance.

During the 1920s, a broad range of corruption issues comprehensively frustrated the electorate until the election of Inukai in 1932. It is useful to understand the types of issues involved, but this won't be a comprehensive list.

In 1925, several politicians were involved in illegal dealings relating to land provided for some well-known brothels. In 1928, the mass arrest of communists was linked to corrupt influence within the prosecutor's office.[35] In 1927, a long standing war minister was alleged to have taken a huge bribe from a rice wholesaler who wished to expand his interests in Korea.

In 1929, another bribery case called the 'Five Private Railway Bribery Incident' implicated officials to the ministerial level in large bribes. Later that year, decorations awarded in the Emperor's name, mainly meritorious service medals, were awarded in return for money.

Between 1927 and 1930, major bribes were paid in the sale of a railway to the government, resulting in a government

---

[35] Mitchell, Richard H. *Political Bribery in Japan.* University of Hawaii Press, 1996, P50.

minister being jailed. In the same period, several *zaibatsu* were implicated in corrupt payments to party officials to "avoid having the party regard [it] with a jaundiced eye."[36]

It is claimed that the connection between the *zaibatsu* and political parties was not made for specific favors but was a continuation of long held relationships, and this remains a sensitive issue, not just in Japan. This will be expanded elsewhere.

Later, in 1932, the election won by Inukai was seen to be the cleanest and least corrupt election since Hara's victory in 1920. This election also saw the largest majority in that period. Inukai was widely regarded as an honorable man, capable of bringing calm and respect to the political scene. In a diabolical blow to Japan's democratic hopes, naval officers and cadets murdered him in 1932. The killers were linked to a radical group called the Blood Pact Group led by a Buddhist priest, and the group had also plotted many other political murders. They had also been responsible for the murder of a former finance minister two months previously.

The two high water marks in the number of prosecutions for political bribery were in 1917, with 22,932 cases, and 1930, with 17,124 cases. The year 1924 also stood out with nearly 14,000 cases. It is doubtful that any democracy could survive this level of revealed corruption. We can only imagine the amount of it that went unreported or charged. Throughout these years, a clear majority of the prosecutions were against Election Committee members, although nineteen of those prosecuted in 1930 were candidates for the Diet.[37]

The view of the prosecutor, Procurator Hirata, was that bribery was so profoundly entangled in the political process that it was not practical to try to reform it. He held that the solution was to eliminate the parties altogether.

---

[36] Ibid P56

[37] Ibid P59

This issue was a colossal disappointment to the idealists who had begun the new century with a platform of seemingly achievable dreams. Yoshino Sakuzo thought that politicians were consumed "so thoroughly in 'connections of interest' that it had become virtually impossible for them to be critical about the institutions within which they operated."[38]

In 1932 he wrote, "The party politicians work under the orders of the paymasters, the plutocrats, and these orders are obviously to serve the interests of big business, while the little man, and particularly the farmer, is progressively impoverished."[39]

We have seen the expansive role taken by the press in publicizing political intrigue. A force almost as pervasive, but more insidious, was to evolve from the creation of a group called the National Foundation Society (*Kokuhonsha*), which grew out of anti-communist elements.

This group formed a comprehensive cross-section of civil and military bureaucrats and justice officials, with more than half of its officials connected to the Justice Ministry by 1928. At its height, the group numbered about eighty thousand, and it became a powerful anti-party pressure group that enjoyed influence across all levels of society. This group was to become one of the tentacles of power that made possible the transformation of a representative government into a totalitarian state.

Although the National Foundation Society saw its role initially to enlighten the public about dangerous foreign ideas, its work expanded to include direct action in undermining the party political structure. Members of the Society reportedly leaked damaging information and photographs that were at the heart of several of the major political scandals of the period.

---

[38] Ibid P60

[39] Sakuzo, Yoshino. *Fascism in Japan.* Contemporary Japan, Sept 1932, P194

In effect, it was a backroom association, which undermined the political process by coordinating misinformation, information, and leaks at various levels of bureaucracy and in the media. We refer to this group again in the chapter on nationalism.

In all these things, we have seen a vibrant and profitable commercial media, strong competition, and lively public debate. In addition, efforts had been made to open the electoral process and to control the excesses of previous times. However, the system as a whole was not resilient enough to resolve the issues of the day. The sheer quantity of these issues and events in combination with government corruption facilitated extremism and intemperance.

An equally extreme reaction was perhaps inevitable. The currents of power that had persisted below the surface throughout the first thirty years of the century continued to interlace at the business and bureaucratic levels. The veneers of liberalism were not core values. A new energy was exerted in restoring order and safety through discipline and the traditional values of paternalism and obedience.

Creating Strength in Industry

The primary needs of modernization and expansion could only be addressed by competitive industry of world size and capitalization. This was backed initially by state initiative and money. Later, it became clear that the military could provide much needed demand and even new markets.

The Meiji period saw the emergence of two powerful pressure groups, the landowners and the urban business classes. In the traditional conception of wealth and power, the landowners held the upper hand, as commerce was not looked upon as particularly honorable, and in fact it carried a social stigma in traditional circles. In addition, the notion of industrialization was not universally welcomed.

The architects of the Meiji modernization created a flurry of activity at a governmental level to nurture industry and take an active role in the development of markets. One of the earliest to develop, for example, was in the spinning industry, which involved the purchase of cotton from India, the construction of facilities, and the creation of markets at home and abroad. Advances were also made very quickly in rail transport, shipping, and in the chemical industry. In turn, these had flow-on benefits to subsidiary industries.

The wars around the turn of the century increased the tempo of all this, as well as introducing the element of foreign debt into the equation. These wars required large capital expenditures to be funneled into essential industries. This expenditure created the need for debt. The new relationship with foreign financial markets and the associated debt was inflationary, but it facilitated further, faster growth.

In the late 19th Century, manufacturing and industry in general were still minor players in the Japanese economy, which remained substantially agrarian. As a force in politics, the industrial-commercial groups were still quite limited. Government had heavily underwritten the hasty modernization, with development initially dependent on intensive government planning, supervision, and subsidy.

State capitalism was in effect the nurturing parent of private capitalism, which was encouraged, but controlled. These factors were critical in creating a pattern of development that defined the structure and philosophy and even the operational methods of Japanese capitalism.

Many of the new industrial leaders were men of the old Bushi class whose future, loyalties, personal friendships, and economic security lay with the government.[40] In pre-restoration

---

[40] Scalapino, Robert A. *Democracy and the Party Movement in Pre-War Japan: The Failure of the First Attempt.* Berkeley: University of California Press, 1953, P251.

times, they were considered to be an honorable, but not noble, class of military personnel, who would often be in the employ of a noble or Samurai. In battle, Bushi would be treated as enlisted men, under the orders of a Samurai officer. The old social class system continued to play a significant role in society. Social mobility was a very foreign, even alien concept.

The political and economic elites were small groups or cliques, but the former did not regard the latter as equals. Despite modernization and a new progressive attitude to industry, there was still a social stigma attached to commercialism. A strong sense of obligation existed in industry to government. This translated into a particular deference to public officials.

The nature of Japanese industrial capitalism is also reflected in its structure. Essentially, and in contrast to most Western models, it was (and is) very centralized, reflecting its state origins, with a small number of high-growth *zaibatsu* closely related to government, financially and personally. By the end of the Meiji era, there was a progressive tendency towards cartelism.

The *zaibatsu* were ideally placed to benefit from the rapid economic growth that sprang from a government policy of neo-mercantilism. In brief, this can be described as a policy that encouraged exports, discouraged imports, and controlled capital movement. It offered greater government control at some cost to domestic standards of living.

Rather than having a large group of small companies each pursuing specialist endeavors, the *zaibatsu* represented a concentrated group, each with associated sub-industries, radiating out from tight governmental fiscal planning. It could be said that this centralized structure represented very low inertia when opportunities for growth emerged, particularly in time of war.

Most observers seem to divide *zaibatsu* into three general groups: those mainly concerned with finance and banking, those whose activities were based mainly in industry, and those whose interests spanned all fields. The largest of them were Mitsui, Mitsubishi, and Sumitomo who were from the third group, and Yasada, which was from the first group. The groups were complex and somewhat fluid over time, so this should be seen as a very generalized view.

As industry developed, the *zaibatsu* formed a vital part of the unfolding economy, especially in their relationship to government. A gulf developed between the huge conglomerates and the smaller industrial concerns, which became increasingly dependent on the new masters of industry for finance and supply.

Despite this, even as late as the Russo-Japanese war, the economic position of the *zaibatsu* was quite uncertain and "their political role was generally marked by great caution."[41] They continued to benefit from government protection and were very particular in repaying obligations, cultivating contacts, and accepting subordination.

The future driving force of the economy and of anti-democratic sentiment was therefore partly born in subservience and obligation and was a unique counter-point of old values and new methods. This image of two paradigms, operating simultaneously, occurred repeatedly at several levels of the modern Japanese story.

To complicate things further, *zaibatsu* were also represented in the ruling elite as members of the House of Peers and had been so since the restoration. The House of Peers and the Imperial Household acted directly on their behalf, and private *zaibatsu* interests interlocked with state interests at all times, ensuring that state capital played an important role in the

---

[41] Ibid P253

development of Japanese capitalism down to and including World War I.

Among its number, the business community included businessmen who had been directly exposed to Western ideas, methods, and education. In terms of modernization, many of them represented a very 'enlightened' group. Their overseas education combined with a general enthusiasm for things modern, industrial, and 'rational' gave considerable pause to members of the establishment 'old order.'

The modern enthusiasms needed to be harnessed but also contained within a traditional, tangible framework. The development of powerful nationalist sentiment was a two-edged sword, and another contradiction emerged, as change and conformity sat unhappily together.

Beyond the drive for profit, the business community was thus caught between the desire for change for the national good and the revulsion felt for foreign ideas, for the preservation of the national spirit. They were ever mindful of their place in the achievement of national goals, working to conform to national purposes. Thus, they were very supportive of political and military leadership of the type offered by individuals with whom they had long-term relationships.

Without wishing to belabor this point, the subservience described stemmed from the stigma of social inferiority mentioned earlier, as landed and intellectual elements continued to look condescendingly upon the commercial occupations and on materialistic values in general. Progress was providing profit, but it was also blamed for greed and corruption.

It is impossible to research the transition from Western style colonial power to Pan-Asian total war without noticing just how 'modern' the methods were in this process. Certainly, parallels exist between Japanese actions then and several actions in the late 20th and early 21st Centuries. Powerful alliances of political, bureaucratic, and corporate interests that supported and profited from a powerful military machine were created. They responded to a clearly stated goal of a 'new order' to face a corrupt racial and cultural enemy. This was pursued through manipulation of triumphal quasi-religious doctrines and a very modern use of the mass media.

As the Japanese economy developed more aggressively toward a military footing, it underwent a kind of second industrial revolution, signaled by an increased development of heavy and chemical industries. A wave of mergers and industrial consolidation followed in financial, industrial, and mass media sectors.

Following the Manchurian expansion in the 1930s, the *zaibatsu* benefited from military contracts and developmental projects. Alongside them, a new sector emerged, which was tailored to empire-building and military contracting. This technologically innovative trend in industry was responsible for the rapid development of state-of-the-art armaments and aircraft. The development was so rapid that the West had little idea of the quality of equipment their armies were to face until the US pacific Fleet had been sunk and the bulk of Southeast Asia had been absorbed into the Japanese Empire.

Control of mass media and industry by a select club of Japanese men was diabolically efficient, but it was at the considerable cost of the Japanese population who suffered from a vast increase in the disparity of wealth and power distribution. Some expansion of these factors is warranted here.

The following paragraph is from an article that appeared in *The Economist*:

"On November 6th 1945, the supreme commander of the occupying forces in Japan, General Douglas Mac Arthur, changed forever the way the Japanese did business. So he thought. He ordered the break up of the *zaibatsu*, the huge industrial conglomerates, which, in 50 years had transformed Japan from a backwater into a world power. The families that owned them were shocked to be blamed for Japanese militarism. But with their concentrations of industrial power, cartels, state-led investment and feudal management, the *zaibatsu* also offended American notions of business. Yet they had served Japan well – and were to do so for decades."[42]

The *zaibatsu* emerged from companies based around family loyalties and feudal traditions. They were able to secure lucrative monopolies, purchase state assets very cheaply, and gain government subsidies. This partly came about because state efforts in establishing industries needed to be privatized in the 1870s to raise revenue. Mataro Iwasaki for instance, founder of Mitsubishi, was granted a substantial shipping monopoly in return for his contribution in ferrying troops to Taiwan during a military expedition in 1874.[43]

In the context of the need to modernize quickly, rapid concentration of economic power among a few families suited the new Meiji regime. The obligations to government, guaranteed by the on-going support detailed above, and close ties in an interlocking social structure ensured that a pyramidal system of interdependencies worked in a disciplined way.

Further concentration by absorption and take-over meant that each family had control across a range of industries, and each of these supported sub-contractors and, later, workers with a culture of lifetime employment in the company and ferocious loyalty to it. In this, the shadows of feudalism were cast over the twentieth century.

---

[42] *The Economist*, 23 Dec. 1999, *Japan's Zaibatsu. Yes General.*The Economist Newspaper Ltd.

[43] ibid

As the Japanese military pressed their national agenda further from home, the *zaibatsu* went with them. By "the time the army secured the oil fields of Southeast Asia, Mitsui had become the biggest private business in the world, employing about one million non-Japanese Asians."[44]

Despite MacArthur's intentions, the *zaibatsu* survived him, partly due to expediency in the post-war period when the new global (Western) concern was communism.

The landed or agrarian propertied groups represented traditional values, as we have seen. Their continued influence came from an electoral gerrymander, which gave them a disproportionate political voice. In the Meiji era, the predominant political struggle was between rural landowners and urban business groups. The power and the vote were substantially in the hands of the former. Before an election law revision in 1900, for example, all but seventeen of the three hundred electoral districts were rural. This imbalance was subsequently addressed, but not substantially.

Early in the century, suffrage laws established electoral representation on the basis of the level of national tax paid, and since rural landowners paid proportionally heavier taxes than urban interests did, government was obviously going to provide most favorable representation for them. Without participation and representation, the urban groups were forced to protect and advance their interests by other means. One result of this was an apparent indifference to party politics and current issues, as business formed close relationships instead with the decision makers and members of the bureaucracy.

They were well aware that if a businessman spoke out against the government, officials carried their custom elsewhere.[45] Herein is the root of much of the corruption of the time. This

---

[44] ibid

[45] Paraphrasing Inukai, 1911 Ibid P258

factor also informs the idea that the national agenda continued to be directed by groups and alliances within the traditional ruling elite, relatively independent of politics, but eventually also joined by the 'new' capitalists, who were increasingly driving the economy.

This brief survey of internal issues reveals vigorous political, social, and economic turmoil within Japan during the period leading up to the 1930s. The media, industry, and an array of political movements blossomed within a growing public sphere, despite enormous governmental control, while also contributing to pressures that ultimately worked against the persistence of democratic and internationalist tendencies.

During the same period, Japan observed, participated in, and benefited from the self-destruction of the old Imperialistic order in World War I. The lessons, challenges, and frustrations that followed, served to make Japan's internal turmoil more difficult to resolve.

5
THE PARIS CONFERENCE, WILSONIAN IDEALISM AND JAPAN

THE FINAL THROES of Western Imperialism (in the old sense) revealed how exploitative world politics had been, how deals and alliances of temporary convenience contributed to a great shedding of blood. A morally, physically, and economically exhausted Europe appeared ready to explore a new vision of international relations.

This was presented by the President of the United States, the most powerful representative of the 'New World,' whose nation was now owed billions of Dollars in War Loans and reparations,[46] and whose claimed authority was backed by her dominant industrial position.

---

[46] This is a very complex issue, but as a simple guide, some of the money's owed to America from 1915–1917 are included here, expressed in dollar values of the time, and the list is by no means the full one;

Great Britain; $1,250,000,000 France $ 686,000,000 Italy $107,000,000 Germany $25,000,000 Reference: Bogart, Ernest Ludlow. *War Costs and Their Financing* New York: Appleton & Co., 1921, P67.

Woodrow Wilson was committed to a profound reform of international affairs. The legacy he left is one of humanitarianism and idealism and yet his role in the frustration of the Japanese after the war can be seen as central in the tensions that ultimately caused Japan to reject the League of Nations. There have also been questions as to his motives in entering World War I when he did. Further, it can be legitimately argued that the harsh terms of the peace created a dangerous imbalance of power in Europe and also the devastating national failure that was at the heart of the birth of Nazism.

Wilson's dream was to design a system in which the processes of negotiation and treaty could become open and transparent, guaranteeing territorial integrity and the self-determination of peoples. This represented a very new language and paradigm from the neo-Darwinism of the previous decades. Conquered territories were to be placed under international stewardship, supervised and agreed upon by the new League of Nations.

One of the background imperatives he had in bringing this to the forthcoming Paris Peace Conference was that under his proposed system, prior claims to conquered territory, including Japan's, could be re-negotiated better to fit his American vision of a healthy balance of power in the Pacific.

This vision was confronted by the old imperial system of diplomacy. The arrangements already negotiated with regard to Pacific territory would not be put aside without difficulty. Australia's claim on former German territory made it very difficult for the US to argue against Japan's similar claim. They both had their sights on former German colonies. Britain was behind both arrangements, but for differing reasons in each case. Both Japan and Australia were calling in favors in return for wartime support.

William 'Billy' Hughes, the Australian Prime Minister, was adamant and energetic in pressing the Australian claim, first as compensation for the Australian blood contribution to the war, but also because of Australia's suspicion and fear of Japanese influence in the islands to her north. Wilson and Hughes both wanted to thwart Japanese claims, but Hughes' parallel claims undermined Wilson. Wilson could hardly oppose the Japanese claim while supporting the similar claim by Australia.

Further, the Japanese had been vigorous in managing their new territories and establishing a strong presence that was anything but theoretical or superficial. In practical terms, the colonies had been Japanese for five years by the time of the peace conference. Their claim seemed ironclad, and there was a general feeling, particularly in the Japanese Navy, that Japan deserved the islands as a reward for its support as well as for the development of its own security.

A Navy document declared: "The newly occupied territories in the South Seas fill a most important position as a link between Japan and the East Indies, the Philippines, New Guinea, and Borneo."[47] This could be the exact argument that Billy Hughes would have given to make his claims both *for* Australian occupation of the islands south of the equator and *against* the Japanese occupation of those north of it. In international security negotiations, what is good for the goose does not apply to the gander.

Many others in Japan argued forcefully for their claims, including the Japanese Prime Minister Okuma Shigenobu who, in the summer of 1914, had flatly asserted that Japan had no territorial ambitions, but now insisted that Japan had earned the right to possess Micronesia."[48] The national press took up the cause as the Japanese people warmed to the idea of islands of paradise for greater Japan. There were liberal and international thinkers who put forward a contrary view, but

---

[47] Peattie, Mark R. *Nanyo: The Rise and Fall of the Japanese in Micronesia, 1885–1945* Honolulu, HI: University of Hawaii Press, 1988, PP51.

[48] Ibid P51

their views seemed increasingly out of tune with the national interest.

In their anxiety over Japanese international stature and the retention of the islands, and suspecting that Britain and America might act as an Anglo-Saxon coalition against them, Japanese delegates prepared and presented the Racial Equality Proposal at the Paris Peace Conference.

In early 1919 the Japanese delegation proposed:

> "Considering the equality of a nation is the basic principle of the League of Nations, its member countries should not set any legal or other discriminations, and should give equal treatments to all the nationals of the member countries despite their race or nationalities."

Speaking at a meeting of The Asiatic Society of Japan in March 2003, Dr. Shusake Takahara, a lecturer and researcher at Doshisha University, Kyoto, made the point that Japan had a direct and an indirect interest in pursuing the issue of racial equality. Directly, he said that Japan was not enthusiastic about the establishment of the League of Nations and undertook to draw up a counter plan. The indirect interest was explained in the on-going problem Japan had with the US in regard to immigration, despite an agreement in 1908 by Japan to prohibit Japanese immigration to America.

"Wilson recognized the importance of the equal treatment of peoples, and hoped to embody this in the universal principles of the League's Covenant. However, as a southerner he was not in favor of the unqualified abolition of racial discrimination, being concerned that this might lead to internal disorder. At the same time, he was not immune to the sense of the threat posed by the 'yellow peril.'"[49]

---

[49] Takahara, Dr. Shusake. *Wilsonian Idealism and its Impact on Japan: The Case of Japan's Racial Equality Proposal,* The Asiatic Society of Japan, lecture given 17/3/03.

Japan did have some supporters in this, including Edward T. Williams, Senior Far East Specialist in the American Commission to Negotiate Peace. His view was an uncommonly inclusive one, and he recommended supporting the proposal for reasons that included the hope that by making concessions to Japanese pride of race, America might find Japan more likely to be conciliatory to China in Shantung. "But he saw this as a separate matter from the problem of Japanese immigration, arguing that just as Japan excluded Chinese laborers, so America should be permitted to exclude Japanese laborers."[50]

As a point of view, this is interesting because it shows a rare contemporary reference to the concept of racial pride and perhaps some understanding of the concept of 'face.' Wilson, Hughes Lloyd George, and others seemed only able to accept Japanese delegates on Western terms, seeing their proposal superficially and through Western cultural filters.

Possibly, they assumed that cultural misunderstanding could only ever occur because of a failure of the Japanese to understand them. The vantage point of superiority was part of their upbringing, but it was not what was needed to keep the Japanese in dialogue with the world. If the League was to become more than a club of well-meaning colonists, it needed to embrace values that were universal, not universally Western. For Wilson's ideals to be meaningful, the Japanese should have come to the conference as Asians and left it as people.

In addition to ambassadorial approaches in America and lobbying in several directions, the Japanese representatives sought direct talks with the Australian Prime Minister. He argued that Japan should certainly be treated as an equal and was already internationally respected, but there were differences between Japan and Australia, and the countries should not interfere in each other's domestic affairs. He referred to the

---

[50] Ibid P2

need to protect his working people, who were imbued with the spirit of 'White Australia.'

The Japanese changed tack by re-wording the proposal to be in pursuit of 'equality of nations,' but this was still rejected by Hughes. Yet another revision was similarly rejected. In a final attempt to be recognized and in order not to lose face and go home rejected, they attempted to get the phrase 'equality of nations' included in the preamble to the League Covenant.

A vote was taken and eleven of the seventeen members voted in favor, while six members abstained. Until that time, every issue had been resolved by a simple majority. In an effort to avoid further complications, Wilson declared that the amendment could not be adopted because it had not received unanimous approval.[51]

Many in America opposed Wilson in his attempt to establish the League. For those opposing him, the racial equality proposal and associated hysteria about immigration became a weapon to undermine Wilson and his dreams. Success was by no means guaranteed, and he clearly saw that his best chance was in acting to guarantee support from the British. We have seen that to achieve that, he would have to support Britain and its dominions in opposing the Japanese proposal. In this context, we can understand how it was possible for Australia so thoroughly to deflect Japanese ambition and pride.

The Japanese failed and were seen by the world to have failed, but from a contemporary viewpoint, it is arguable whether the failure was theirs.

Neo-Darwinism could not be put aside easily in a world that was organized around material practicalities. Racism was a representation of the huge technological gulf between the haves and the have-nots, as much as it was an elaboration of the same fear of, and competition with, 'the other' that defined communities, gangs, states, and nations. It was also an

[51] Ibid P3

underlying, seldom discussed, assumption that allowed for the wholesale exploitation of entire countries.

People in the West were still under the influence of the nineteenth century concept of racial difference that claimed to be qualified by respectable scientific theory and regarded "racial differences as biological, a matter of fact, not prejudice."[52] These theories weren't seriously challenged until the 1930s in the United States and Britain, and although we now understand that as a concept, 'race' is scientifically untenable, it still exists widely as a social category.

Japan was really pushing the idea of racial equality between great powers, seeking an affirmation of status *despite* racial difference. Naoko makes the point that this is in essence a political demand, "imbued with a sense of insecurity but also arising out of national pride and sensibilities."[53]

As Takahara put it, "The Racial Equality Proposal issue became a measure of the level of Western commitment to liberal democracy, and ultimately one must conclude that it was submitted and rejected under the international and social limits of the time."[54]

It is fair to argue that the Japanese intentions were never properly understood, or were at least misread. The Japanese approach to race was every bit as complicated and 'of its time' as the Western one, and it is most unlikely that their proposal represented a desire for complete international equality between peoples.

They certainly regarded themselves as being the natural leaders of 'lesser' Asian groups. They were later to distinguish between race according to color and race within color, in their

---

[52] Shimazu explores this beautifully in his conclusion. Shimazu, Naoko,. *Japan, Race and Equality: The Racial Equality Proposal of 1919.* London: Routledge, 1998, P184.

[53] Ibid

[54] Ibid P3

attempt to rationalize a perceived equality with the West, despite color, and superiority to the Koreans and Chinese of the same color, for example.

The Japanese had made extraordinary military and economic progress and were ready to step up to the plate. These were the measures by which they judged their readiness for world status. Their country needed to be recognized as one of the major players. Certainly they needed to be recognized as being members of the same 'club.'

The proposals most likely represented this need to be openly and publicly acknowledged as World leaders, alongside those of the West—or more particularly—those that were 'white' and had traditionally controlled the World agenda.

There has obviously been debate about the relative importance of the issue of immigration in the creation and meaning of the proposal. There is no doubt that it was understood by The Powers to be about immigration, but it appears that if it gained that flavor, it did so partly from the bureaucratic input in its drafting and partly from practical recent experience by the West, in its reading.

In his book, *Japan, Race and Equality: The Racial Equality Proposal of 1919,* Naoko Shimazu emphasizes the priorities of the Foreign Ministry in drafting the proposal, and "in the absence of detailed guidelines from Tokyo," it was worded to reflect "the particular perspective of those with an immediate input into its drafting in Paris." He continues, "immigration was such an important issue for the Foreign Ministry which tended to perceive it not only as a practical problem, but also a symbolic manifestation of Japan's 'unequal' status"[55] and a cause for the loss of face and humiliation of the Japanese people."

---

[55] Shimazu, Naoko. *Japan, Race and Equality: The Racial Equality Proposal of 1919.* London: Routledge, 1998, P165.

Although Naoko acknowledges immigration as a key issue in the minds of some, he places most emphasis on the need for recognition of Japan's great power status, a result of Japan's sense of insecurity as a non-white power.

The proposal came about as a consequence of internal conflict over Japan's engagement with the West. Prime Minister Hara and his supporters held the view that participation in the League of Nations would represent an important signal of Japan's intention to co-operate with the West, in preventing Japan's further isolation from the international community. This pro-Western, internationalist foreign policy was called *obei kyocho*. Hara and the *obei kyocho* supporters were vigorously challenged by at least two groups for whom the League appeared to be a thinly-veiled attempt to maintain Western, and particularly Anglo-Saxon, dominance in World affairs.

Under the pressure of the imminent conference, Hara sought a compromise from his detractors at home. They agreed that participation was to be allowed in exchange for some sort of assurance that Japan would not be subject to racial discrimination within the League. This became an important issue in the minds of the public in Japan, and many argued that it was a *sine qua non* of Japan's joining the League.

These issues were to provide the impetus for the intellectuals of Japan to search for a new way to see themselves in the world. But at the conference, both Hughes and Wilson probably felt so constrained by the expectations of their power bases at home that their support was never likely to be given.

The consequences of these events reverberated throughout the 1930s, largely unnoticed by people in the West. Following the conference, Japanese governments pursued what came to be called 'Shidehara diplomacy,' seeking to emphasize international co-operation, especially with the United States and Britain, despite another loss of face on the World stage and despite angry and often violent repercussions at home.

Those who favored this co-operative engagement looked increasingly wrong-footed as Britain turned more openly to the United States for hegemony in East Asia and the Pacific. The 1924 American Immigration Act further undermined the moderate position, showing how willing the Americans were to humiliate the Japanese. This Act replaced a general quota for immigrants with individual national quotas, according to which Japan was only allowed one hundred persons per annum, on the same level as tiny countries such as Samoa. The Japanese people felt that they had been stigmatized and marked as unworthy.

In the minds of many in Western governments, the racial equality proposal had raised fears of unmanageable emigration from Japan. In this there is a tragic irony that the racial equality proposal, created by Japanese internationalists, ultimately led to the undermining of the internationalist, pro-Western position.

Upon his return from the Imperial conference in 1921, Mr. Billy Hughes addressed the House of Representatives. In part he said:

> "For us, the Pacific problem is for all practical purposes the problem of Japan. Here is a nation of nearly seventy millions of people, crowded together in narrow islands; its population is increasing rapidly, and is already pressing on the margins of subsistence. She wants room for her growing millions of population, and markets for her manufactured goods. And she wants them very badly indeed. America and Australia say to her millions 'Ye cannot enter in.' Japan, then, is faced with the great problem, which has bred wars since time began. For when the tribes and nations of

the past outgrew the resources of their own territory they moved on and on, hacking their way to the fertile pastures of their neighbors. But where are the overflowing millions of Japanese to find room? Not in Australia; not in America. Well, where then…?

"These 70,000,000 Japanese cannot possibly live, except as a manufacturing nation. Their position is analogous to that of Great Britain. To a manufacturing nation, overseas markets are essential to its very existence. Japan sees across a narrow strip of water 400,000,000 Chinese gradually awakening to an appreciation of Western methods, and she sees in China the natural market for her goods. She feels that her geographical circumstances give her a special right to the exploitation of the Chinese markets. But other countries want the market too, and so comes the demand for the 'Open Door'…

"This is the problem of the Pacific—the modern riddle of the Sphinx, for which we must find an answer…Talk about disarmament is idle unless the causes of naval armaments are removed."[56]

This speech gives some idea of the oratory quality that brought Hughes to world attention at the time. He was very popular in Britain and argued very forcefully for Australian interests after the war. This is quite a prophetic speech in many ways, and military preparation in Australia would have been better served if it had been taken aboard as a genuine warning. But of course it is also the insecure argument of an insecure people who had not long ago themselves been 'hacking their way' to other people's fertile pastures, and claiming them for themselves. The colonies of Australia had, by the time of this speech, been a Federated nation for not quite twenty years,

[56] Wigmore, Lionel. *The Japanese Thrust*. AWM Canberra, 1957

and it had its own stories of dispossession. Hughes was born a Welsh man.

Can we identify a significant change in Japanese direction as a result of the failed proposal? In general terms there is certainly evidence cited elsewhere in this book of a general sense of disillusionment with the international scene as perceived in Japan of the 1920s. The internationalist *obei kyocho* were intellectual, liberal, and sophisticated in a Western sense and may have had their ideas cast aside as being representative of the worst of modernity anyway.

But the popular reaction to loss of national face as portrayed in the contemporary press suggests otherwise. If there was a pivotal point in the making of The Pacific War, this may well have been it.

In fractionally re-orienting the nation, giving credibility to those who wished to resist Westernization, and in mobilizing public suspicion of Western intentions, the failure of the proposal represented an awful victory for the irrational. Despite idealistic intentions and rhetoric at the conference, the Powers were only prepared to deal in structural, practical adjustments. In order to feel able to take part, the Japanese needed symbolic affirmation. The Powers misread the Japanese need for empathy, seeing only the threat of emigration.

Years later, many Japanese figures involved in these events would look back on the failure of their proposal as a pivotal moment in the direction taken by their nation.

Konoe Fuminaro became one of the most important thinkers and politicians during the 1930s, and he was Prince Saionji's private secretary throughout the conference. In 1933, only a month before Japan withdrew from the League, he wrote, with obvious regret:

"In thinking about it, the Paris Peace Conference was the ideal opportunity to correct the existing irrationalities in the world and to establish a true world peace. This conference was held immediately after the war and the politicians who attended it had all experienced much pain with the horrors of the war. However, the Paris conference did not recognize the blatant irrationality of discriminating against people by skin color."[57]

The Japanese people had their suspicions confirmed that the Anglo-Saxons could not be relied upon to live up to their ideology and that international justice was just another power game.

Ambassador Ishi was prepared to re-submit the proposal even as late as April 1921, but his government instructed him not to, on the basis that it could further strain relations with Britain, America, and Australia. Naoko says of this: "All in all it was considered best not to disrupt the rather 'delicate' relationship between Japan, Britain and the United States by resubmitting the proposal. It was this sort of 'weak-kneed' (*nanjaku*) attitude of not wanting to upset the allies which later became the focus of criticism of the 'Shidehara diplomacy' in the late 1920s."[58]

By 1922, Japan's formal empire had been completed but the inherent problems remained. Insecurity and ambition within the ruling oligarchy created a hunger for more. The pursuit of this happened despite the passing of the imperialist world order that had provided the model for Japanese expansion and which had tried to manage Japan's expansion within its own strategic limits.

It also happened despite, and perhaps being blissfully blind to, the growth of nationalism in Asia, a force Japan would later try to harness for its own purposes.

---

[57] Konoe, Fuminaro. *Seidanroku,* Tokyo, Chikra shobo P263, quoted in Shimazu Naoko 1936, P179.

[58] Shimazu,, Naoko. *Japan, Race and Equality: The Racial Equality Proposal of 1919.* London: Routledge, 1998,P171.

6

THE WASHINGTON
CONFERENCE 1921–1922

T HE ONGOING RACE for naval superiority was hugely expensive, so after the war, the leading naval powers were able to agree on a number of limitations that attempted a readjustment of world naval strength and a reduction of expenditure by powers still being crushed by war debt.

Britain had long enjoyed clear naval superiority and had built its vast empire on the ability to control the oceans and its trade routes. On the face of it, the conference was a positive and idealistic American initiative first proposed by Senator William E. Borah, Republican of Idaho. President Harding took the idea to other nations, perhaps with idealism tempered by the promise of the application of some restraint upon Japan, which had become a regional player of formidable and growing strength.

Some would argue that the main goal of the US at the conference was to contain Japanese expansion and allow it to put its own stamp on the region. Given the growing suspicion that existed between the two powers, it is not unreasonable to suggest naval supremacy over Japan in the Pacific was its prime goal. A defensive Japanese attitude was not surprising as the area of US interest was Japan's own backyard.

It should be remembered that this relationship was not just friendly rivalry. Both countries had each been to war in the region in the recent past. Japan went to war with China in 1894–95, securing Taiwan, and the USA fought Spain to take control of the Philippines and Guam. These two events saw Japanese and American interests in potentially threatening positions geographically.

The defeat of the Russian fleet by Japan in 1905 had caused the US to view the threat of Japanese naval power more seriously than it had. To match the Japanese would be costly in financial and political terms, and it is in this context that the American initiative at the conference must be seen.

Unlike many diplomatic initiatives, this one began with the presentation of a fully detailed plan submitted by the American delegate Charles Evan Hughes, the Secretary of State. Over the following weeks, the major allied powers—Britain, France, Japan, and USA—worked on a series of nine separate agreements that covered strategies for the settlement of disputes.

This work included the creation of a moratorium on naval building for a period of ten years; pledged mutual respect for the sovereignty of Pacific possessions and mandated territories; agreed on the return of Kiaochow in Shantung province by Japan to China; placed a limit on the tonnage of capital ships; agreed on a set of rules for the use of submarines in warfare; and outlawed the use of poisonous gases in warfare. Agreements were also made with regard to the development of cable laying and location for international communication purposes.

The presentation of these ideas met with considerable skepticism by representatives of Japan, in particular. Their delegate expressed significant reservations about the allocation of shipping tonnage, but all these agreements were ultimately ratified. The conference was seen as a broad-brush initiative for peace and international understanding.

It is hard to see at first glance how Japan gained anything through its continued participation. Britain, too, had signed away its traditional dominance of the world's oceans. These two factors were to take on major significance in the twenty years that followed. For Japan, this was to be another in the accumulating series of incidents, which undermined its ability to maintain a moderate foreign policy by causing the moderate international negotiators loss of face at home. Their willingness to engage with the West had cost the Japanese significantly in ships and Naval strength.

The Japanese had demanded parity with USA and Britain but were denied. They saw this as naval inferiority and, having not been *spent* in the World War, they were not happy to accept these limits, until it was pointed out that the US would not develop any naval bases west of Hawaii. This referred to Guam and the Philippines.

It became apparent later that the US willingness to sign away the right to fortify island bases in an effort to gain easy fleet superiority actually represented a significant change in the power balance in favor of Japan. The US was now dependent on treaties to hold Japanese expansion. Japan was already poised over several strategic areas and could access US defensive bases very quickly, if it was so desired. The American fleet conversely had a very long sea voyage from its western base at San Diego to reach and reinforce its interests in the region. When the time came, the instant loss of Hawaii not only cost lives, it cost a great deal of time while the US industrials rebuilt the fleet.

Japan was mollified for the moment but withdrew from the treaty in 1934. As to Britain, this fundamental shift in the importance of its naval capacity went unnoticed in Australia. The failure to grasp the potential consequences of this caused strategic planning failure throughout the 1930s and contributed to the serious lack of preparation for Australia's potential role in an Asian/Pacific war. Churchill and his supporters in Australia perpetuated the old worldview right up to the fall of Singapore, which based the integrity of the Empire and its Dominions on British naval supremacy, leaving the Dominions free to send their armies to support British interests in Europe, as required. The potency of British Naval power was not only diminished by negotiation, it was more significantly diminished by the tremendous vulnerability of old ships to modern aircraft.

Naval Strength, 1922 Agreed Limits;[59]
USA 525,000 tons
Britain and Dominions 525,000 tons
Japan 315,000 tons
France 175,000 tons
Italy 175,000 tons

Before all of this, the pre-eminent power in East Asia was represented by the Anglo-Japanese alliance. The decision by Britain to terminate that treaty was felt in Japan as a strategic blow and a significant loss of prestige. It was also widely and powerfully represented in Japan as a major betrayal. From the British point of view, the maintenance of the treaty was incompatible with the perceived need to strengthen ties with the United States.

The result of the Washington Conference however only served to compound the betrayal, as Japan found itself not one of two major players in its own backyard, but one of five. To the new generation of leaders in Japan, the effect of the conference was to confer an insult in the form of dual hegemony for Britain and the US in the Pacific.

---

[59] Ibid

The conference caused more than a ripple on the islands of Japan, but its effects were felt equally on the mainland of China. In February 1922, a nine-power treaty was declared whose signatories included China. It bound the Powers to respect China's sovereignty, independence, and administrative integrity. The powers were required to relinquish and abandon spheres of influence, pursuing instead the principle of "equal opportunity for the commerce and industry of all nations" within China. This was a clear endorsement of the American preferred policy of 'Open Door' and a rebuttal of the Japanese position.

What the treaty didn't address was the Chinese often repeated request that all existing "special rights, privileges, immunities or commitments be deemed null and void."[60] It also failed to address Chinese demands for the cessation of foreign leases. The neglect of these issues undermined the possible meaning and value of those agreements that referred to 'Chinese sovereignty.' The process, which was to be gradual and incremental, involved a reduction by the Powers of the rights of the exploiting nations but on terms and at a pace that suited them. Many people in both Japan and China did not support this but for very different reasons.

The Japanese sense of 'mission' that was applied to the enlightening and reforming of a 'decaying' Asia created an energetic modernization and Westernization after World War I but developed into the very different Pan-Asianism in the 1920s and 1930s, which aimed to unify the Asian peoples and reject Western imperialism in Asia. The change was no doubt accelerated by the perceived failure of the internationalists to engage with the West on acceptable terms.

---

[60] Beasley, W. G. *Japanese Imperialism, 1894–1945*. Oxford: Clarendon Press, 1987, P168.

After the negotiation of the naval agreements in the 1920s, Japan's ultra-nationalist groups had become increasingly proactive and aggressive, considering their nation's direction to be far too moderate to meet their perception of Japanese interests.

The Japanese public had very little experience of being able to express dissent concerning foreign events or to participate in policy making. Yet there is plenty of evidence of dissent in general. The Cabinet had no direct control of the military, which could act independently, even forcing the resignation of a Cabinet with which they disagreed.

The people felt more linked to the Emperor than to the process of his government and were almost guaranteed to support him. The military were able to conduct their policy conferences in his presence, and he was therefore identified with military decisions. The Cabinet was seldom seen to have that sort of relationship.

The complexity of this situation meant that parliamentary democracy was in effect a charade made more emphatic by state Shinto religion that encouraged devotion to the Emperor. Japanese national leaders had never been responsible to the people in a way that would be recognizable to people in western democracies. In fact, in the cultural period before the Meiji restoration, the individual had no rights enshrined in law at all. The smallest unit to have rights in law was the family. The individual owed honor to the family and the Emperor.

In exploring the role of the 'public sphere,' some historians maintain that the public had for centuries been docile, and that dissent was not a factor in the public acceptance of the actions of an authoritarian government. This is not the predominant view, however, as there is plenty of evidence of dissent in country life and towns, in philosophical debate, and cultural circles. If there was a public sphere able to provide a platform for debate and disagreement, how did the transformation to ultra-nationalist authoritarianism occur?

We need to approach the question, not assuming that the Japanese endured a poor quality version of democracy, the aim of which was full participation, but by considering it on its own terms. With the exception of the Left, the pre-war public sphere sought neither popular rule nor unconditional popular rights. The values embraced were "not partial or immature variants on democratic themes but the very inverse of democratic values."[61] This transformation is examined more fully in a later chapter.

In elevating the state above social control, authoritarianism assumes the superiority of rulers to the people. This is better understood when it is remembered that the history of Japanese thought and philosophy are based on Sinitic and Confucian values and not on Western ones. Implicit in this is the belief that societies are based on relationships of varying status. Importantly, the people can be said to have been more suspicious of popular sentiment than of leaders, "the polity was founded on the values of responsibility and expertise in officials, clarity, and transcendence in decisions."[62]

In a democracy, probably the reverse is true. It is based on pluralist values of debate and pragmatic compromise. It must consequently "tolerate a high degree of division and indecision, review, and reversal. It must concede disparate visions of the good and multiple centers of value."[63]

But despite the setbacks presented in politics and on the world stage, Japan advanced into the 1920s careful not to adopt any policy or undertake any action that would jeopardize its

---

[61] Berry, Prof. Mary Elizabeth. *Public Life in Authoritarian Japan*, Daedalus Vol. 127, 1998. Issue 3, P133+. American Academy of Arts & Sciences. At the time of writing, M.E. Berry was professor of history at the University of California at Berkeley.

[62] Ibid

[63] Ibid

international relations. 'Shidehara diplomacy,' as it was called, sprang from firm belief in some circles that Japan's future progress could best be guaranteed through industry, trade, and international economic relationships.

The Washington System of International Relations

Japanese internationalists had gained a great deal of personal and national prestige by taking the world stage as leading players in global diplomacy within the system that had become known as the Washington System. The Japanese inclusion in the treaties and the more ephemeral agreements represented the nation's full participation in the new international idealism, through which it was hoped that a peaceful world could be nurtured within a spirit of co-operation and agreement.

The pursuit of an internationalist agenda necessarily involved costs and compromises for each participant nation. In the period after the war, these costs were willingly shouldered, but as national economies all over the world suffered a slide into economic depression, national interests worked against the spirit of co-operation. The new idealism represented an attempt by the 'old order' to become more inclusive and less imperialistic, but under economic pressure, their difficulties were borne from a starting position of strength and market control. For emerging economies like Japan, the same pressures represented a more difficult burden, even the possibility of complete national failure and political implosion.

The economic cornerstone of the system was the adoption of the international gold standard by the major trading countries. This allowed predictable currency convertibility and ease of trade for all. For the Japanese, the focus for the application of the system related to international access to the resources and markets in China. Indeed, China was the central factor in the successful functioning of the system. The plan was to enable the gradual stabilization of China to allow it to play an independent part in regional politics and trade. To begin with, Chinese nationalists adamantly opposed the system, but as their hold became firmer on the country, their attitude to international co-operation softened. National infrastructure needed to be constructed to allow for the growth of industries. For this they needed foreign capital and technical advice, and much of this came from America.

Shidehara Kijuro was a career diplomat, the ambassador to Washington, and several-times Foreign Minister for Japan. His wife was from the family that owned the Mitsubishi Company, and this no doubt informed his views on the power of commerce.

While Shidehara's words may have reflected internationalist and moderate intentions, their effect when amplified through military and adventurist filters on the frontier, was still offensive to many Chinese, who felt economic conquest as keenly as they did military domination. This fed into the rising violence within China, between factions and also against foreigners of all persuasions.

From the Paris Conference onward, it became very difficult to typify the allegiances and agendas within China. In general terms, nationalists and communists wanted to strip away the layers of privilege and exploitation enjoyed by all foreign powers, but they had to play one off against the other merely to maintain the struggle to become representative of their own country. Other warlords were prepared to work in a more structured way with foreign powers to develop their own interests, as it later transpired in Manchuria.

The United States and Britain moved towards recognition of the Chiang Kai-shek regime in 1928, accommodating some of his demands. In doing so, they highlighted the entrenched position of Japanese interests. Shidehara's global view was of

Japan being widely engaged and mutually dependent on the West and on China for continued development. However, the emergence of the nationalists in Chinese government threatened Japan's colossal economic and human commitment in Manchuria. Chiang's forces could move in that direction at any moment. China announced that extra-territoriality would be abrogated by 1932 unless a negotiated agreement could be reached by that time.

Gradually, the Shidehara government agreed to negotiate on the issues of tariffs and extra-territoriality. It was hoped that Japan's position in Kwantung and south Manchuria could be reserved in the same way that the British interests had been, with regard, for example, to Shanghai.

There were many divergent forces within Japan that perpetuated the contradictory nature of Japanese impulses at the time. The exquisite Japanese culture of humility, understatement, and beauty, which was formed over centuries of intimate relationship to an ancestral landscape also by this time, embraced worldly intellectuals who had been exposed to the ideas and the free intellectual spirit of the West. Many worked idealistically in government and the bureaucracy with genuinely inclusive objectives. These were the parts of Japan that interfaced with international politics most gently. In contrast, on a separate but parallel path, economic and military agencies represented by overbearing officials, callous policemen, and rapacious traders and others are remembered for a general viciousness, particularly in Korea. Then, of course, there were the armies.

Shidehara reluctantly followed Britain and the United States in pursuing a negotiated reduction in special privilege and influence, which represented the end of the treaty port system, but in attempting to do so, he was unwittingly emasculating the very structure that kept militarism subservient to, or at least outwardly obedient to, the internationalist aims of the Foreign Office.

Before negotiations could be concluded the army made its move.

On the pretext that Chinese elements had bombed a section of the south Manchurian railway line that Japan controlled, Japanese forces occupied strategic centers in the Mukden area. An event like this would now be called 'false-flag terrorism,' where, in the absence of a real provocation, the aggressor simply creates one. The 'incident' created problems for the League of Nations as well as for more liberal elements within Japan. In a growing climate of militarism, anyone speaking against the army actions could easily be labeled as unpatriotic and therefore discredited. The inability of moderate Japanese voices to re-commit to the Washington system at this point heralded a new era for Japanese foreign policy, in which Japan was to become increasingly isolated.

The following chapter further explores the reasons for the failure of moderate voices to prevent the 'Manchurian Incident.' This major turning point in Japanese foreign policy will be detailed more expansively in a later chapter.

7

POST-WAR LIBERALITY
AND THE LEFT LOOKS WEST

I N THE PERIOD after World War I, even the population of
Japan was swept up in the momentum of war weariness,
and this allowed some room for democratic and liberal
ideas on the national stage. The moderate left had made inroads
in the battle for suffrage and representation, but party politics
was not able to capitalize on its gains.

The left looked westward (as opposed to *West*ward) at the
apparent success of the Russian Revolution, but they weren't
the only ones looking. More than a few alarm bells rang within
the military groups. While factional disputes and unbridgeable
gaps existed between sections of the left, conservative forces
in business as well as the military acted to ensure Japanese
insulation from the threat of communism.

By 1920, the Far Eastern branch of the Soviet Comintern
had been located in Shanghai in order to export communist
ideas and programs to China and Japan. Japanese communists
began direct involvement with Russian elements culminating
in the creation of the *Gyomin Kyosanto* or Enlightened People's

Communist Party, and a subsequent distribution of leaflets in various cities in Japan. Soon after that, the first of a long series of arrests was made.

An international conference of communist delegates in 1923 created disunity in the Party over the level of foreign interference likely from subservience to Russian communist policy control. Even at this point, national identity and fear of its loss were significant concerns for the radical left, as they were for the radical right.

Further arrests created even more disruption. However, the foreign source of their leadership did give the Japanese communists an advantage over the moderate leftists, providing an ideological framework and some semblance of party discipline. But the little progress they made was repeatedly punctuated by further mass arrests, followed by mob violence, martial law, and the murder of several radicals by police.

By 1924, total union membership was concentrated in two main groups of associated unions, one comprising some thirty-five unions, with a total membership of 20,000, and the other comprising thirty-two unions, with approximately 12,500 members.[64]

Several attempts were made to disband, reform, and reconfigure groups within the radical left. Although the numbers of participants were not big in national terms, this clearly was a movement with serious intentions. In 1925, the main social-democratic elements combined in the formation of the *Shakai Minshuto,* or Social Mass Party, with a leadership from such notable moderate intellectuals as Yoshino Sakuzo and several others. The three basic tenets of the new party are cited in Scalapino as follows:[65]

---

[64] Scalapino, Robert. A. *Democracy and the Party Movement In Pre-War Japan: The Failure of the First Attempt.* Berkeley: University of California Press, 1953, P327.

[65] Ibid P331

1. Firmly believing that the basis for setting up healthy livelihood conditions for the nation-people lies in the creation of a political and economic system, which has its base in the working class, we pledge the realization of this.
2. Recognizing that healthy livelihood conditions of the nation-people are damaged by the production and distribution laws of capitalism, we pledge the reform of these by legal methods.
3. We reject both the presently-established political parties, which represent the privileged classes and the extremist parties that ignore the process of 'social evolution.'

This party, perhaps more than any other, attempted to advance socialist democracy and parliamentary representation of the working class in the pre-war era, but it too was subject to internal dissent and on-going factionalism. By 1926, there were five national leftist parties and many smaller district parties.

The protracted story of the fragmented communist parties and their unhappy relationship with the Soviet policy dictators is very complex and beyond the scope of this chapter, but the few references given here can serve to demonstrate the presence of a muscular and determined resistance to Japanese ultranationalism over several decades.

By 1928, there was an attempt by the moderate left to forge some sense of unity in preparation for the elections to be held that year, but the squabbles continued, and unity eluded them throughout the campaign. This was the first election since the Universal Suffrage law, but voters were faced not with one unified proletarian party, but four of them, and a guaranteed failure.

Largely because of 'wedge politics,' the lower economic classes failed to vote for any of the labor parties in any significant number. Of the eighty-eight leftist candidates who ran for election, only eight were elected. This powerful defeat was repeated in the 1930 election. The continued existence of the extreme left enabled the nationalists to marginalize the moderates, and it became easy to 'divide and conquer.'

The Right was able to capitalize on public dissatisfaction with party politics and on unrest directed against Westernism and internationalism. At their most dynamic, they were seeking to "combine a program of drastic social and economic reform along socialist lines with a nationalist platform of race consciousness and foreign expansion."[66] For reasons given earlier, it then became possible and expedient for some members of the radical left to merge into what was really the radical right.

The Left in Retreat

The 1932 election, under the cloud of the Manchurian War, reduced the representation of the left even further. This defeat was sufficient to cause the two main leftist parties, the *Shakai Minshuto* and the *Zenkoku Rono Taishuto,* to merge into a new party called *Shakai Taishuto*, or Social Mass Party. This party attempted to represent moderate leftist elements and unions until its dissolution in 1940. It represented anti-capitalist, anti-communist, and anti-fascist agendas, but even in expressing their goals in this way, the party seems to have been reactive, even negative, and certainly on the back foot.

In looking at these decades, we are given reason to wonder how much support the West offered to the moderate left in its attempt to control the radical right and militarism in general. The consensus seems to be that there was no support.

American strategists seemed to equate all leftist movements with communism, how ever moderate their aims. The only

---

[66] Ibid P344

active outside support against militarism in Japan came from the Soviets, whose communism was also militaristic. In effect, the decline of moderate forces left Japan having to play the role of the inevitable enemy, whether fascist or communist.

The Anarchist Movement

Like the communists, the various anarchist groups represented a very broad spectrum of beliefs and strategies. For some, assassination was an acceptable method of operation, while for others, pacifism was pursued, sometimes at great personal risk and without compromise.

In researching this, it is difficult to find much, in reference to the various forms of resistance to Japanese militarism, and most of that which has been written concerns the communists. Anarchism was a part of a global idealism, which directly threatened capitalism and formed a part of the radical left that unwittingly and unwillingly provided the springboard for militarism to win the battle for control of the Japanese government.

Whereas the communists were aligned with the Soviets and their military machine, the anarchist groups in Japan never became aligned to other nations and were constant in their opposition to militarism. The anarchist opinion of the liberal left was as dismissive as was their view of the communists. They took the position that the liberal left was compromised by adopting the anomalous policy of accepting capitalism, yet opposing military force in the creation of new markets, which a Marxist viewpoint would see as an inevitable consequence of capitalism.

There were many important players in the movement, but we will concern ourselves with just a few here. One of the earliest foundation anarchists in Japan was Kotoku Shusui, who was a dedicated campaigner against the Russo-Japanese War. His newspaper columns did not last very long but had an on-going influence into the early century. In 1926, two nationwide federations were established, *Kokushoku Seinen Renmei*, or the Black Youth League, and *Zenkoku Rodo Kumai*, or National Libertarian Federation of Labor Unions.

These organizations published newspapers between the mid 1920s and the mid 1930s. The Libertarian Federation example presents an anarchist perspective very coherently.

The following extract is a translation attributed to John Crump, a well-known British socialist and academic in Japanese studies. It was part of a paper presented at the annual conference of the British Association for Japanese Studies in Sheffield, England, in April 1991. Sections are taken from a November 1931 edition of the Federation newspaper, *Jiyu Rengo Shinbun*.

> "The Japanese militarists have mobilized their army to China on the pretext 'for the peace of the Orient' or 'to defend the Japanese people in China.' They always use, whenever a state crisis occurs, such beautiful expressions as 'For Our Fatherland' or 'For Justice' and try to stir up the people's patriotism. But what is the fatherland? For whom does it exist? Never forget that all states exist only for the wealthy. It is the same with war. War brings injury or death to the young men of the poor and hunger and cold to their aged parents and young brothers and sisters. But to the wealthy it brings enormous riches and honor.
>
> "The true cause of the mobilization to China is none other than the ambition of the Japanese capitalist class and military to conquer Manchuria. Japan has its own Monroe doctrine. Japanese capitalism cannot develop, or even survive, without Manchuria. That is why its government is inclined to risk anything so as not to

lose its many privileges in China. Therefore it has approved the enormous expense of the mobilization, despite the fact that it is experiencing a deficit in the current year's income of the state treasury. American capital has flowed into China in larger and larger amounts. This represents an enormous menace to the Japanese capitalist class. In other words, now Japan is forced to oppose American capital in China. In fact this is the direct cause of the mobilization.

"…The military have engineered the opportunity to demonstrate and establish their strength, which has been weakened of late by disarmament and pacifist public opinion. Of course, a secret agreement has been reached between the military and the capitalists, because they both belong to the ruling class.

"In this situation, what must we do? The Communists say 'Defend and come to the aid of the Chinese revolution!' But who will benefit in China when Japanese power is totally eliminated from that country? It will be none other than the newly rising Chinese bourgeoisie and the capitalists of other countries. We must keenly observe and criticize all that takes place. In the face of war, we must not make the mistake, which our comrade Kropotkin and others made during the World War. Of course, we opposed the mobilization. But we found that merely one-sided opposition is a very feeble response. The sole method to eradicate war from our world is for us, acting as the popular masses, to reject it in all countries simultaneously. We must cease military production, refuse military service and disobey the officers. Complete international unity of anarchists would signal our victory, not only economically but in the war against war…"

This article comprehensively expresses the core philosophy of the group. They were profoundly idealistic and internationalist but were subject to the same divisions and factions that fractured the moderate left. In criticizing Japanese militarism, they claimed its actions to be inevitable and consistent with all capitalist states.

This point of view, incidentally, was not verified by subsequent history, with post-war Japan becoming both economically powerful and pacifist, although the viewpoint can arguably be seen to hold true in the case of some others.

The article makes the point that the Manchurian Incident was not just an action by an army out of control but an expression of the needs of Japanese capitalists to secure resources and create markets. This may be true on one level and false on another, and the writer does allude to this.

At a governmental level, it does seem that the actions in Manchuria were a significant embarrassment, causing a loss of face to the Prime Minister. On the other hand, the powers underpinning the government were tied both to the military and to the industrial/commercial sectors in a back room, old boys' club sort of way, behind the public face of power.

Interestingly, the article identifies the clash in China as being a clash of economic interests between Japan and America. In this they make no distinction between the actions of a democracy and the actions of Japan under an Emperor, the economic forces within both states dictating their actions more than their means of government. Both were aggressive in pursuing and securing their economic interests. Obviously, a conservative, even liberal view would be that America was acting strategically and in support of China, and not as an economic aggressor, but this may be hard to defend as a proposition when the events of the 1930s are examined.

The anarchists stood in opposition to the Naval Arms Limitation Treaty, and even the League of Nations was dubbed 'the International Capitalist League.' Many of their pronouncements were brave, even foolhardy, given the government reaction to criticism. Many were arrested at demonstrations. Members were known to infiltrate the military in order to subvert discipline.

There were reports of anarchists being court-martialled for refusing to obey orders. They also organized strikes in facilities such as munitions factories. In general, they were so opposed to the very core of capitalist statism that they were virtually written out of history.

A later result of these decades of turmoil was an attempted coup d'état in February 1936. This involved 1,400 officers and men of the Army, attacking the Prime Minister's residence, the Tokyo Police Board, and several private houses belonging to officials. It is likely that this incident was inspired by fascist ideology, specifically the publication of *The Fundamental Principles for Reconstructing Japan* by Kita Ikki in 1919, referred to below.

The consolidation of military power by 1936 involved active participation by many of the old economic and political elites. There was an element of coercion in all of this, but the creation of a muscular military state did hold the promise of an economic potential for some.

The cumulative effect of domestic unrest in and out of politics only served to emphasize the insecurity and fears among civilian conservatives, and this allowed the perception of military groups and their dogmas as a potential shield against chaos. There were few viable alternatives offering a coherent vision, and this encouraged a general conformity and concurrence, but never to the point of unanimity around a single figure or group.

Fractured Politics and the Rise of a New Nationalism

Writing soon after the war in 1953, Scalapino considered that even had the Japanese won any sort of victory in the Pacific War, their political system would have fractured anyway, because despite the decline of the party system there was no great unanimity of purpose among the elites, and, he claimed, no clear mass support.[67] He maintained that the imminent collapse of the parties "was for a time forestalled by political forces more powerful than they." Parts of the bureaucracy and a section of Inner Court officials maneuvered in such a fashion as to delay the parties' complete capitulation. The maintenance of a public sphere was considered as a desirable component of a modern state.

On the other hand, the phenomenon of nationalism was one of the factors contributing to the demise of the democratic process due to the ways in which the Japanese example evolved in comparison to the earlier-developing models of Europe. For example, nationalism in England came to be associated with the advance of democracy for historical reasons. As power gradually shifted from an absolute monarch towards greater representation, the middle class associated the parallel growth of national prestige with democratic values.

The Japanese nationalist movement, unlike some in the West, grew out of agrarian-military elements, not a comfortable class who saw hope in national success and wealth in democracy. In Japan, the commercial class was weak in every respect except in economic terms, enabling the Japanese agrarian forces to raise a nationalist movement to counter the

---

[67] Scalapino, Robert. A. *Democracy and the Party Movement In Pre-War Japan: The Failure of the First Attempt.* Berkeley: University of California Press, 1953, P347.

inroads of commercialization by emphasizing the superiority of their own primitive institutions.[68]

Their nationalism drew on the soldier-peasant union, Shintoism, and the divinity of the Emperor, and these foundations persisted, finding nationalist purpose both in anti-foreign sentiments and in the 'mission' to create 'an Asia for Asians.'

As the century progressed, nationalism also came to include anti-Western, anti-capitalist, and anti-democratic sentiments in the bundle of things against which they could rebel. Through all this, they never adopted the 'state nationalism' of the business class that was generally supportive of democracy, if only because it was seen to be subject to foreign influence.

The growing centrality of capitalism helped produce a new variant of nationalism, casting off some of its agrarian elements while maintaining its link with rural-military forces. This really complex and fragmented path towards a totalitarian style of nationalism began in earnest after World War I, but for the sake of staying on topic, we will examine only a fraction of the many societies and individuals concerned, concentrating on several that represent significant threads in the tangled web of Japanese pre-war politics.

The Rosokai (The Society of Mature Men) was established in October 1918 and, although never a major force in itself, several groups that formed from it did so under the guidance of two important figures. The Yuzonsha (Society to Preserve the National Essence) began as a fragment of Rosokai around 1921 under the leadership of Kita Ikki and Okawa Shumei, both of whom were to become living symbols of Japanese militarism.

Okawa had become fiercely anti-Western after the 1924 US Immigration Act and had published a book in 1925, Asia, Europe and Japan, in which he foretold the inevitability of a war between the United States and Japan. He was particularly

---

[68] Ibid P349

forceful in advocating the emancipation of the Asian nations from Western domination, under the leadership of Japan.

Kita is well known for his famous book, *The fundamental Principles for the Reconstruction of Japan* (or *A General Outline for...* depending on translation of *Nihon kaizo hoantaiko*). Ikki was an egocentric and impetuous personality who probably came closest to being a father figure of the Japanese radical right. Initially influenced by Chinese revolutionary thinkers, his path to radical nationalism was via socialism. Wishing to create a 'true' socialism with the primacy of the state as a central theme, "his writings were imbued with that heroic interpretation of history which was so important in Western Fascism. He played upon the thesis that an inspired man or group could change the history of a country and of the world."[69]

Nihon kaizo hoanaiko described a utopian vision of tight, nationalist government. The plan of action called for the Emperor to suspend the constitution, dissolve the Diet, and declare martial law. The Emperor would thereby demonstrate his centrality to the government of the state, and a military junta would be established to redistribute wealth and land more equitably. The old elites would be swept away and a new council would sit in support of the Emperor.

Ikki put forward foreign policy ideas that were aggressively expansionist.

> "Japan was to undertake the task of fostering the immigration of Chinese and Indians to Australia, and also Chinese and Koreans to Siberia. Eventually the Japanese reform measures could be extended to these areas, and with the unification of races would come an equalization of standards. A special administrative structure would be used to carry out reforms overseas.

---

[69] Ibid P354

But since Japan's objectives of helping India attain independence, maintaining security in China and occupation of South Pacific islands would affront the West, particularly the United States, a large naval force was also justified."[70]

Thus, expansionism is expressed in matter-of-fact terms, with a sense of mission, purpose, and moral 'rightness' that equals similar, previous Western expansion in its presumptions.

Pan- Asianism

In combining the redistribution of wealth with chest-thumping foreign expansion in his platform, Kita Ikki appealed to many levels of discontented elements within Japan. This kind of thinking fed into what became known as the Pan-Asian movement.

The transition into Pan-Asianism involves some 'creative' realism in which embellishment and repetition give the appearance of truth to an impossible contradiction. In this, it predicts the modern idea of forcing a people to be free and democratic by occupying their country. The rationale at home is expressed in terms of defensive needs. But in the Japanese case, they took the divine relationship of the nation to its Emperor as a starting point, enabling them to imply in colonial policy that, on the one hand, they could claim racial superiority, and yet, on the other hand, they proclaimed racial brotherhood and union of all Asian peoples.[71]

---

[70] Tanaka Sogoro. *The Source of Japanese Fascism- The Thought and Career of Kita Ikki,* Tokyo 1949, P245 cited in Scalapino, Robert. A, *Democracy and the Party Movement In Pre-War Japan: The Failure of the First Attempt.* Berkeley: University of California Press, 1953, P356.

[71] Duus P. *Economic Dimensions of Meiji Imperialism,* in Myers, Ramon H., and Peattie Mark M. (ed) . *The Japanese Colonial Empire, 1895–1945.* Princeton, NJ: Princeton University Press, 1984, P122)

This contradiction was not lost on other nations but became entrenched as a quasi-religious justification for leadership. Leadership was then able to evolve into other forms of control. In both the Japanese and modern American examples, infrastructure and economic management was imported and imposed from outside.

The Pan-Asian brotherhood also allowed the Japanese government to develop a position of anti-colonialism with regard to Western interests in Southeast Asia, while maintaining the fiction that Japan was not a colonial power.

The Pan-Asianists drew a sense of vindication from the failure of the Japanese race equality proposal at the Paris conference leading to a series of energetic public campaigns. The various pressure groups involved used this momentum to confirm in the public mind the very reasonable proposition that the West was not treating Japan with adequate respect. In this, they seem from our vantage point to have been correct. A view developed of Japan as a 'wronged' nation that should turn from the West and to its Asian brothers.

Parallel to this global-thinking type of group, and with some confusing overlap, the agrarian causes were rekindled in a different branch of the radical nationalist movement. An on-going rural crisis and the continued national dependence on urban business and industry sparked a revitalized agrarian nationalism, demanding the restoration of rural political and economic rights. One of the leading spokesmen for this movement was Gondo Seikyo, whose writings energetically put forward the case for the return of agrarian autonomy and an economy based on traditional rural employment and production. He was very critical of the Prussian-style centralization and bureaucratic controls, appealing to traditional values as well as racial supremacy to counter the perceived evils of Westernism and capitalism. Gondo's establishment of the *Jichi Gakkai*

(Self-Government Institute) in 1920 fostered the creation of other associations pushing similar agendas in rural districts.

In summary, the three main expressions of organized Japanese nationalism up to the 1920s consisted of a conservative establishment movement and two revolutionary movements differing in their emphasis, especially by the rural/urban divide.

The conservative nationalism included several political parties, bureaucratic groups, and military cliques around the ideas of the Meiji constitution and 'national polity.' Although tending towards the anti-democratic, their platforms aimed at only minor changes to the status quo.

The two main revolutionary groups—and this is a significant simplification of the events—were represented by the ideas of Kita Ikki in one case and Gondo Seikyo in the other. Kita emphasized a highly centralized industrial state, while Gondo strove for a decentralized agricultural society, although there were many points of agreement, impossible though that may seem, and membership was fluid.

It is an interesting point that differences between groups were not always ideological, because personality and group dynamics were often the cause of disagreement, rather than points of belief or conviction.

8

THE BEGINNINGS OF THE SHOWA PERIOD

F EELING PARTICULARLY EXPOSED to international economic panic in 1929, and without sufficient natural resources to modernize to the extent felt necessary, Japan was vulnerable to growing anti-Japanese sentiment and disorder in China. The growing presence of Soviet forces in the Far East was also seen as a threat by the military leadership. Power struggles in domestic politics were very de-stabilizing at this point, and while politics in general lost the confidence of the people, it was in direct proportion to the perceived integrity of the military. Yoshimitsu Khan expressed it this way:

"In this context the military began to manipulate its residual command authority which, in the deepening crisis, many were coming to see as invested with an unsullied purity—even a spiritual power. With the first signs of a favorable reception to this cause, the military now not only pursued its own interests but began to expand its sphere into the domestic arena."[72]

The Depression therefore contributed to the rise of the military, if only indirectly. This is not unexpected; tough economic conditions often bring law and order issues to the fore, as well as issues of xenophobia. Two conflicting forces operated in the era.

Speaking very generally, social justice and equity issues may arise from poverty and loss of hope, and this can prod a national agenda to the left. On the other hand, economic insecurity increases susceptibility to fear of 'the other' and suspicion of competitors, with a consequent move to the right. Broader and more complex social and historical factors determine which force gains the ascendant. The tendency to inclusiveness, internationalism, and egalitarianism has been exceptional rather than normal.

In the case of Japan, much of the population sought reassurance, hope, and national pride in the military. A change to an offensive position, independent of government policy, produced a perception of their military decisiveness in Manchuria, paradoxically providing a sense of safety at home.

While the rest of the world looked on in horror as parts of the Japanese Army flexed its muscles in Manchuria in 1931, at home they seemed to offer confidence and optimism to a public jaded by political ineptitude. Known euphemistically as the 'Manchurian Incident,' this action was really an invasion of north- eastern China by the Japanese Kwantung Army.

In need of an excuse for military action, the Japanese bombed the South Manchurian Railway line and promptly blamed the Chinese Army. They responded to the provocative

[72] Khan, Yoshimitsu. *Inoue Kowashi and the Dual Images of the Emperor of Japan,* Pacific Affairs vol 71, issue 2, University of British Columbia. Gale Group, 1998, P221

bombing by invading and occupying Manchuria, despite Prime Ministerial statements maintaining the Japanese position involved no plans for expansion. The situation around which this event unfolded are dealt with in greater depth in the following chapter.

How is it possible that a civil government can represent certain ideas internationally, and yet these ideas are contradicted by the actions of its own army? The question requires a closer look at the duality already mentioned in the design of the constitution and also the concept of supreme command.

The core idea at the center of Japanese militarism was this notion of *iaku no gunmu*, or supreme command. As a concept, it was embedded with sacred and mysterious qualities for militarists, and it represented absolute control of the Empire's armed forces as it was vested within the constitution. Articles 11 and 12 determine that the Emperor has the prerogative of the sole jurisdiction over the armed forces and the Empire.

The authority described in Article 11 is called *gunreiken* or authority of military command, while that in Article 12 is called the *gunseiken* or authority of military administration. Combined, they formed the *gunjitaiken* or supreme military authority.

In many parliamentary systems, this power is based in a ministry that is responsible to parliament, and which decides the size, training, and deployment of the army, navy, and air forces. In the Japanese system, the separate, direct relationship between the Emperor and the armed forces was explained as essential to the prosecution of a successful war. Any interference from the Diet or by the cabinet would seriously impair the efficiency of the military forces.

In common language, *iaku no gunmu* means "the military affairs of the curtain and screen,"[73] alluding to the profoundly

---

[73] Colegrove, K. W. *Militarism in Japan*. World Peace Foundation, 1936, P18.

private and unique power of command shared between the Emperor and his military advisers.

An example of the seriousness of this esteemed relationship is as follows. The young officers who assassinated Premier Inukai in 1932 were given sentences of four years imprisonment. In contrast, the would-be assassins of Premier Okada in 1936 were given death sentences as well as popular condemnation because, although they were unsuccessful in their task, they disobeyed the Emperor's command to surrender immediately.

The Emperor's military camp and his civil government were therefore separated by law, and if the Emperor really had the sort of powers and capacities imagined in the idealized language of the constitution, and the quasi-spiritual power attributed to him by his subjects, there might not have been a problem.

The reality, however, fell far short of this. Fact and fantasy diverged in the actual humanity of the Emperor. Rather than two arms of government united through him, Japan and the world had to deal with a semi-autonomous military with its own agenda. An interesting complication in this is that ministers for war and the navy straddled both arms of government, with soldier-politicians having a unique opportunity to influence the character of the civil arm. This became more than an interesting complication as the 1930s progressed.

It is not difficult to imagine that the dual arms of government were sometimes in conflict, but as the pre-war decade advanced, the constitutional weapons available to the military made any conflict less evenly balanced. Because it had been legislated in 1898 that civilian government could never control the military, and because the ministers of the army and navy straddled both arms of government, they had the capacity to bring down a cabinet. Having done so, they also had the power to dictate the terms of a new government.

This happened on several occasions but only when the army and navy worked together, and there is one famous occasion when they didn't. The 1930 London Naval Conference not only brought tensions to a head between the services but also within them. In this, the navy failed to block the cabinet in its co-operation with the great naval powers in limiting world naval strength. There was disagreement even among naval officials, and the result was a victory for representational government, perhaps its swan song. Shortly afterwards, Premier Hamaguchi was shot and died of wounds.

Just as the military could and did bring down cabinets, they could also influence the composition of them. This occurred in the Saito (1932–1934) and Okada (1934–1936) cabinets. In 1936, they also blocked Premier Hirota's choice of three or more members. They refused to permit Shigera Yoshida to become minister of foreign affairs because of his relationship to a family known to be staunch defenders of the parliamentary system.

They also prevented the appointment of Naoshi Ohara as Minister of Justice because of his role in pushing for the prosecution of the assassins of Premier Inukai. Another appointment was blocked because the candidate was editor of a progressive newspaper, *the Tokyo Asahi*.

This dual form of government must have been alarming for other countries in their efforts to have diplomatic relations with the civil authorities, while also trying to predict the future actions of the military.

In media terms, the military found plenty of popular support. In contrast to the *Asahi Shimbun*, the *Yomiuri Shimbun* began as a small circulation paper struggling with a declining market share, and it found the solution to its survival in glorifying military aggression in Korea and in Manchuria. The causes of military adventurism were found to be capable of inspiring a generation, and generating sales.

During the 1930s, 'thought control' became a very real phenomenon when groups of right-wing extremists raided and closed bookshops and news agencies with tacit encouragement from the military. Further restrictive media laws were enacted after the beginning of the war with China in April 1938, effectively the start of the Pacific war.

When assessing the impacts of these curbs on the media, it is easy to overlook the relative sophistication of the various groups in the population. Although Japan has always enjoyed high literacy rates in world terms, the mass of people in Japan of the period, as in the West, were unlikely to be very critical of the material placed before them in the media. Japanese soldiers were often drawn from poor rural areas, especially during the depression, and had very limited experience of the world.

As we have seen, in this period, negative controls of the media persisted, but a particular bureaucratic relationship also encouraged positive programs designed to meet the propaganda needs of various governmental arms. These were called Inter-Ministerial Control Committees, and they were instrumental in formulating and implementing details of policy. In them, military officers and bureaucrats were able to revolutionize the regulation of the mass media.

By means of 'consultations,' media outlets were encouraged to meet the needs of the committees. This was subtle on one level, but was very specific in being able to 'suggest' descriptions of subjects and events in acceptable ways. The film industry, for example was *assisted* in the inspiration of greater dedication to national goals, and newspapers became *responsible* for improving public morale.

Many chauvinist groups worked in a clandestine way to develop imperialism and totalitarianism. Several involved people of wealth and privilege working behind closed doors to further goals not compatible with representational government. One example was the *Genyosha* or Black Ocean

Society, which had as its aim the development of a continental policy. It received secret support from various members of government and was involved in terrorist activities in several regional areas.

Another group, the *Kokuryukai* or Black Dragon Society is said to have been active in making the Russo-Japanese War possible. Out of many societies in the early 20th Century, the *Yusonshu* was formed to unite the various factions in society to "fulfill Japan's great historical mission in Asia."[74] They recognized that aggressive foreign policy required unity at home, and they focused on the emperor as the central point of that unity.

They held that "modern capitalism should be disciplined by absolute nationalism" and that "revolutionized Japan will cause the white race to retreat from Asia."[75] Yet other groups sought to rationalize the 'independence' of Manchuria and China under the 'guidance ' of Japan.

In 1931, a new party was launched called *Dai Nippon Seisanto*, or Great Japan Production Party, calling for the usual nationalist things but also a massive increase in the size of the military forces, the abandonment of all arms limitations agreements and the end of white supremacy. Another group, The Society of the Spirit of Great Japan, had a long record of violence against workers meetings and against unions. Its stated aims included the promotion of harmony between capital and labor.

During the 1930s, The *Kokuhonsha* or National Foundation Society advanced the case for fascism, specifically to allow Baron Hiranuma to become Premier. He had been very successful in public life and had been associated with *Kokuhonsha* since 1919.

Hiranuma was instrumental in Japan's withdrawal from the League of Nations, the abrogation of the Washington Naval Treaty, and the signing of the Anti-Comintern Pact. After the

[74] Ibid P29

[75] Ibid P29

abortive military coup of February 1936, he became president of the Privy Council. He was prime minister for eight months in 1939, resigning after the Russo-German pact was signed. He continued as president of the Privy Council and was home minister in 1940.

Ultra-nationalist Momentum After 1930

In the period leading up to the Manchurian Incident in 1931, nationalism gained momentum as discontent grew in response to the corruption, rural poverty, and the depression as outlined previously. Whereas in Germany and Italy a single mass movement ultimately acted to unify disparate agents of discontent against socialism and selected out-groups and for a coherent national agenda, in Japan, the period saw continued factional competition in a fluid morass of political hyperbole.

We can identify three major trends emerging. First, the proliferation of popular nationalist societies persisted. Second, we can identify a merging of civil and military forces and, third, by 1931, there was a significant increase in terrorist activity and attempted revolution.

The *Kokuhonsha* was perhaps the most coherent and influential society to emerge in the 1920s. Under the influence of Hiranuma, it went on to represent the interests of many of the country's most important and influential military, bureaucratic, and ministerial leaders. The membership also included *zaibatsu* representatives.[76]

---

[76] Some of the important names include: Suzuki Kisaburo, Field Marshalls Togo Heihachiro and Uehara Yusaki; Generals Ugaki Kazushige, Kato Kanji, Araki Sadao, Mazaki Jinzaburo, Koiso Kuniiaki, and Hata Shinji; and Admirals Arima Ryokitsu and Saito Makoto. Zaibatsu included from Mitsui, Ikeda Seihin, hara Yoshimichi, and from Yasuda, Yuki Toyotaro. From Scalapino, Robert, A. *Democracy and the Party Movement in Pre-War Japan: The Failure of the First Attempt.* Berkeley: University of California Press, 1953, P360.

This was a complex alliance of people and opinions, including some apparently irreconcilable differences evidenced in the fact that the radical nationalists marked some of its members for death, while others were actually affiliated with the same nationalists. Despite this, however, the agenda of the organization symbolized the future power orientation of Japan.

In this period 'patriotic' labor unions were also being formed in an effort to bring the masses into the national socialist 'camps,' but they were never successful in this and, instead, the power base increasingly developed from the middle class including small industrialists, contractors, shop owners, small land owners, and lower-class officials, especially those in rural areas.[77]

There had always been a close association between selected top generals, admirals, and high-ranking officials in the bureaucracy, but through the *Kokuhonsha,* the significance of the mingling of powerbrokers took on a new significance.

Yet another type of productive alliance also developed between civilians and military men in the radical nationalist movement. We have seen how conscription brought military experience and its associated values to the poor rural communities and that the military presented some of the only opportunities for advancement by merit rather than by birth.

These factors, combined with the ethics of self-sacrifice and fanaticism, made a fertile seedbed for hatred of those who proposed disarmament and engagement with the West. Against this background, we can understand the potential for influence of these young soldiers and officers, by figures such

---

[77] Maruyama Masao. *Nihon Fascist no shiso to undo* (Japanese Fascist Thought and Action) Sec 2, in *Sonjo shiso to zettaishugi* (Revere the Emperor - Oust the Barbarian Thought and Absolutism), Tokyo 1947, P48, cited in Scalapino, Robert. A. *Democracy and the Party Movement In Pre-War Japan: The Failure of the First Attempt.* Berkeley: University of California Press, 1953, P362.

as Kita, whose personal charisma had a tangible effect on many future military-political leaders. One outcome was the 'Young Officers' movement and, despite constant army-navy rivalry, sufficient commonality existed among them to add weight to the general military influence in politics by 1930.

By this time, a group of young rightist radicals had gained tacit support for extreme action from some fairly senior military figures. With the radicals gaining support at the expense of the conservatives, a fundamental shift occurred, giving them the initiative in a new level of challenge to democratic politics.

We need to keep in mind the context for this. The world was struggling with a deepening depression, the Japanese rural economy in particular was receding in importance and was almost economically insolvent, and party politics was fragmented and in disarray.

Some historians attribute the enormous volatility and violence of the period between 1931 and 1937 as an expression of agrarian frustration and unrest. The young officers came through the conscription system from very poor rural areas and had very little to lose. Their explosive anger at the poverty and the failure of the rural economy was focused on business interests and representatives of foreign ideas perceived to be at the core of their troubles.

The parties were at the heart of their grievances, as they represented so many of the interests that were symbols of injustice. The period is littered with plots, attempted coups d'état, and assassinations.

The event that became known as the 'March Incident' in 1931 marked a major turning point in the Japanese political experience. This was a plot that involved members of a group called *Sakurakai* but also included various high ranking military officers. The plan was to overthrow civilian rule by violent means and install General Ugaki Kazushige as military leader. The project was actually abandoned before it began when senior military people made it clear that sufficient support would not be forthcoming.

Okawa had created the plot, and it is said that around three hundred bombs had been acquired for the purpose. The planned coup d'état heralded the beginning of the militarist era. As they took a more offensive position, the parties lost membership and support. Military press censorship intensified, and writers who displeased the military were threatened with violence.[78]

Following the outbreak of violence in Manchuria, pledges were given by the top-ranking military men that "discipline would be restored" and only a limited number of troops would be used against the Chinese. Some young Foreign Office officials were in support of the army, sabotaging efforts in opposition to it. The cabinet was split in the turmoil that followed with only Shidehara and Inoue Junnosuke, Minister of Finance, openly defiant of the War Office.

When the army moved large numbers of troops contrary to its promises and without Imperial sanction, Premier Wakatsuki had no alternative but to authorize payment for the expenses incurred. The opposition party Seikyukai openly supported the military aggression.

It was in this setting of confusion that the 'October Incident' was revealed. The planners of the 'March Incident' had reinvented the plot this time to assassinate the whole cabinet during a meeting, with other power-grabbing measures outlined previously. The plan was discovered in time, and the whole matter brushed under the military carpet with a few light sentences given to ring leaders.

The fear created by these plots brought a great deal of power to the militarists, strengthening the feeling that only

---

[78] IMTFE, Document No. 110500, Exhibit No. 140 (Affidavit of Maeda Tamon, editorial writer for the Asahi Shimbun, 1928–1938) cited in Scalapino, P366.

the military could control the military. Members of the Inner Court Circle rationalized that some appointments be made of 'conservative' military figures to help prevent revolution. This mindset is crucial in our understanding of the creation of Japanese governments throughout the decade leading up to the attack on Pearl Harbor.

The conscription system and the reversal of rural fortunes in society together had provided the motivations as well as the manpower for a revolution. The Court Circle must have been very nervous that a really dynamic leader might emerge from among the many groups of violently dissatisfied radicals. A revolution would be very destructive, but worse, there was no way of predicting the outcome.

If there is one point that any Western reader should be able to find empathy with, it is this: The Inner Court Circle demonstrated repeatedly over subsequent years that they would do whatever was necessary to maintain a government that was capable of keeping order. Japan was never to be left exposed and vulnerable like the many other Asian peoples who had become tools of the West. History had shown with great clarity up to this point that in the absence of strong, effective central government, Asian people fell under Western control or internal unrest.

Not surprisingly, the series of coups and incidents served to split the established parties and move politics into a more nationalist and radical direction. The left-wing parties were crippled by dissent, defection, and disillusionment, with the last remaining party of the left, the Social Mass Party (*Shakai Minshuto*), after years of opposition to fascism, communism, and capitalism finally supporting the China war, if in a dispirited way.

This left the Japan Proletariat Party (*Nihon Musanto*), a socialist group led by the likes of Suzuki Mosaburo, but the government forcibly disbanded it in 1937.

There was an element of fatigue in the dissolution of the left, but also a strong element of disillusionment. Robert Scalapino noted that "prominent among the reasons for recanting given by democratic socialists and communists was their disillusionment with the 'false' internationalism of democracy and communism."

He went on to emphasize the impact of foreign nationalism on the rise of Japanese nationalism: "They pointed to Russian and American discrimination against Japanese fishermen and workers, Western imperialism against the Asians, and Russian imperialism under the guise of the Comintern."[79]

The role of the Emperor as 'Supreme Commander' was established and the brief flirtation with party politics appeared to be over. How ever hard Inoue had tried to keep the role of the Emperor above the rough and tumble of politics, the direct relationship with the army was ultimately too powerful to allow the legislature to steer the country on a liberal course.

It is worth noting that it was about three hundred years before this that the English parliament challenged the divine right of the English King to rule alone. Although Cromwell's victory shed a lot of English blood, from that time, neither King nor Army has been able to sustain a challenge to the people's right to be ruled by a parliament. The containment of regal power was later cemented in the bloodless intervention,[80] which saw William of Orange installed as the first really 'modern' monarch.

In the 1930s, the checks and balances available between most Westminster style legislatures, judiciaries, and armed forces were not available to the Japanese. Their evolution into

---

[79] Scalapino, Robert. A. *Democracy and the Party Movement In Pre-War Japan: The Failure of the First Attempt.* Berkeley: University of California Press, 1953, P374.

[80] It could be regarded as an invasion by invitation of parliament.

modernity was made quickly in historical terms and not over the course of centuries.

Democracy was never more than a fondly held dream even for the most Western-looking of liberals, who had been made to appear unpatriotic in their attempts to be heard. What transpired was a convergence of factors that seem in retrospect to have been inevitable.

The layers of constitutional government that stretched over the ruling, vested interests were gradually drawn back, peeled like an onion, until a streamlined military and industrial machine was revealed. This seemed tailor-made to build economic power in perfect pragmatic harmony with military expansion and an ethos built upon the myth of racial superiority and a quasi-religious mission.

9
CHINA EMERGING

THERE HAD BEEN a steady growth of nationalism inside China during the 1920s and 1930s, challenging Japan's special position there while anti-Japanese sentiment grew in intensity. In effect, this played into the hands of Japanese militarists who were able to capitalize on the view that legitimate Japanese interests in China were being threatened and that Japanese residents were in danger. The people were not told that a program of imperialistic expansion was taking place in China, but that the Japanese army was simply protecting Japanese rights and eliminating radical Chinese groups who were standing in the way of peace.

Despite efforts by the League of Nations, Japan gained complete control over Manchuria in 1931, setting up a puppet state called Manchukuo with an act that would be described euphemistically now as 'regime change.' Following this, further expansion was made into the Chinese province of Jehol, the effect of which was to put some two-hundred million Chinese people under effective Japanese rule. This heralded the new phase in Japanese expansion and military power, occurring within a context of the collapse of centralized state control and widespread political disorder in China.

The Japanese people had never known a war fought on their own territory; for them, the terrible destruction and human carnage of war was only ever represented through the purifying filters of official propaganda designed by the militarists and sensationalist coverage in newsreels and the popular press.

The 'adventures' against Russia and China were presented as a succession of glorious manly deeds, of sacrifices for the sake of honor and the nation, and in every sense, an opportunity for men of loyalty. It is arguable whether the build up to the start of the China war was based on the need for defense, but it was presented as such.

We will be looking at China from several viewpoints because, like most of the causal factors of the Pacific War, the Japanese actions in Manchuria were grounded in a context or continuum involving other powers. We have seen that Japan defeated Russia in 1905, and this was a significant redefinition of the balance of world power. The culmination of that war took place at Mukden, the capital of Manchuria.

During the battle for Mukden, over 26,000 Russians were killed and over 40,000 Japanese were killed or injured, but the Japanese prevailed. This action in this place saw the birth of the Japanese Kwantung Army, which had the job of protecting Japan's Manchurian possessions, and which later became very aggressive in pursuing those interests within Japan itself.

By 1930, Manchuria had therefore been a significant frontier against the Russians for over twenty-five years at the cost of a great deal of blood. It is significant that the traditional enemy was also 'foreign,' not Chinese. During the following years, the Russian Revolution did nothing to reduce the Japanese conception of Manchuria as a security threat, as much as an opportunity to survive and develop.

How the Japanese should deal safely with the challenges and opportunities in that frontier was hotly debated politically at home and militarily within the armed forces in Manchuria. The inability of the Japanese to reconcile the agendas represented by these two separate debates could be seen as one of the most important issues of the 1930s within China, within Japan and, ultimately, across the entire Pacific Rim. The inability or disinclination of the West to assist Japan in this compounded the failure of Japanese diplomacy.

Eventually, this 'Manchurian Incident' of 1931 enabled the various factions of the governing circle to coalesce around the *Tosei-ha*, the 'control faction,' which was later led by General (later Prime Minister) Tojo Hideki. The fatal streamlining of the powerbrokers into a reasonably coherent force meant that it was finally possible to reconcile the divergent streams of domestic and international policy for the single military agenda. But the 1930s were to throw up plenty of deviations from simple militarism as the Japanese relationship with China became more complex, and Japan reassessed its relationship with democracy and the West.

Assassinations of prominent figures provided a very real impetus for socialists, communists, and anarchists to recant their beliefs and devote themselves, at least outwardly, to the service and veneration of the Emperor. As soon as blood had been spilled in China for the Emperor, the nation owed a 'blood debt' to the war dead, and dissent became much more difficult.

Japan's actions in China did not take place in isolation. China has its own enormous story, and during the early 20th Century, the Chinese struggle for a stable, central, and national government involved a redefinition of its relationships with what were then called 'The Powers.'

We have seen that, after the Russo-Japanese War, Japan bristled with a new found sense of importance as it proclaimed its arrival in joining the great powers. In this it was a bit like Bismarck's newly unified Germany only a generation earlier. The latecomer to the club of Imperial powers was insistent on her rights to treaties and concessions and the acquisition of spheres of influence.

This early position on the world stage was a self-conscious attempt to re-make Japan in the image of the Western Powers as they were in the 19th Century. After a time, this aim seemed to sit uncomfortably within the developing nationalism in Japan, first because Western Imperialism was changing, and second because the Japanese saw the continuing Western cultural influence in Asia as an issue against which they alone could make a stand.

Rather than simply having an exploitative share of China in combination with other powers, it was felt that Japan could protect and defend China while, at the same time, avail herself of the markets and resources available there. It is difficult not to see this attitude as self-serving from a Western perspective, but it seems less so from the perspective of Japanese survival as an autonomous nation, wishing to be surrounded by sympathetic nations governed with Asian rather than Western values. Indeed, the expression of this type of foreign policy has been typical in the West throughout the post-war era, with covert and overt destabilization of 'unacceptable' governments by agencies of the United States, most particularly in the countries of South America. It is difficult to defend either example, but it is easy to understand both.

We will see that the American attitude in the 1920s was remarkably balanced and humanitarian with regard to the Chinese difficulties and may, in fact, represent an idealistic high-point in US foreign policy. But it had the luxury of geographical distance in its perspective: China wasn't in America's backyard, and its interests then were more commercial than strategic.

The nature of Japanese capitalism changed, too. Beginning as primarily commercial activity super-imposed on the traditional rural economy, it was transformed fairly quickly into an industrial economy. The early stages of industrial expansion were funded by capital from London and New York, but it evolved to rely on contributions from areas under Japanese control.

Japan could never escape the fact that its capitalism developed late and had to develop quickly. In a parallel sense, Japan came late to Imperialism, too, and the pie was already sliced and on several other plates. The treaty port system was an elaborate international framework, and to push the metaphor further, the pie was already crumbling at the edges by the mid 1920s.

In becoming involved in the international rivalry for influence, Japan had to find a place within either of two groups. The British and American approach was to insist on equal opportunity for foreign interests in China under what was referred to as the Open Door. The Russian and German approach was autarkic, with a preference for monopolistic rights within spheres of influence.

We have seen that Japan was open to ideas from both German and British influences in the past. There was no denying the admiration held in Japan for the Prussian or Germanic style of governance, but on the other hand, Russia was a potential threat. Traditionally, Japan had developed trade links with Britain and America, but they would be major stumbling blocks to increased influence in China. In true Japanese style, they managed to maintain treaty links in China alongside Britain and America but also advanced their own strategic objectives by achieving a sphere of influence in Manchuria.

This two-pronged approach to China not surprisingly created two separate power bases within the Japanese leadership. The army had traditionally concerned itself with northern defense in general and against Russia in particular, and they maintained an aggressive control of Japanese interests in dependent territories with the backing of colonial officials and business interests.

Treaty privileges were more concerned with Japan's relations with Britain and America and so came under the influence of the Japanese Foreign Ministry, along with banks and exporters.

In his work, *Japanese Imperialism, 1894–1945*, W. G. Beasley typifies the change in Japanese policy between 1905-1930 as "being a gradual strengthening of 'informal' and 'economic' imperialism at the expense of the 'formal' and 'strategic' variety. The growth of overseas trade and investment during that period parallels the greater weight attributed to commerce and industry in national life."[81]

A consequence of this was military disaffection as the army strove to maintain its autonomy in pursuing 'defense' policies without interference from civil authority. The perceived need for this increased as the Foreign Ministry acted to change the treaty port system, better to suit the trading needs of the country.

The traditional restraints on the army dissipated with the death of the elder statesmen. The growth in power of political parties representing the needs of the newly emergent bourgeoisie further emphasized the gulf between civil and military interests. The army objected to the treaty port system as an unwarranted foreign influence that could only act contrary to Japanese interests.

For some others in Japan, the system placed Japan in the same exploitative role as the Western powers when a

---

[81] Beasley W. G. *Japanese Imperialism, 1894–1945*. Oxford: Clarendon Press, 1987, P165.

co-operative one was more desirable. There were yet other groups that anticipated a relationship in which China's contribution to Japanese industry could be achieved in the name of resistance to the West. It was from these that the notion of 'co-prosperity' was first given expression.

By the time of the Wall Street crash, the Japanese Empire represented three distinct elements. The first consisted of the original colonies and spheres of influence providing a protective ring around the home islands and guaranteeing basic foodstuffs. The second involved participation in the international system based on treaty privileges for trade and investment in East Asia, and related to its membership of the League of Nations. The third saw them adopt a complex position in China amongst the international community whose interests were represented there, involving a military presence and commercial arrangements.

The presence of the foreign powers in China was already under some pressure. Before going on to explore the development of the Japanese position, it is advantageous at this point for us to examine the Chinese situation from other perspectives.

Having had a dynamic, multi-national presence in numerous Chinese ports and cities, the growing nationalist movement in China began to question the unequal relationship enjoyed by the foreign powers. By 1925, the change seemed quite emphatic as the nationalists made it clear that treaty rights were open to question and even the lives of foreigners might be in jeopardy.

America and Britain Face the Rise of Nationalism

"Japan stands little chance of industrial survival unless she can obtain control over the resources of China." –From a British Foreign Office Report 1920.[82]

---

[82] Ibid P166

At the Washington Conference in 1922, the 'Powers' had made it clear that they did not wish to change the treaty system in any meaningful way. It suited their combined purposes to have foreign enclaves in China feeding from the frontier of such cheap labor and sources of supply.

There was a willingness to explore tariff reforms by convening a tariff conference, but they were as one in expressing the Western view that for China to achieve more equitable treaty arrangements she would need to "put her own house in order." In this they referred to the regional and provincial control by warlords who undermined national stability.

The one stabilizing element within China was the nationalist Kuomintang, centered mainly in Kwantung. They were responsible for a rational program of political, social, and economic reform but were seen to be under Soviet influence and, therefore, treated with some suspicion by foreign powers.

An incident in Shanghai on 30th May 1925 brought matters to a head. The demonstrations that followed the shooting of Chinese at the Police Station in Louza unleashed a bout of public anger that went on to represent the popular resentment of the unfairness of the treaty system.

The mass expression of unease at the presence of wealthy foreigners, who were maintaining their privileges in ways not available to the local population, gave foreign governments reason to consider their positions. A compliant population had made commerce very comfortable, but it could be quite a different matter to defend or enforce the treaty system in the face of mass objection or resistance.

At this point, American Secretary of State Kellogg followed his rather humanitarian instincts in taking the lead on the issue of extra-territorialism. He maintained that a nation of four-hundred million people should not be expected to admit foreign control of its rights and its economic development.

He argued further that the present system was old-fashioned and no longer relevant. His preparedness to convene the tariff conference seemed to be a genuine expression of a desire to work in co-operation with the Chinese rather than dictating policy to them.[83]

Generalized expressions of anti-foreign sentiment soon gained pace and merged into the Chinese Nationalist Revolution. Foreign interests soon realized that even treaty reform would not be enough to placate the growing Kuomintang, who were beginning to assert the sort of power that could break the provisions of the treaties without consideration to diplomatic niceties. Further, if the Kuomintang were able to achieve concessions, the government in Peking would have to address the anti-foreign sentiment by responding in kind or risk losing its own popular support.

In any case, as bitter fighting intensified between the warlords and the nationalists, the treaties were likely to be overlooked or broken in the confusion. The foreign interests were not the only things at risk. As the situation intensified, it became clear that large numbers of foreign nationals resident in China would also risk their lives by staying there.

Kellogg's response to the deteriorating situation was cautious, as he believed that the United States should not use force to protect the rights of its interests, but it should maintain strict neutrality with regard to the various factions there.

The difficulty in this position was that it made any useful negotiations unlikely, because there was no single authority with whom to deal. Until 1928, the outcome of the Revolution was in considerable doubt and, before that, it was feared that to establish negotiations with the governments in Peking and Canton separately might lead to a permanent division of the country.

---

[83] Borg ., *American Policy and the Chinese Revolution, 1925–1928*. New York: American Institute of Public Relations, 1947, P420.

Kellogg's caution in the unstable conditions had an interesting consequence. In December 1927, the British sent a memorandum, which effectively took the initiative with "the first imaginative and courageous public statement made by any foreign government since the beginning of the Nationalist Revolution." It asserted that, in the new reality of the situation, the Powers should "abandon the idea that the economic and political development of China can be secured under foreign tutelage" and "disclaim any intention of forcing foreign control upon an unwilling China."[84]

Mr. Kellogg and his Department were unsettled by this loss of initiative as they regarded themselves as the leaders of the pro-Chinese lobby, particularly since the British memorandum echoed almost precisely his own long-held, personal views.

In the midst of this, it became apparent that events in America had caused a shift in the public and business attitude that, in turn, caused Congress to push for a less timid approach in securing concessions. In response, Kellogg announced that, for the first time, he was prepared to act on behalf of United States alone in the absence of co-operation from the other powers.

The urgency of the situation increased sharply on the 23rd of March 1927 when the swaggering Kuomintang army not only approached Nanking but also entered the city, looting foreign owned property and killing foreign nationals. The situation resulted in the shelling of the Chinese troops by Japanese and Western warships, which were on the river at the time.

The mayhem and loss of life cast British and American conciliatory policy in an entirely new light. Questions were raised about the wisdom of letting the murder of foreign nationals go unpunished. The concern was that inaction would further encourage attempts to rid the country of foreign interests.

---

[84] Ibid P421

Kellogg held his line. In his view, there should be no military response, no punishment, and no sanctions. This must have been a difficult line to hold. Kellogg felt that his best course of action was to give whatever support possible to the 'conservatives' within the Kuomintang in their struggle with the more radical elements.

Remarkably, his President immediately supported Kellogg. Coolidge made a speech in April 1927. "Ultimately," he said, "the turmoil will quiet down and some form of authority will emerge which will no doubt be prepared to make adequate settlement for any wrongs we have suffered."[85]

This was a 'big picture' view, which acknowledged the nationalist movement in the wider context of China's journey towards modern self-realization. The Far Eastern Division of the State Department who were pushing the line that China's struggle should unfold without foreign intervention probably influenced this view. The echoes of it, though, ten years later, were to create a less positive foreign policy with regard to Japan, whose needs and desires became dynamically linked to the development of its interests and its threats in China.

When the Kuomintang under Chiang Kai-shek overthrew the Northern regime, the nationalists had control of China, at least in principle. Kellogg was quick to support the new regime, and Mac Murray concluded a new tariff treaty within two months of nationalist troops reaching Peking.

For its part, the new government made it clear that their expectation was for unconditional termination of extra-territorial rights. Despite demonstrable good will, the United States was not prepared to take those demands seriously, even given Kellogg's personal inclinations. The reason for this was in a fundamental difference of viewpoints between Mac Murray, the American Minister in China, and Kellogg in Washington.

---

[85] cited in Ibid P423

Whereas Kellogg was not interested in maintaining the treaty system, Mac Murray was adamant that the situation did not warrant a relinquishment of the safeguards that came with the treaties. Mac Murray had a strong sense of the anti-foreign feeling within the country, and his judgment was that it would take very little agitation for all foreign interests to be ousted. He regarded the Washington policy as being of unnecessary appeasement, and he wanted the nationalists to be dealt with from a firm position. He feared that if they were unrestrained initially, they would resort to provocative actions that would ultimately escalate out of control.

Mac Murray was in favor of a muscular policy, backed by military action if necessary to defend America's 'rights' in China. After the Nanking Incident, he strongly advised sanctions.

The strongest advocates for the abolition of extra-territoriality and issues of Chinese independence within America were the various church and missionary groups until the time of the Nanking Incident. If the Incident silenced those groups—for many complex reasons—it animated business groups in the cause of American intervention.

The American Chamber of Commerce of Shanghai called on the United States Government to co-operate with the other Powers in armed intervention to maintain American interests and to ward off Soviet influence.

The Chamber of Commerce saw the struggle in China as one between Western Powers and the Soviet Union, arguing that the nationalist revolution was neither "spontaneous nor native" but was "Soviet managed and engineered." Further, they held that Chinese misery was the result of the avarice of the warlords, not the 'unequal' treaties created by the Powers.

Dorothy Borg wrote in *American Policy and the Chinese Revolution*:

"As China's disorder had, in the Chamber's view, reached a state where the Chinese people were unable to protect either themselves or foreigners from the 'militarism, brigandage and Bolshevism' with which the country was saddled, it thought that the only solution was intervention by the foreign powers. The conciliatory policy of the foreign governments, the Chamber stated in its declaration of April 1927, 'had merely strengthened the position of the lawless elements and encouraged outrages like that of Nanking.' Firm and concerted action by the foreign Powers was, therefore, necessary not only for the protection of foreign interests but also for the ultimate good of the Chinese people."[86]

These arguments could almost be substituted for those of the Japanese government for its position, if not its policies, in China. There is very little effective difference. Both portray the revolution as a proxy battle between Soviet and Western influence. Both carry within them assumptions that economic prosperity for foreign interests would be for the ultimate good of the Chinese. The difference was in the preparedness of the two countries to act on these issues. More significantly, the perceived risks for Japan were adjacent, inescapable, and urgent.

In American eyes, Japan had undergone a transition from co-conspirator and ally, to competitor for hegemony in China. US policy would therefore become as much about limiting Japanese influence as it would be about the needs of the Chinese or the threat of communism.

Despite this, the Coolidge Administration pursued a policy that was more in line with the missionary view than that of the Chamber of Commerce. The point in emphasizing the Chamber's view is to cast Japanese policy in another light

---

[86] Ibid P430

and to show that, in other circumstances, Japan and the US might have become more closely linked in an alliance based on ideology, rather than becoming enemies in competition for power. But that is an essential tension within capitalism: competition is by definition uncomfortable with co-operation, despite ideology.

The Ishiwara Road To Manchukuo

A 21st-Century reader who has grown up with the reality of a unified China will find the repeated brief references to the Manchurian Incident baffling.

It really isn't possible to understand Japan's relationship with the World without some understanding of the events that led to the creation of Manchukuo and the meaning of these events in the unfolding of the 1930s.

The following outline will draw upon events covered elsewhere in this book, but from the reference point of China. It was there that it first became evident that the Japanese attempts at co-existence with the West were causing a reactionary shift within rural, military, and deeply traditional sectors of Japanese society.

Orthodox imperialism within Japan began to appear soft and individualistic, and therefore Western, to some observers. Modernization had created new wealth in groups formerly without status. Landlords were no longer the protectors of villages but their absentee exploiters. To some observers, politics was run by the self-serving, and the universities were too liberal. The nationalist drive was to recreate the steel of Japanese character by re-embracing tradition.

The nationalist view of the outside world was colored by the humiliations of recent events, particularly in treaties and conferences. Kita Kiki described Britain as a "millionaire standing over the whole world" and referred to Russia as the "great landlord of the northern hemisphere." He added that, "our seven hundred million brothers in China and India have no path to independence other than that offered by our guidance and protection."[87]

Similarly, Prince Konoe Fuminaro, who would become Prime Minister several times wrote that Western policies professed to be for the maintenance of World stability were "attempts by the 'haves' to keep out the 'have-nots.' They intended to ensure that late-comers like Japan 'remain forever subordinate to the advanced nations,'" and he argued that without changes such as "equal access to the markets and natural resources of the colonial areas," Japan would be compelled to re-create the status quo by force to ensure its own survival. He was later to claim that it was the failure to break Anglo-American control of international trade that had forced Japan to move into Manchuria. [88]

How these nationalist sentiments transformed the nature and reality of Japanese Imperialism can be illustrated in the career of Ishiwara Kanji who came to be associated with the *Tosei-ha* or Control Faction. He served in China during 1921 and 1922, returning to Japan with a pessimistic view of China's potential to be a worthy partner.

He then studied in Germany with a view to understanding the technical and strategic demands of modern warfare, and in the process, he gained powerful insights into Japanese deficiencies in these areas. More than anyone, he undertook a rational redesign of the armed forces to create a remarkably modern and efficient force.

The vital move that followed his experience in Germany was his appointment to the staff of the Japanese Kwantung Army, where he played the central role in planning the operations in

---

[87] Tsonoda, *Sources*,776 cited in Ibid P178
[88] Oka Yoshitake, *Konoe Fuminaro*, P10–13, cited in Ibid P179

Manchuria between 1931 and 1932. These operations represented a radical shift in the Japanese interface with the world.

Ishiwara's thinking was almost messianic in that he believed the Japanese Army was the instrument destined to save the world from Marxism and Western materialism. His vision included a series of wars fought to achieve Confucian righteousness across all of Asia. Japan would be the liberating force, and Russia, Britain, and the United States would be subdued, each in turn, to that end.

These aims were not just an eccentric whim. This was his life's ambition, and he was more aware than most of the preparations needed to accomplish these aims and the expected human cost of their execution. Preparation for total war required total unity at home in a controlled economy. The population would need to be mobilized in such a way as to focus their energies and resources on the national task.

Greater Japan would need to absorb the areas of danger closest to the Home Islands first, and this would enable further achievements. Ishiwara saw that each objective achieved made the next one easier. His was a long-term plan in which the major player in national security and development was not the government but the army. Although his thinking was never universally supported even within the army, the implicit challenge of his ideas reverberated throughout the 1930s.

Background to the Manchurian Incident

By 1921, the Hara government in Japan had decided that supporting the local warlord, Chang Tso-Lin, could protect Japanese interests in Manchuria. This was intended to be a mutually beneficial relationship. For Chang, it offered the possibility of greater power and security—possibly even outside Manchuria. In return, Japan expected protection of the hundreds of thousands of Japanese subjects and substantial investments and assets held there.

Chang had national ambitions and, in time, these came to undermine Japanese interests, primarily by threatening Chiang Kai-shek whose nationalist movement had the possibility of being a valuable ally against communism, despite the continued threat they posed for Japanese forces. These complexities inherent in the Chinese situation made for very subtle and delicate policy maneuvering.

Chang Tso-Lin's determination to play a national role created challenges for the Japanese when, in moving his headquarters to Peking in 1926, he created the possibility of a confrontation with Chiang Kai-shek.

There was broad agreement amongst various Japanese factions that their primary policy aim was the establishment of a Chinese government that was not only capable of maintaining peace and order, but one which could do so through economic and social organizations similar to those of Japan. It was also considered necessary that it should be a robust, durable government. Insulating Inner Mongolia and Manchuria from the political instability and violence in China was also considered to be essential.

The Army view tended toward the idea that China should be made to recognize Manchuria as a self-governing state. The Foreign Ministry was not prepared to go this far, and they continued to have reservations about Chang and his potential role as a leader.

We have seen that the Foreign Ministry had a more global perspective, and in fact was represented by men who, in many cases, had been educated in the West or had spent time there. This broader perspective also included an understanding of international trade.

In contrast, the Army perspective grew out of a tradition forged through decades of campaigning on the Chinese mainland, particularly against Russia. The business interests they were more inclined to support were the ex-patriots' interests in their everyday experience within the very large Japanese communities living in China.

Other views were that Chang should be supported as a warlord provided he withdrew north of the Great Wall, while yet others argued that Japan should have nothing at all to do with 'puppets' of any kind.

Beasley puts Tanaka's 1927 view of the situation this way:

> "China proper and Manchuria-Mongolia must be regarded separately. In the first, Japan was willing to give countenance to any Chinese regime that was moderate, friendly, and likely to preserve stability. In the second, because of the importance of Japanese strategic and economic rights, it might become necessary to take direct action in the event of disorder. Short of that, however, Japan would support any effective Chinese leader who was willing to respect its special position."[89]

During 1927–8, unofficial negotiations led to an agreement giving Japan new railway rights in Manchuria and further economic co-operation between Chang and the Japanese interests there. The Foreign Ministry was unhappy about this private diplomacy, but after further official deliberations, a somewhat modified agreement was signed in May 1928.

Premier Tanaka saw benefits from this agreement but needed to find a way to remove Chang from his continued unsuccessful involvement in China's civil war. Chiang Kai-shek was moving towards Peking; so public warnings were made that the Japanese were ready to intervene to prevent hostilities reaching Manchuria. Chang was offered passage

---

[89] Beasley, W. G. *Japanese Imperialism, 1894–1945*, Oxford: Clarendon Press, 1987, P186.

back into Manchuria if he and his army moved before fighting reached the capital. At the same time, it was made known that Chang would not be allowed to move into the southern frontier again.

At this point, in trying to placate the British and Americans, Tanaka stated that he had no intention of invading Manchuria as a protectorate. He maintained that Japan would observe the Open Door there. But he expressed limits in this and was not prepared to have the area penetrated by communist groups, which would destabilize the political landscape all the way to Korea, potentially even threatening the emperor-system in Japan. Nor would he allow the Kuomintang to extend its authority north of the Great Wall.

Tanaka was a dynamic Premier with a background in the Army, but his subtle position amidst the two sets of expectations within his own instruments of national policy was too subtle for some. Attending the recent policy conference was a Colonel from the Kwantung Army staff, Colonel Komoto Daisaku, who concluded that what Tanaka really wanted was the total, forceful occupation of Manchuria. He was confident that his own Army superiors also wanted to support Tanaka in this.

Komoto used his initiative to create a pretext for the execution of this unspoken policy by arranging the placement of a bomb under the train on which Chang Tso-lin was traveling from Peking to Mukden. The bomb was detonated on his direction and Chang died hours later.

What is really significant about this is that no attempt was made by Tokyo or anyone in the Kwantung Army to exploit the opportunity offered by the fabricated 'incident.'

Worse for the Colonel's co-conspirators than the failure "to restore order," was the counter-productive effect the incident had on their own militant cause. Chiang Tso-lin was replaced by Hsueh-liang, his son, who was quick to demonstrate his position by aligning with the Kuomintang and repudiating the agreements signed the previous year by his father. His anti-Japanese sentiments and actions were also mirrored elsewhere, particularly in the south where Japanese goods were boycotted and trade was badly affected.

These trade and other difficulties in China had a ripple effect as Japanese businesses suffered and, in turn, exerted pressure on Tanaka to create a better trading position. Gradually, Japanese policy shifted. In February 1929, he established a tariff agreement with Nanking; in March of that year, he withdrew forces from Shantung, and he formally recognized the Kuomintang as China's central government in June. These were not the actions of an old soldier looking for a stoush, but the actions of a politician looking for trade, prosperity, and international acceptance.

The Foreign Ministry had reason to feel vindicated at this point, as army action had been shown to have negative economic consequences.

Despite this, the Tanaka cabinet resigned en masse in July 1929 because it was the Emperor's perception that Tanaka had not been severe enough in his punishment of Komoto for the assassination of Chiang Tso-lin, and on the other hand, militants had resented his attempts to punish Komoto more severely.

Meanwhile, the groups that had been sympathetic to Komoto saw inadequate preparation as the reason for their loss of face rather than misguided action. The recently appointed chief of the operations section of the Kwantung Army began to ensure that the next opportunity would not be wasted. His name will be familiar to the reader. It was Ishiwara Kanji.

During 1931, the pressure on Shidehara to overcome Japan's increasingly disadvantageous position in Manchuria increased as anti-Japanese elements became more vigorous within Manchuria and global trade issues made Japan appear more vulnerable. Shidehara attempted to find a mutually beneficial settlement with the Kuomintang, but this was not acceptable to the Kwantung Army operational staff. Itagaki Seishir and Ishiwara Kanji began to plan a military operation justified on strategic and economic grounds.

In general, the operation was intended to consist of an invented incident on the railway, which would necessitate the occupation of key points in response, followed by the rapid expansion of operations throughout Manchuria. The element of surprise was considered necessary because Kuomintang forces heavily outnumbered the Kwantung Army.

Planning for this involved War Ministry officials as well as General Staff, and co-ordination with Japanese commanders in Korea was discussed. By September, enough was being said in Tokyo for it to be widely known in military circles that the army was proposing to pre-empt any likely agreement between Nanking and Tokyo over the Manchurian question.

This talk caused some anxiety in the imperial court with Prince Saionji Kimmochi urging caution. Senior army officials responded by deciding to lay some careful political groundwork before any action was to take place. Tatekawa Yoshitsugu was asked to convey this warning to Mukden. In turn, Itagaki and Ishiwara were secretly informed that a restraining message was on its way and resolved to act on the night of Tatekawa's arrival, before his message could be delivered. There is debate about the level of complicity amongst various players in this conspiracy and whether responses to the 'emergency' on the railway were manufactured or made in ignorance, but the effect was to have the military occupation of southern Manchuria well under way by the following day.

The Creation of Manchukuo

The most senior army men, including the War Minister, decided that there was to be no going back. Japanese interests in Manchuria would have to be formalized in a way that recognized the position of the Kwantung Army. Reinforcements were ordered for the 10,000 men on the spot, but particular care was taken to restrain their forces from moving too far north in provocative engagements that might inspire Russian intervention. But 'operational necessity' on the ground made it very difficult for Tokyo to control commanders in the field.

Protests from the West and from China were met with official denials of territorial ambition. The Foreign Ministry persisted with its line that Japan was merely repressing terrorism and trying to maintain law and order. They insisted that Japan respected the Open Door and China's integrity. The reality as seen by the outside world was of military action running at cross purposes to Foreign Office declarations, and the conclusions available to be drawn were either that the Japanese were unwilling to reveal their true intentions, or their army was out of control.

The consequences of the military operation in Manchuria rippled through Japan's relationships with the Kuomintang, Britain, America, and ultimately the League of Nations. The actions of the Kwantung Army profoundly affected the reactions of the Powers to Japan's stated ambitions. The militarists and nationalists who sought to undermine internationalist aims of Japanese foreign policy had achieved a significant victory.

Itagaki and Ishiwara always intended that a Japanese military administration would follow the occupation, but the War Ministry and the General Staff were not prepared to go that far. They insisted on a Chinese led government, and in September 1931, they ordered that the army stay out of the raising of taxes, customs, and local government. Beasley explains this as seeing "the way forward as being through an extension of treaty rights and a reinforcement of the system of Japanese advisers."[90]

---

[90] Ibid P194

While the new cabinet was in agreement with this, the Kwantung Army was not, but given rigid opposition to their position, the Ishiwara group put forward a proposal for the creation of an 'independent' Chinese state with a Chinese figurehead. In their characteristically confident way, the plan was implemented before official sanction had been given.

Pu Yi, the last of the Manchu emperors had abdicated at the time of the revolution. He was to be installed as figurehead, but his control would be limited to internal administration, while defense, foreign policy, transport, and communications were to be run by Japanese authorities. The administration, under a Chinese Prime Minister, represented a complex combination of interests designed to foster a population sympathetic to its Japanese neighbor and economic partner.

To the Chinese in general, and to the international community, Manchukuo was a pariah state, universally shunned. But to many Japanese, it became a place of opportunity and inspiration. Capitalists and industrialists found a place to develop heavy industry. The South Manchurian Railway Company employed large numbers of trades and professions as it provided expertise in logistics and the connection of materials manufacture and markets. Intellectuals and liberals under increasing police observation and interference in Japan saw an opportunity to create a more ideal society than that from which they had come. [91] The Japanese military learned to deal with all of these in order to create and protect Manchukuo.

Thousands of poor farmers were sent into the Manchurian countryside to start a new life and establish a viable agricultural industry. The economic and political adventure lasted until the Soviets advanced into the area in 1945. Manchukuo disappeared overnight, but not without on-going consequences.

[91] Young, Louise. *Japan's Total Empire: Manchuria and the Culture of Wartime Imperialism* Los Angeles: University of California Press, 1998

It would be easy to typify the creation of the Manchurian Incident as the beginning of a fifteen-year domestic crisis, ending in 1945, but to do so would be a serious oversimplification. The crisis of 1931 was without doubt a turning point, but it represented a shudder in which the futures imagined by various forces at work within Japan settled a little more firmly and clearly into place. But none of those imagined futures were inevitable, yet.

Reading the report of the International Military Tribunal for the Far East, one gets a strong impression that from 1931 the crises and various incidents were inexorable, inevitable, and cumulative. This was written soon after the Pacific War with a view to apportioning blame and understanding the flow of events. It emphasizes the militant speeches and writings of the time, creating the impression that the mood of crisis was a relentless, mounting one. More recent writers generally give some emphasis to other less militant forces at work and the continuing struggle to maintain civilian government. The army had been difficult, even at times impossible, to control, but the battle continued.

In fact, the crisis was a major turning point for China, the West, the Imperial Armies, and most particularly for the Washington system of international relations, but less so for the people of Japan, who remained substantially preoccupied with domestic concerns. However, the 'adventures' in Manchuria did produce a wave of popular support for militarism and 'China bashing' and the problems of poverty and unemployment made for a receptive mass audience.

This interest was enabled by sensationalist coverage in the popular press, which extended into a series of media events very similar to embedding journalists in the recent Iraq war. Journalists and filmmakers were flown to hot spots and shuttled back to Japan for mass screenings of newsreels, exhibitions, and lectures. The tens of thousands of people who went to these events were influenced positively and actively by hysterical and commercial popularism, but also negatively by the pervasive controls that prevented more responsible or moderate voices from being expressed.

However, there still remained the expectation that politics and elections would return to normal, and reactions to the exploits of the army in Manchuria were not universally positive. The limits of pluralism had been defined, though, and the capacity to criticize the state openly had dissipated emphatically from this point.

With many soldiers returning home by 1933, and economic recovery beginning to soften conditions, at least in the cities, the sense of crisis subsided. A British member of parliament on a visit to Japan in November 1935 felt that the Japanese parliamentary process was starting to reassert itself, militarism was subsiding, and the Japanese cabinet was exerting pressure on the more wayward elements in the army, which itself was becoming more moderate.[92]

At this point, and despite the powerful state controls referred to elsewhere, the Japanese people had not been mobilized or reorganized for the 1931 crisis, partly because the crisis was created 'from the ranks,' but also because the nation had still not set itself on a course that would inevitably lead to war. Despite the growing perception of nationhood and a growing willingness to make sacrifices for the nation, there was still no clear conception of the national purpose, or rather, there were many contradictory ones.

While nationalistic individuals and societies made good use of this and other events that were elevated to the level of crisis, the most profound change came about not through their actions but from the throttling of other, alternative voices. The

---

[92] Pickering, Ernest H. *Japan's Place in the Modern World*, London: George G Harrap, 1936, Pp 223–4.

lasting legacy at home in Japan of the 1931 crisis was therefore reductive and cumulative in ways not apparent until 1937.

For the Kwantung Army, the crisis of 1931 became a reminder to the population of what it could achieve and a powerful bargaining tool for increased funding and resources. Their agenda was expressed in terms of security and prosperity, and in this they played a critical role in refining the national identity, further developing links between the need for security and the concept of nation as victim.

The global criticism that arose from the crisis only served to convince many Japanese that the West was determined not to see the 'true' situation in Asia, in which the Japanese were doing what the disorganized Chinese were not able to do: develop Asia for Asians. In this conception, the misunderstood nation was again being reminded of its place, in the same way they had been after the Triple Intervention of 1895 and at Versailles in 1919 through the defeat of the racial equality clause.

Tragically, if the recent crisis showed that the international community could be ignored, it also made it harder for the Foreign Ministry to cite diplomatic concerns in seeking restraint from the army.

10
JAPAN TURNS AWAY

I N 1932, JAPAN gave notice of its intention to resign from the League of Nations and, in 1934, to abandon the Washington treaty. Despite various overtures from the West, it was to Germany that it turned, when the Anti-Comintern Pact was signed, as a statement of solidarity against communism in 1936. The aggressive nationalism implied in the terms of the pact proved a powerful inhibitor to other anti-communist countries, who might otherwise have wished to be included. The US had looked to Japan as a regional anti-communist force, especially in its proximity to the unstable regions of China. Western needs and intentions, however, were much more subtle than they seemed.

Since the start of the century, the most powerful fear among British imperialists was that Germany might combine with Russia to form a Eurasian bloc that would reduce Britain to a position more in keeping with its land mass and population size. This was a very real possibility when the war began to degenerate into what many thought might become a world revolution. Socialists seemed able to take hold in Germany, and the revolutionary spirit seemed to be undeniably international in its reach, spreading like embers blowing ahead of the conflagration in Russia. While being outwardly anti-communist, Britain encouraged and benefited from the ideological schism that ultimately developed between Russia and Germany and there is plenty of evidence that both Bolshevism in Russia and reactionary fascism in Germany were materially encouraged by elements within the British and United States governments.

Fear of communism within Japan itself strengthened ties between Japanese industrialists under pressure during the economic hardships of the depression and the militarists. As communism gained international strength, the Japanese reaction to it blossomed. Just as Japan was able to motivate its people in a struggle against the perception of an international communist threat before the war, America was able to harness fear of the same threat as a pretext for regional influence and aggression in Asia and South America after the war.

In Japan, any form of liberal thought was often portrayed as communistic, and therefore criminal. Western culture, liberalism, and communism were all cast as part of the same evil. The concept of individualism was increasingly seen as a manifestation of selfishness.

Further, internationalism had brought with it an economic system in which the future of Japan became tied to the goodwill and success of Western economies, and from a 1930s perspective, this may have looked very dangerous. Together with the other powers, Japan struggled to deal with problems in supply of raw materials as well as with markets. Rural poverty hit very hard at a time when suffrage became available and the popular Press was bourgeoning. It had been in this setting that elements of the army, through its actions in Manchuria, had made persistence within the Washington system almost impossible.

Graphic and sensational newsreels of the time gave no hint that the fracas in Manchuria was a home-cooked conspiracy. What was portrayed was a nationalist Chinese attack on legitimate Japanese commercial interests. The Cabinet was unwilling to risk trying a full reversal of the army's gains, with the opposition party joining in the public support of the 'punitive' army actions. Although the Emperor and the Inner Court were in accord with Shidehara, he became increasingly isolated and powerless in his opposition to what amounted to an attack on internationalism.

Although the attempt to negotiate a settlement of some kind directly with Chiang appeared from the Japanese perspective to be a demonstration of its good intentions, the West saw such moves as unilateral and therefore against the spirit of international diplomacy, which had applied since Washington. What the Japanese creatively represented as a police action within accepted international boundaries, the West saw as a flagrant violation of the Nine Power Treaty.

This provided Chiang Kai-shek with a perfect opportunity to recast his regime as internationalist and inclusive, suffering under an attack by a rampant lone aggressor. Much of his subsequent rhetoric was therefore delivered with the force of international backing. His appeal to the international community represented a considerable reversal of the revolutionary Chinese attitude to the Powers. Some would describe it as cynical while others see it as an act of tactical genius.

Had it not been for a general preoccupation by the major capitalist powers with the spreading failure of their economies as the depression started to bite, the Chinese appeals for justice might have gained some real traction. It is even conceivable that the Kwantung Army's bluff might have been called. However, the international system was in disarray economically as well as diplomatically.

The good intentions that typified the 1920s had degenerated into a trend towards protectionism, control of foreign trade, and a substantial failure of the use of the gold standard. Disastrous unemployment subverted internationalist sentiment, with a growing focus instead on domestic issues of labor, welfare, security, and poverty. The international community to which the nationalist Chinese had hurriedly turned was able to listen but not able to do very much at all. In fact, the advanced economies had to respond to the same sort of insecurities that had led Japan from the international bosom.

Although preoccupied with their own problems, Britain and the United States remained hopeful that the situation in Manchuria could be resolved in such a way as to keep the two combatants within the international community. In the process, it might be possible to re-assert the strength of internationalism. The two powers therefore gave the Tokyo government an opportunity to act in accordance with its stated commitment to the processes of peace within the frameworks of the Washington system.

In a sense, this was an impossible challenge for the moderates in Japan who were faced with far worse internal consequences should the army's will be challenged by a demand to return to the pre-September 18th status quo. A significant loss of face for the military would be explosive.

By October, the Kwantung Army began to build upon the absence of external restraint from Tokyo and from the international community. The isolated skirmish evolved through further aggressive acts into an occupation of Manchuria.

By mid October, the situation could no longer be ignored and neither could the Chinese pleas for international support. The consolidation of the Japanese position in Manchuria only served to amplify the appeal of Chiang's new position. His transformation from leader of a radical, nationalist, anti-foreign and revolutionary movement to internationalist was complete, despite the fact that there was still no unified China and communism was still yet to be dealt with, or as it happened, not dealt with. It is particularly ironic that the powers to which he now appealed for help were among the very ones that had previously exacerbated the national disintegration that lurked at the heart of China's troubles and Japan's concerns.

The League of Nations and the powers acted by denouncing Japan's lawlessness as being against the spirit of the 1928 Paris treaty, and from this point, Japan no longer had the upper hand diplomatically. The League Council passed a resolution calling for a return to the positions held before the September incident. Japan was the only dissenting voice. Although not a member of the League, the United States aligned itself firmly with the League on this issue, and therefore joined the community of supporters of the Chinese nationalist position.

With foreign encouragement, China agreed to a Japanese proposal for a League commission of enquiry to explore the causes of the incident and to make recommendations for a settlement of grievances. The Chinese hoped that Japanese aggression would be recognized and stopped, while the Japanese hoped that Chinese attacks on Treaty Rights would be highlighted and stopped.

The commission was headed by the Englishman Lord Lytton, who had firm hopes of smoothing the gritty situation, but the optimism born of collective agreement within the League was dampened by the toppling of the Wakatsuki cabinet and the resignation of Shidehara from public life soon after that. By the time the Lytton report was presented, condemning Japanese actions as well as Chinese violations of treaty rights, the Japanese government had recognized the new state of Manchukuo.

During 1932, the Saito cabinet was still anticipating continued trade in China in collaboration with the Powers, despite the new role played by Manchukuo, but by 1933, this attitude had changed. In March 1933, Japan asserted that "in its present chaotic condition China could not be regarded as an organized state" and the conclusion was that "the general principles of international law which govern the ordinary relations between nations" had to be "considerably modified in their operation as far as China is concerned."[93]

Further, the Japanese position reflected a sense of resolution growing from a truce of sorts with Chiang's commanders, which drew a line roughly along the Great Wall. As a military arrangement, even a temporary one, it delivered to Japan the practical Chinese recognition of a very special influence across a vast northern area.

By late 1934, the Japanese position had therefore changed again. Officials from the Army, Navy, and Foreign Ministry drafted a document for the cabinet, which maintained that it would be "necessary to abandon the pretence of non-intervention in Chinese politics." Japan must "exploit internal strife" as a means of dealing with anti-Japanese attitudes, encourage Nanking to appoint more sympathetic officials within its government, and seek to "detach local leaders from their allegiance to the Kuomintang."[94] Hirota's new diplomacy was also then directed towards gaining a more general recognition of Japan's new position of influence, particularly by the United States.

Somewhat optimistically, or perhaps naively, Hirota proposed a two-power agreement with the United States to recognize the perceived new reality of two centers of regional influence, each on its own side of the Pacific. Hirota felt that with clearly delineated regional interests, the two nations would never need to go to war. The response by the United

---

[93] Beasley, W. G. *Japanese Imperialism, 1894–1945*. Oxford: Clarendon Press, 1987, P200.

[94] Ibid P201

States was of course negative, but more obliquely, it became involved in economic aggression aimed at Japan's energy security and independence.[95]

The US actions illustrated a very modern use of power involving manipulation of markets and materials from a position of strength, without it being necessary to use military control or expand a formal empire. To some observers, this was the actual purpose of the Washington system. Diplomats could maintain the peace, allowing business to build upon its colossal economic advantage. Increasingly outside the system, Japan had only the military option available to it to maintain its markets and guarantee supplies when pressured by economic aggression.

Within China, Chiang was active in lobbying for more American support, but the United States expressed concern that the nationalists were not wholehearted in fighting the Japanese but were pitting their best units in the war against the communists. Stanley Hornbeck of the US state department felt compelled to remind Chiang that it was not America's job to fight China's battles, and that the purpose of US policy was to serve American interests. Moreover, the US was hampered by the Neutrality Act, which stemmed from the Nye Congressional hearings in 1935.

The American Tokyo Ambassador Joseph Grew expressed US options at this point as being either to pull out of the East Asian region or insist on the continued adherence to the Open Door. The latter would need to be backed by a build up of military and naval power in the Pacific.

A third, somewhat confronting view was expressed by a state department official who had served as minister to China and had also participated in the Washington Conference during the previous decade. John Mac Murray maintained that Japanese expansiveness in China was a direct result of

---

[95] Expanded in Chapter 11

the actions of others, including the United States. He held the view that it was the actions of the Chinese and the Americans that had undermined the Washington system, warning that a war with Japan would result from a continuation of the American policy of supporting the nationalists in China and ignoring legitimate Japanese grievances. Chinese disunity, he argued, undermined legitimate Japanese commercial, railway, and other rights in Manchuria.[96] These were under threat by bandits and warlords who had continued to attack Japanese people and property. He further argued that even should the US win a war with Japan, it would then have to compete with the Soviets, instead, for the mastery of the East. Mac Murray's remarkably prescient views thus expressed were consigned to the archives, safely out of view.

The Japanese Navy agitated for parity with the US as part of the recognition of the new situation, and during 1934, preliminary talks were held in London to establish a new naval agreement, and it was hoped that Japan's needs would find recognition there. The US was adamant that the existing ratios set in the previous decade should be maintained, and this ultimately led to the Japanese abrogating the Washington Naval Treaty.

During 1935, the Kwantung Army used considerable unsanctioned initiative in setting up a regional government in northern China, together with political councils to 'harmonize' relations between Manchukuo and surrounding areas. At the same time, it became increasingly evident that the two military arms had divergent views as they each assessed future security in terms of their own capacities.

The navy wanted to secure its oil requirements and saw economic penetration of Southeast Asia as their primary objective. The naval men urged caution in northern China

---

[96] Gelber, H. G. *The Dragon and the Foreign Devils, China and the World, 1100BC to the Present.* London: Bloomsbury, 2007, P276.

and Inner Mongolia, which should remain "special regions under Chinese sovereignty."[97] In contrast, the army view was grounded in China as a project—with the army firmly centered within it—and with the new China as the key in the administration of East Asia. In addition to these views, the Foreign Ministry was still concerned with achieving some kind of on-going accommodation with the Kuomintang.

The improbable task of reconciling these vastly contrasting worldviews sat heavily with the Hirota cabinet. In August 1936, a statement was produced called the 'Fundamental Principles of National Policy,' which attempted to do just that.

This statement gave voice to the shared view that Japan needed to counter the Powers in their assumed superiority in East Asia by creating a new set of relationships built upon co-prosperity and shared values. It was intended that a strong coalition between Japan, Manchukuo, and China would allow Japan to extend its interests into Southeast Asia in "gradual and peaceful ways," but this was conditional on the preservation of basic needs for the army and the navy. For the army, this consisted of sufficient forces in Korea and Kwantung to afford protection from Russia. For the navy, it consisted of a fleet sufficient to maintain superiority over the United States in the western Pacific.

Further, in Japan, steps would need to be taken to promote the right attitudes in the people for the tasks ahead, to improve economic organization and to achieve self-sufficiency in essential resources.

Many scholars maintain that, from the point of view of the Tokyo government, these statements were not meant to bring about territorial expansion. "They still thought in terms of informal empire, that is, of securing an increase in Japan's

[97] Beasley, W. G. *Japanese Imperialism, 1894–1945*, Oxford: Clarendon Press, 1987, P200.

privileges through pressure exerted on Asian governments, including that of China."[98]

Mainland Chinese read Japanese inclinations differently, however, seeing Kwantung Army negotiations at the local level as an attempt to undermine the Kuomintang and dismember the country. From 1936, Chiang Kai-shek reached an agreement with the communists and resistance to Japanese actions became more resolute.

Trade, Industry and Regional Power

The Great Depression did much more than simply put national economies at risk. By the mid 1930s, the effects of it on international trade, power and, therefore, wealth, threatened the basis for maintaining peace and order. Poverty created discontent that challenged governments, which then moved to protect their workforces, threatening trade. Trade disruptions undermined agreements over markets and therefore threatened regional stability, and if the wealthy economies suffered, the most marginal ones suffered much more.

For example, during the depression, growing exports to Japan of Australia's foodstuffs and raw materials was very important to Australia's eventual recovery, particularly when other traditional markets were contracting. By 1935–6, the trade balance in Australia's favor made up one third of the amount needed to pay annual interest on the Australian debts owed to other countries, from its effort in fighting for the Empire in World War I.[99]

The flood of cheap Japanese goods caused some concern among local manufacturers, but the population, which had suffered reduced incomes and pensions, welcomed these economical goods.

---

[98] Ibid P202

[99] Wigmore, Lionel. *The Japanese Thrust*. Canberra: AWM. 1957, Sec.1 P5.

Banks and economic strategists saw a growing and continued trade with Japan as being logical and beneficial to Australia, but English manufacturers were increasingly unhappy with the trend. Of course, there was a human face to this unfolding tragedy, too, as the manufacturing cities of Britain suffered under the collapse of British competitiveness in its traditional staples, for example in Manchester. By 1935, Australia imported more textiles from Japan than from Great Britain—for the first time. This caused the appearance on Australian shores of a very assertive trade delegation from Manchester, which had the desired effect at the government level. The result was a licensing system that worked against the importation of certain Japanese (and other) goods. This example is representative of many such pressures on emerging exporters such as Japan. The Japanese had been so successful in adopting modern production methods they out-competed the British, who were still using first- and second-generation equipment in an aging infrastructure. The British solution was to shut the Japanese out of the markets within its empire by blocking Japanese exports with selective tariffs.

These things all occurred at a very sensitive time for Japanese manufacturers who were struggling with what we now call a credit squeeze. There was increasing alarm in Japanese industry as it became harder to find markets for its products. At the same time, Japan's fuel supplies were under serious pressure from a cartel of Western suppliers, outlined in Chapter 11. Japanese expansionists were able to build on this fear, stressing that the West was making it impossible for Japan to exist—let alone thrive—as a manufacturing nation. If it was impossible to trade fairly in a world market, then it seemed logical to find regional groupings that could provide self-sufficiency. Any hint of autarky by the Japanese, however, was seen as a threat to the system of free markets in which, it seems in retrospect, winners were grinners and losers could make their own arrangements. That might be regarded as fair in open competition, but hardly so when alternatives such as attempts at self-sufficiency were actively discouraged and when even the British Empire behaved like an autarkic bloc. Many modern observers including Noam Chomsky trace the roots of the Pacific War substantially to these issues at this time.[100]

Increased industrialization had caused Japan's dependency on imported raw materials to increase, and this contributed to a strengthening of control over its colonies in an attempt to compensate for a corresponding subordination to Western imperialism.

Market problems created the need to increase state aid to local capital in securing the home market and to make local products more competitive as exports. This form of protectionism was a state-managed solution for overcoming the international status quo that furthered Western economic interests at Japan's expense.

Japanese industry grew rapidly throughout the period of the First World War, improving levels of self-sufficiency, but throughout the 1920s, problems were encountered that seemed to prevent further expansion and development. The Japanese iron and steel industry can serve as a good example of a co-operative relationship between government, the military, and industrial sectors, which went a long way to address these issues, overcoming inherent limitations.

The South Manchurian Railway Company held a virtual monopoly of coking coal and iron ore. Domestic steel production capacity always exceeded demand causing steel manufacturers to operate inefficiently, making it impossible for them to be competitive. By 1929, up to thirty-two percent

---

[100] See for example, Chomsky, N. *What We Say Goes, Conversations on US Power in a Changing World*. Crows Nest NSW Aust: Allen & Unwin, 2007, P146.

of Japanese plants had been shut down due to cheap imports from China, Korea, and British India.[101]

In response to this, *zaibatsu*-related iron and steel companies created defensive cartels to resist foreign imports and, at the same time, exerted pressure on the government to provide helpful relief measures. The state responded by increasing military demand for iron and steel and overcoming the problem associated with the supply of iron ore in part by restructuring the industry into the Japan Iron and Steel Works (*Nittetsu*) in 1933. This was in effect a giant state capital trust representing a fusion between private *zaibatsu* capital and the largest of the government-operated steel works.[102]

This late developing private industry was perceived to be central to Japan's economic future, and it is no surprise to see the heavily assisted success of the 'monopoly bourgeoisie' in the 1930s as being thoroughly meshed with the rise of totalitarian control, and in some eyes, fascism. The capacity for private-state capital to advance domestic and foreign agendas meant that the increasing power of the *zaibatsu* occurred at the expense of small landholders and poverty-stricken agrarian workers whose needs were cast aside. By the time of the Manchurian Incident of 1931, Japan's industrial leaders began to by-pass the political parties "in favor of a relationship with the militarists that was far more dynamic, mutually profitable, and institutionalized than anything yet seen."[103]

---

[101] Bix, H. P. *Re-Thinking Emperor-System Fascism: Ruptures and Continuities in Modern Japanese History*, Bulletin of Concerned Asian Scholars Vol14:2 1982 P12.

[102] Nagura, Bunji. *A Study of the Japanese Iron and Steel Industry in the Interwar Period*, Journal of Historical Studies No 489, Feb 1981 Pp1-9, cited in Bix P12.

[103] Bix, H. P. *Re-Thinking Emperor-System Fascism: Ruptures and Continuities in Modern Japanese History*, Bulletin of Concerned Asian Scholars Vol14:2 1982 P12.

Military initiatives gave the *zaibatsu* an advantage more than comparable to earlier government assistance, building on the mutually beneficial aim of creating an economic force that was capable of expanding Japanese power throughout Asia. The beginnings of this relationship in the building of power, the creation of markets, and the solution of earlier supply problems enables us to see the 'desirability' of the start of the China War in mid 1937 in a different light. It was this war after all, which became the Pacific War and culminated in a crescendo of industrial-military co-operation until 1945.

The Japanese aim of the creation of a 'Greater Asia Co-Prosperity Sphere' was to embrace Korea, Indo-China, Malaya, and Indonesia in such a way as to insulate the region from depression, with raw materials flowing to Japan for conversion into goods for the huge Chinese markets.

Despite the plan, ultimately over a million Japanese soldiers throughout China could not bring the Chinese Nationalists to their knees. Market demand therefore remained difficult on one side of their dream ledger, while the supply side was limited by their reliance on foreign metal and fuel from sources that became increasingly intolerant of the Japanese operations in China.

Changing the Guard

Following World War I, any worthwhile assessment of the changing Asian situation would be based on an understanding that Britain's enormous power and influence there were bound to decline. The dominant force in creating a new power balance would involve the United States and others. The question was, which others and in what form of balance? The salient point here is not so much Britain's decline, but the power vacuum it could create. Leaders in expansive nations see a power vacuum as an opportunity, while those in vulnerable nations see it as a threat. Japan was both expansive and vulnerable.

Having been the greatest of creditor nations during the 19th Century, Britain came out of the war and into the Depression owing a vast debt to America for supplies bought during the course of the war. The amounts owed to Britain were nearly as vast, but were unlikely to be repaid by devastated European nations. Britain had also sold about half of its overseas investments, which had the effect of reducing its ability to fill the gap between the cost of imports and the value of exports.

The most serious threat to British wealth, however, was the loss of markets. Many pre-war customers could no longer afford British products, and many also used tariffs to protect their own recovering industries at the expense of their old suppliers. Despite this, Britain tended by and large, to be a supporter of free trade until 1931.

Japanese exporters had market worries of their own. By 1931, for example, in a desperate situation, too, the British were becoming vigorous in restricting Japanese trade to its former dominions. We have seen that this included textiles that competed directly with those produced in Manchester. In a more comprehensive sense, Japanese industry was also about to be threatened directly by the determination of Euro-American oil companies to perpetuate the dependence of emerging nations on Western controlled sources of fuel.

Militarily, Britain still had a lot of ships and cannon on the high seas, but the apparent might of the fleet was increasingly becoming an illusion. Navies built by newer, more efficient economies produced the next generation of naval weaponry. The decline of Britain may have been obvious to some in Japan, but the British Empire seemed confident, even complacent, in outposts such as Singapore, Australia, and Hong Kong.

The situation in Europe became increasingly important in the British estimation of the balance in Asia. If Hitler became too great a threat to the balance of power in Europe, a consequence would have to be a moderation of British policies towards Japan in China, because it was recognized that British power could no longer maintain a controlling interest in both spheres. At the time, Hitler appeared to have less expansionary goals than Japan, and it seemed possible that an accommodation with the former with regard to Europe might enable a more controlling hand to be played against the latter in Asia and the Pacific.

Britain was realistic about the capacity of the treaty system to control Japanese expansion and was more prepared than the United States to explore other avenues. To that end, British efforts were made to engage with Soviet Russia, maintain good relations with Japan, recognizing as far as possible its expanded role in China, while at the same time, providing help to the Chinese. Chamberlain even advocated the recognition of Manchukuo, but this never became policy. Chamberlain has been chiefly remembered for the failure of his appeasement of Germany and this is historically quite unjust. He was vigorous in trying to keep the powers engaged with one another, and he was also creative in searching for alternatives to war.

While a general view of the actions of the United States through the 1930s gives the impression of a solidifying support for the Chinese nationalist cause, there are instances of American action that undermine the view that this was for moral or principled reasons aimed at Japan. For example, a massive loan in 1933, which amounted to $50 million from the Reconstruction Finance Corporation was for funds to purchase American cotton and wheat. Outwardly a supportive gesture, this was a one off response to Congressional pressure to find a profitable way in which to dump domestic surpluses for which there was no longer a market.

Similarly, but more cynically, Congress passed a Silver Purchase Act in 1934 that authorized the Treasury to buy the metal at rates that were higher than the world market rate. This caused a serious depletion of Chinese silver reserves as it flowed to the United States, despite pleas from Chinese officials.

China was forced off the silver-based currency system in 1935, undermining its ability to restructure industry and rehabilitate its struggling economy.[104] Such muscular economic policy had the same capacity to produce misery as an invading army did. For many people, poverty meant early death, whether by gun, ill health, or starvation. Surely this informs a view more consistent with those expressed by Prince Konoe on the real purpose of the Open Door policy favored by the managers of world economics.

By contrast, the British attempted to assist China, but in doing so they aimed to involve Japan in addressing the chaotic repercussions of the American silver purchase policy. With knowledge and support at fairly high levels in London, Frederick Leith-Ross had the idea of extending aid in co-operation with Japan in the hope that China might be persuaded to offer *de facto* recognition of Manchukuo. This initiative represented the British willingness to accept a new situation in the region within certain limits, if the nations concerned could be kept within the Washington system. The British had acted in a similar way towards Italian and German revisionist tendencies. These ideas were presented to Hirota and others, but the Japanese response was fettered by implacable army resistance to any notion of Anglo-American co-operation in Asian affairs.

The shift in economic power to the United States was mirrored in its military power. The difficulty in Japan was that there were those for whom a long-term alignment with the US made perfect sense. It pays to be in the good books of the most wealthy power, especially if they have become your banker, but it became clear that this would not be possible while Japan was also attending to the needs of home defense and economic

---

[104] Eastman, L. E. *The Abortive Revolution: China under Nationalist Rule, 1927–1937*, Cambridge, MA: Harvard University Press, 1974, P189.

security, as perceived by those most suspicious of Western intentions.

The recognition of the Soviet Regime by the United States in November 1933 further muddied the waters. Roosevelt clearly showed by his actions in this regard that an engagement with the Soviets might be useful in containing Japanese ambitions, to their mutual benefit. The ramifications of a possible *rapprochement* between these two countries must have received serious consideration in Tokyo. While this was only diplomatic recognition and not a treaty, it is part of the context for the later grouping of nations that would see Japan aligning with Germany: an event that was never a foregone conclusion.

The Washington system of international diplomacy had become refracted by the depression, including infringements created by the Japanese determination to improve its position in Asia on one hand and trade tensions created by advanced economies on the other. In 1935, the Comintern sought to offer a simpler, binary lens through which to view the world, by calling for a united effort to resist fascism and its attempted disruption of the status quo, chiefly represented in the policies of Japan and Germany. In this, the Soviets were attempting to re-join international politics as a stabilizing and unifying influence, and they joined the League of Nations in 1934.

The United States and Britain were not interested in joining either an anti-communist or anti-fascist cause, preferring to work with the Soviet Union, China, Japan, Italy, and Germany, in an effort to keep them engaged within the Washington system. On a commercial level, however, power was exercised without the same level of responsibility.

11

PREAMBLE TO A FUEL WAR 1934

THE EMBARGOES THAT were ultimately used by Roosevelt to punish and possibly provoke Japan had a turbid and very complex history going back to the mid 1930s. During that period, the interests of huge petroleum conglomerates converged with those of national governments, resulting in an attempt to control the regional power of 'new' economies, while at the same time securing maximum profitability for an industry suffering from over-supply and falling prices.

Of course, in the 21st Century, we now face problems concerning the supply of oil, too, but from the other side of the equation. Since US oil reserves peaked in the 1970s, the problem has been one of securing future supply, rather than of securing current markets. Western foreign policy has therefore tended to move its focus from the Far East to the Middle East. In both regions, the populations came to see themselves as victims of Western Imperialism. Attempts to resist this have resulted in Western aggression in both regions, but it has been carried out under the guise of regional security.

Despite the parallels between the Japanese position in the 1930s and the American position in the 2000s, Japan was denied then what America has since had the power to maintain. Today, a Middle Eastern type of 'nationalism,' taking the form of fundamentalist Muslim resistance, has threatened or perhaps given the appearance of threatening security of supply. Western wealth and comfort has been increased and sustained by the policies that ensured control of both sides of the supply equation. Western populations need to acknowledge this reality and consider the implications of it continuing. China, no doubt, already has. The West prevailed as controllers of the market in times of glut, and it is seeking to do so also in times of impending shortage.

On March 16, 1935, Stanley Hornbeck wrote to the American Secretary of State, Cordell Hull, "the termination of the naval treaties having been given, both Japan and the United States are making special efforts to increase their naval forces and the American Government and American interests are engaged in the making of plans and the launching of enterprises which, from the Japanese point of view, are a menace to Japan's sense of national security."[105]

He continued, noting that, in many ways, Japan now regarded herself as a major power, but recognizing the need for secure fuel supplies, was endeavoring to improve her position with regard to accumulation and regulation of the handling of petroleum. He then wrote, "The American Government and American interests—along with [the] British are opposing Japan's efforts in that direction."[106]

---

[105] Hornbeck to Hull, March 16, 1935, P3, *Hornbeck Papers* Box 184, File Joseph Grew Correspondence, 1935 Hoover Institution, Stanford Calif, cited in Breslin, Thomas. *Trouble Over Oil: America, Japan and the Oil Cartel 1934–1935*, Bulletin of Concerned Asian Scholars. Vol 7 Issue 3 1975 P41

[106] Ibid

These comments from the middle 1930s are in stark contrast to the orthodox versions of pre-war history such as that by Herbert Feis, in which the Americans "refrained from threats and coercions, either alone or with other countries" until 1940.[107]

By this time, it was widely acknowledged that energy security was vital in warfare and national security. It was in 1912 when Churchill made the decision to convert the British Navy from coal- to oil-powered ships that were faster, more economical, and flexible in operation. From this point, he had committed Britain to oil dependency and a foreign policy to match.

World War I was concluded through the actions of a blockade on Germany's fuel supplies as much as by trench warfare. Lord Curzon, a member of the British War Cabinet, commented "The Allied Cause has floated to victory on a wave of oil."

In a 1975 Journal article, Thomas Breslin presented a very well-researched case that the informal embargos by oil companies—American and Anglo-Dutch—produced tensions that contributed to further deterioration in the sensitive relationship that was unfolding between the Japanese and American governments. In it, he maintains that the Western oil powers were involved in "low level economic warfare against Japan, with what can be termed semi-official sanction."[108]

In what ways was this semi-official? Breslin cites official documents that reveal that American authorities were happy to encourage any restraint on Japanese growth, allowing their aims to be pursued by commercial interests, without the dangers and embarrassments associated with a potential

---

[107] Feis, Herbert.1950, *The Road to Pearl Harbor. The Coming War Between the United States and Japan*, Princeton University Press, P7

[108] Breslin, Thomas. *Trouble Over Oil: America, Japan and the Oil Cartel 1934-1935*, Bulletin of Concerned Asian Scholars. Vol 7 Issue 3 1975 P41

failure of a government-sponsored action. The oil companies were acting to maintain their monopolistic and profitable position in the entire Pacific region and did so against several Asian governments. In Breslin's words:

> "With the encouragement of government officials who saw the companies' moves as a way to achieve national goals through private means—with the added benefit that the government would not be embarrassed if the policy failed—the oilmen carried out an embargo on shipments of oil to Manchuria, resisted Japanese oil storage regulations, kept alive the possibility of an official American embargo against Japan itself, and prevented Japan from obtaining oil-bearing lands." [109]

The context for this is rather complicated, involving supply issues and the failure of open competition to provide sufficient profit to satisfy the largest companies. Following World War I, the American petroleum industry had enjoyed the best of times with huge demand on limited output, and a consequent rapid rise in prices. Aggressive attempts by the British to secure their own supplies in Iran, Iraq, and Trinidad led to a significant reduction of the American share of reserves outside Russia, shrinking from 46% in 1923 to 30% in 1943. [110]

Discoveries of further reserves in America off-set anxiety about this to a degree, but the consequential fall of well-head prices only served to emphasize the importance of foreign markets to maintain profitability.

The late 1920s saw fierce competition develop between Dutch, British, and American companies for foreign market share. A dispute that involved the purchase and cheap sale of Russian crude oil in Asian markets, and the refusal by

---

[109] Ibid

[110] Unpublished MBA thesis by Charles E. Sumner cited in Ibid P41

Standard Oil to participate in a boycott of Russian petroleum, led to a deterioration of relations between the oil giants and consequential price wars and overproduction.

The inevitable fall-out from that was reduced profitability until an agreement was reached in 1928, which "established a precarious peace by *allocating global markets* outside the United States, *setting export quotas, and fixing prices*."[111] Price fixing might seem alarming to the modern reader versed in the theory that the market is always right. The market is only considered to be right when it suits those who control it.

The situation in America as the Depression deepened was exacerbated by further discoveries in Texas and a sharp decline in prices, while foreign demand for the American product declined further with the increase of production in Asian and Latin American countries. This was made worse by the development of foreign refinery capacity, making the most profitable fuel share even lower for US companies.

Petrol and petroleum-product export from America dropped by almost two-thirds in dollar terms between 1929 and 1932—from $562,116,000 to $209,000,000.

The formerly cozy club was facing disruption from many fronts as emerging economies sought to have some control of the energy they required to modernize and develop. In 1930, a push within China to rouse popular support for a local refinery company and the stated expectation that it should be supported over foreign interests, was magnified by the appearance in China of very cheap Russian kerosene. As a by-product of the refinery process with a limited world market, the loss of the kerosene trade in China was a serious threat to profitability for the Western companies. It was felt that Russia was dumping its product in China specifically to undermine the Western interests there.

---

[111] Williamson, H., et al, 1963. *The American Petroleum Industry: The Age of Energy, 1899–1959*, Evanston. Northwest Uni. Press, Pp528-32 (my italics).

The Russian threat spread from China to Manchuria and Siam. Western market share was further challenged, especially by the potential loss of the Japanese market and Japan's capacity to operate in Manchuria under very preferential terms of trade.

By the end of 1933, Japanese officials had made the decision to follow the lead of France and some other European governments in taking control of the fuel industry with a view to achieving self-sufficiency. In effect, this amounted to a very rational three-tiered solution. The first step was to develop refining capacity and rationalize distribution. The second involved the exploration of technologies for the production of alternative synthetics. The third concerned acquisition and experimental drilling.

All of this only served to intensify the global price war, and even the Japanese importers were under pressure, but whereas the pressure on the Chinese resulted in an official back down, the Japanese acted positively to secure their control over supplies. In 1934, new Japanese legislation required suppliers to be licensed and gave the government the power to regulate and supervise the operation of importers and refiners. It even empowered the government to set prices if it was deemed to be in the public interest, and as an added safeguard, importers were required to maintain a given minimum stock on shore.

Although entirely within its rights as a sovereign state, and despite this being a rational, non-aggressive program designed for national and industrial survival, it was enough to send Western oil executives to seek help from their own governments. The Japanese were too big a market to be allowed to enjoy such independence. Meanwhile, Japan, not unreasonably, was working towards gaining increased import quotas from Netherlands East Indies. The oil companies saw their domination of Asian markets under substantial threat and looked for ways to thwart the legislation.

In March 1934, *Business Week* described the potential loss of the Japanese market as the 'ultimate problem' for US interests in the Far East and went on to say that "there is brave talk in New York and London of forcing Japan to a showdown."[112]

The problem, as expressed by American Ambassador Grew in Japan, was that a successful monopoly in Manchukuo might lead to similar successes elsewhere in China thus encouraging the Japanese government to act in other ways unfavorable to US business interests.

To simplify a very intricate set of negotiations, the Japanese demands caused the American and British to make joint representations to the Japanese government, while at the same time preparing for an embargo on oil shipments to Japan and Manchuria. While these negotiations were commercial rather than governmental they were conducted with the knowledge and implicit support of key figures in the US State Department, and others. State Department advice was that if smaller oil producers under-cut the embargo they could be "brought into line."

The achievement of a disciplined and united embargo was more difficult than it was first thought. Ten thousand tons of California crude from smaller independent refineries made its way to Manchuria despite the refusal of the large companies to make supplies available, underlining the fierce competition between suppliers, even from the same nation. But the pressure was mounting, and the Japanese became increasingly aware of the possibility of governmental assistance in stopping their trade altogether. This implied threat was used forcefully in negotiations.

British co-operation in a multi-nation embargo was offered as long as it remained a 'private affair,' because some elements in Britain favored reduced trade barriers over protectionism.

---

[112] *Business Week*, editorial, "Foreign Trade." March 17, 1934, "Business Abroad: The Far East," April 28, 1934, cited in Breslin.

Despite everything, during 1935, the Japanese were able to secure an increase in petroleum imports by finding willing suppliers in California, Ecuador, the East Indies, and Mexico. Pressure continued from both sides throughout the period 1933-1936 without any clear signs of victory for either. The Japanese were denied alternative technologies and supplies, but the oil companies were pressured into consideration of meeting Japanese storage requirements.

While a successful, complete embargo was never achieved, State Department and government-level negotiations were sufficient to create the very real possibility of one. This threat unfolded over the decade leading up to the Pacific War. The growing Japanese insecurity can be understood in this context as they sought to find reliable future energy supplies and independence in ways already enjoyed by countries such as France and Italy, but which were denied them by Anglo/Dutch/American companies who showed a determination to act together. This challenge to Japanese safety and independence goes right to the heart of the fear and insecurity inherent in Japan's engagement with the West. Yet it was Japan that had to carry the stigma of aggression, having been backed into a corner.

The Japanese situation was made immeasurably worse by the global changes that saw many other countries attempting to create energy independence or find viable markets for their reserves. The importance of the Japanese and Manchurian markets and their apparent vulnerability made them targets for a protracted campaign. Japan had to maintain supply from sources beyond its shores. Its role as a potential enemy amplified the existing connections between industrial and political objectives.

American oil companies faced a deteriorating situation in East Asian markets after 1936. Ambassador Grew's view was that all Japanese-controlled markets would be lost as that nation worked towards achieving self-sufficiency. Anglo/American oil interests in Korea and China were being discriminated against, and Latin American crude, having been nationalized, was competing for a shrinking market. Discrimination was not supposed to travel in both directions.

There is little doubt that powerful Western forces were not acting with good will or in the interests of peace. Where a market existed for exploitation, all possible pressure was exerted to control the terms of trade and the level of supply to ensure maximum profitability with no accountability in regard to the ultimate costs. After all, even a war would bring commercial and industrial benefits.

The Heroes of Freedom were becoming agents of freedom from responsibility. An inter-relationship of business and foreign policy interests of the kind illustrated here would be called ultranationalist when applied to Japanese actions, in marked contrast to the orthodox description of American ones, which would simply be called free market capitalism.

12

THE 1930S. AN UNRAVELING OR A CULMINATION?

"*T*HE PEOPLE CAN *always be brought to the bidding of the leaders. This is easy. All you have to do is tell them they are being attacked, and denounce the pacifists for lack of patriotism and exposing the country to danger. It works the same in every country.*" Hermann Goering in *Nuremberg Diary*, by Gustave Gilbert, 1947

Certainly, the events of the 1930s within Japan do give the impression of the kind of cynical exploitation of human fear and frailty expressed in the quote given above, but the advance of repression was an incremental attempt to keep the most radical elements under some kind of restraining influence, as much as it was a nationalistic response to international frustrations and national paranoia. It could be argued that the Japanese ruling oligarchy represented the central position, between radical left and radical right. Many democratic nations even in the 21st Century have been subjected to the successful application of Goering's formula with none of the fundamental challenges to their national survival that threatened Japan from the 1920s. The causal issue in these modern examples is the persistence of ruling interests, whether in government or not.

One view of the Meiji restoration is that the oligarchs "were able to transform their private class interests into the general interest, effectively counteracting demands from the peasant majority for basic bourgeois rights and liberties" in the process.[113] In this view, they managed to do it by consistently finding foreign policy crises and exploiting popular fear and insecurity.

In retrospect, Japanese actions do give that impression, but some would argue that this is a cynical view of a nation driven by so many conflicting forces that almost any outcome was possible. It also assumes that the Inner Court Circle was in accord with the most radical elements within the army, but the actions of the Circle don't support this view. However, the ruling class was very sophisticated, and their power was cleverly reinforced by romanticizing and utilizing the mystical charisma of the imperial institution, creating the emperor role as an abstraction so central to the national story that in his name extraordinary power could be wielded, but by whom?

This closed power system remained essentially unchallenged until industrial capitalism created conditions and opportunities sufficient for the traditionally oppressed to challenge the regime. We have seen that the nature of the 'restoration' has been described as 'revolution from above,' and to a certain extent we can see the 1920s as a period when many groups with conflicting interests tried to 're-jig' the revolution to meet their own particular needs. Democracy and pluralism represented the needs of a large number of these groups,

---

[113] Bix, H. P. *Re-Thinking Emperor-System Fascism: Ruptures and Continuities in Modern Japanese History*. Bulletin of Concerned Asian Scholars Vol14:2 1982 P3.

while the needs and aims of capital, National Socialism, and inherent militarism were represented by many groups of anti-democratic persuasion.

If the 1920s saw an opening of a political can of worms, the 1930s saw the forces that had created the Meiji restoration expand to include a wider power base and put the lid back on. In achieving this, the Home and Justice Ministries played a similar role to that which in Germany was played by the fascist 'Nazi' party.

The 'Manchurian Incident' of 1931 can be seen as the cause of a new state of mind in Japan rather than the effect of one. However, the possibility of that event to create that state of mind was itself established earlier, by the work of the Home and Justice Ministries. We have seen that the incident was 'created' by elements of the military to expropriate China's three Eastern Provinces, and we shouldn't underestimate the effect that it had in the West.

The effect in Japan, however, was also very powerful right through the decade, creating the necessary mentality for the total mobilization in the nation for war. This did not come from the population, nor outwardly from the government, but from a group of army officers imbued with ideas of national mission and reconstruction. Some would argue that their main aim was to achieve change at home rather than control in China, for the simple reason that to achieve larger foreign objectives, those at home would need to be made receptive to self-sacrifice and self-denial.

Whether or not we agree that the young officers acted in that conspiratorial way, they created several domestic consequences that played out over the succeeding years, in the context of growing repression in domestic Japan.

First, they created fear, a common enemy and 'blood debt,' which in that society were significant agents for unification. Second, they built upon the motivation for self-denial, sacrifice, and the willingness to fund military 'needs' created by the propaganda and other Home Ministry projects. Third, the military was able to consolidate its power, independent of the civilian government. Fourth, the freedoms of the population could be further repressed in the interests of security.

In his journal article, Herbert Bix[114] argued that a very significant change occurred as a result of the 1929 Peace Preservation Law. It was this he argued that signaled a shift from the Meiji police state to a qualitatively different, composite fascist state as distinct from a 'merely' militarist one. This view is open to debate and will be examined in greater depth in a later chapter.

The cabinets of the early 1930s were supposedly apolitical, 'national unity' ones, but by 1933, political arrests had risen to 18,397.[115] The increased press censorship explored earlier was combined with a campaign to suppress protests and strikes by rural labor in farming and fishing villages.

Aggressive foreign policy was maintained to achieve strategic and economic objectives and as a tool for "forging domestic integration while giving the appearance at the same time of working to contain more radical demands for a national restoration and reconstruction."[116] The Okada cabinet began distributing pamphlets and propaganda material preparing the population for an impending war in 1935 or 1936.

This sense of crisis and national tension was further heightened by the political assassinations that occurred in 1932 and which grew out of the same militarist fanaticism. Those assassinated included Finance Minister Inoue Junnosuke, Mitsui chief Baron Dan Takuma, and Prime Minister Inukai

---

[114] Bix, H. P. *Re-Thinking Emperor-System Fascism: Ruptures and Continuities in Modern Japanese History*, Bulletin of Concerned Asian Scholars Vol14:2 1982.

[115] Ibid P6

[116] Ibid P6

Tsuyoshi. This is an extraordinary amount of carnage for a nation to absorb, and it must have created a deep sense of alarm. The following year, Japan withdrew from the League of Nations, further isolating itself from foreign influence.

Bix also makes a very strong case that it was the police, under the centralized control of the Home Ministry, that played the major role in achieving the causes of industrial capitalism and 'emperor ideology.' In this, they paved the way for the military by nurturing "public hysteria and fear over issues such as anarchism, communism, and radicalism."[117] The police had complete control over freedoms of speech, association, and assembly.

In addition to legislative controls, in 1928 they were given special powers in a move to decentralize repression through expanded roles within the ministries of Home, Justice, and the armed forces. All prefectures were given 'thought procurators' (*shiso gakari*), 'special higher police' (*tokko keisatsu*), 'military thought police' (*shiso gakari kempei*), Home Ministry police officials (*keimukan*), and specially deputized police assistants (*keimukanho*).[118]

By the time of the Manchurian Incident, sufficient fear and hysteria had been created by the police in all its forms, to create a compliant population in the face of demands for spending on armaments. At the same time, the arrests and fear caused by the internal security apparatus managed to deflect some of the public focus from the effects of the Depression, while increasing fear of external dangers.

By the middle of the decade, no anti-war or anti-militarist public opinion was openly expressed. Having effectively silenced the left, the Home Ministry persisted in its efforts to press its advantage. In 1935, it adopted a 'heresy annihilation' policy (*jakyo serimetsu*), further tightening its control over

[117] Ibid P7

[118] Ibid P7

religious practice, and this heralded a number of laws that systematized the reorganization of the legal system further towards a fascist model without pre-emption by civil unrest or provocation, except perhaps by the perceived external threat of international socialism.

In the struggle to maintain the party system, unexpected support was provided by the Constitution itself. The very institution that had created so many difficulties for the parties protected them from radical and fascistic streamlining of the political process. The radical and militarist deification of the Emperor made criticism of the Meiji constructed constitution rather difficult. The Diet and the party system were granted to the people by Imperial edict and could not be challenged without sacrilege. This partly explains why Japanese authoritarianism remained less radical than its equivalents in the West.

Having said that, elected governments were not capable of creating the kinds of change that would meet the real needs of the largest sectors of the population. That power was beyond the democratic process, and the capacity to replace a cabinet perpetuated real power within the Inner Court Circle, the military, bureaucratic, and industrial interests.

In one view, whenever a substantial increase in repression was needed to maintain this control, an 'incident' was created, or was allowed to occur, which would herald a change of cabinet and the tightening of laws for the further restrictions of freedoms and rights. This assumes that Japan was on a course pre-set by a ruling group. On the contrary, the centers of most entrenched power continued to act in support of the party system of democracy.

Despite the bitter factionalism and the daily condemnation and ridicule of the parties in the popular press, the system was to some extent protected by elements of the Inner Court and even the Emperor. Prince Saionji also worked behind the scenes to protect the parties in general and the more antimilitarist elements within them in particular. His attitude and that of the Inner Court Circle was representative of a more global perspective, a less bombastic and chauvinistic view of the West, and a fear of the consequences of militaristic aggression.

These fine tendrils of balanced conservatism bound many elements of Japanese leadership together, even from within the military. It was always intended that the power in Japanese politics be spread among the oligarchy since the Meiji 'revolution from above.' The nobility, the military, the bureaucracy, and the industrialists competed and plotted, and while power fluctuated over time, the interdependence of these groups acted to prevent the utter dominance of any one of them. This factor inhibited a descent into the singularly concentrated power structure associated with fascism, particularly in Europe.

A third factor acting to the benefit of the parties was the war weariness of the general public. While there was no mass movement, and probably could never have been, the elections of 1936 and 1937 produced some surprising results. Despite these factors working for the party system, its final winding down can be explained in part by the failure of successive cabinets to address the growing difference between expansionary foreign policy with regard to Asia and the need to maintain a peaceful trading relationship with the United States.

The party system and labor unions had provided outlets for the expression of discontent and for the needs of those outside the oligarchy. They were gradually wound down, as external expansion increasingly became the focus for energies that, under other circumstances might have been directed towards internal issues of state. By 1940, both had been abolished.

Russian Dolls in the Politics of Militarism

Within the military at this time there was a sense that early attempts to force their goals onto the national agenda had been counterproductive, and by the late 1930s, many were working to achieve their aims through the medium of politics. To do this, they needed to work with what had become a new generation of bureaucrats in the ministries who had grown up with a pan-Asian view of Japan's 'mission' but who were also determined to keep political power from military hands.

Under the influence of the renovationist faction organized by the new bureaucrats, the Ministry of Foreign Affairs maintained that Japan was the best placed power to provide stability in East Asia and that Western powers should recognize this. This can be said to apply to the foreign ministries of Hirata, Arita, and Shigemitsu. [119]

The younger, more radical members within the renovationist group held considerable sway over the more moderate ministers. For example, Minister Arita was forced to declare Japan's determination to "fulfill her mission as the stabilizing power in Asia," and Minister Matsuoka was supported in his refusal to accept the influence of the army in his negotiations with the French in Indochina.[120]

With regard to factional elements within the army, leadership or control was in the hands of the Control Faction (*Tosei-ha*) between 1936 and1941. With support from bureaucrats with socialist leanings, the Control Faction sought to change the national free economy into a more controlled one during 1938.

This rang alarm bells among financial and ruling elites, causing them to brand the Control Faction as Marxist and generally building anxiety and fear. This was geared to bring

---

[119] Murakami, Sachiko. *Indochina: Unplanned Incursion*, in Conroy, H., Wray, H. (eds) *Pearl Harbor re-examined: Prologue to the Pacific War.* Honolulu: Univ. of Hawaii Press, 1990, P144.

[120] Ibid P144

the Imperial Way Faction (*Kodo-ha*) back to a dominant position.

The Imperial Way Faction was mainly concerned with the potential Soviet threat from the north and was adamantly opposed to the southward advance and the Greater East Asia Co-Prosperity Sphere. General Minami and General Ugaki, notable for his role in the arms reduction of 1925, led another renovationist group. They stood in solid opposition to the Control Faction for the chaos caused in relation to Manchuria and Mongolia.

The complexity of these factions and groups can partly be explained in historical and regional terms. The Minami and Ugaki group were the successors of the once all-powerful Chosu Faction of the original Imperial Army, and it was still regarded by many as the mainstream of it.[121] Other rivalries existed as remnants of Imperial service or favor from the Meiji restoration and involved armies raised in particular provinces or regions.

In contrast to the other two factions, the leaders of the Control Faction were younger and lower in rank, but they held powerful positions in the army's general staff and the war ministry. The three-way pull of these groups caused confusion, indecision, and embarrassment in several campaigns overseas. This division can in large part explain the conflicting views of Japanese intentions in Indochina.

From this very simplified account of a huge military organization, we can see how difficult it is to typify the actions or intentions of 'the Japanese Army' when their internal divisions were so pronounced.

Further, the traditional friction between the Army and the Navy continued, perhaps exacerbated by the growth in power of the Army. The range of opinion from radical to moderate in the armed services created a specific need in government

---

[121] Ibid P145

of any persuasion. Whoever ruled the Government had to be able to control the military. This explains why several navy men succeeded Inukai as Premiers: slightly moderate but still military. Significantly, though, the final Premier before Pearl Harbor was from the Army.

Flying the Flag and Folding the Parties

By 1936, the trends begun at the time of the Manchurian Incident were resolving themselves climactically. We have seen that the unraveling of the party system was in many ways a culmination of forces inherent in the system since Meiji times. There had not been an election since 1932 and, since the *Seiyukai* opposition had put aside their internal squabbling for a major challenge to the Okada government, it was decided to dissolve the Diet and call an election.

Although the radical right had not entered the party contest in any substantial way, the election was still a surprise in the distribution of votes. The *Minseito* Party won 205 seats on a slogan of "what shall it be, parliamentary government or fascism?" The *Seiyukai* did not do as well as expected, dropping to 174 seats from 303. The big surprise, looking back on the era, was the percentage gain of the *Shakai Taishuto* which, as a labor party, was expected to decline in support. In fact, it more than doubled its vote from that of the 1932 election but still gained only eighteen seats.

This was still better than the national socialist groups who managed only six seats.[122] Here was a visible triumph for the democratically inclined and a very poor showing for the ultra militarists. These results also revealed large-scale public apathy and voter absenteeism, but the Okada government survived.

---

[122] Scalapino, Robert. A. *Democracy and the Party Movement In Pre-War Japan: The Failure of the First Attempt.* Berkeley: University of California Press, 1953, P382.

Only days later, the militarists had their revenge on the parties. The 'February Twenty-sixth Incident' involved more than 1400 soldiers under the command of young *Kodo ha* (Imperial Way Faction) officers whose attacks were spread throughout Tokyo.

Okada's residence was occupied and he was reported killed. The former Premier and Keeper of the Privy Seal, Saiko Makoto, was killed. General Watanabe, the leader of the *Tosei-ha* (Control Faction) and Inspector General of Military education was killed. Several other key figures were wounded or fatally wounded.

There were others who, having been marked for death, had escaped, and Okada himself was found alive. The man killed by mistake in his place was his brother-in-law.

The confusion lasted for days as rebels erected barricades, and the military leadership recoiled from perpetuating the bloodshed. It emerged from the chaos that the militants wanted to achieve the destruction of the old ruling cliques and the salvation of Japan under a 'new order.'[123] Ultimately, surrender was achieved partly through the command of the Emperor. The nation had to digest the implications of the greatest domestic crisis since the Satsuma Rebellion of 1877, fifty-nine years previously.

This incident provides a crucial insight into the events that were about to take place in China and the subsequent political problems. The group involved in the attempted revolution were members of the First Division whose younger officers had been associated with the Kita-Nishida group and who were about to be posted in China. Their posting and the repercussions at home created a situation where the most radical militants in the forces were overseas, essentially unrepresented or controlled in Japan.

[123] Ibid P383

Thirteen army officers, four civilians, including both Kita and Nishida, were executed. Generals with any connection to the radicals were transferred to the reserves. *Kodo-ha* was no longer a force at home. But what had been unleashed in China?

The aftermath on the domestic scene predictably saw a consolidation of military power in the hands of *Tosei-ha* generals, one of whom was Tojo Hideki. The remnants of the Okada government resigned, probably grateful enough simply to be alive.

The Inner Court Circle approached Konoe to be Premier, but he declined at this point due to ill health. Hirota Koki was appointed instead when it was judged that he would be acceptable to the military. Being acceptable was not apparently enough as he learned when he tried to assemble a cabinet. The military had very specific requirements as to personnel and policies. The thrust of their demands was acceded to, including expansion of armaments, tighter economic controls, and censorship.

The Hirota Cabinet set about finding rational ways in which the various factional aims could be reconciled into policy. The Army was absolutely committed to rebuilding China into a stable, sympathetic neighbor with accessible natural resources. The General Staff were concerned with protection of the north from Soviet invasion, and the Navy were primarily concerned with economic expansion into South East Asia to secure the raw materials for defense. The Foreign Office was concerned with Japan's international relationships and was adamant that no engagement in China should be undertaken that could threaten Japan's international standing.

Hirota achieved a statement of principles called the Fundamentals of National Policy, and it was from this document that the New Order and the Co-prosperity Sphere were to develop. The thrust of this document was to achieve the replacement of the 'tyranny' of the Powers with cordial relations based on principles of peaceful co-existence and co-prosperity. Economic expansion would flow from the strong coalition of Japan, Manchukuo, and China, and by peaceful expansion of economic influence into South East Asia.

The price for all this rhetoric of peace was to be in providing the armed forces with the tools to protect their interests. Forces would be increased in Korea and Kwantung to defend against the Soviet threat. The Fleet must be developed to maintain "ascendency in the west Pacific" against that of the United States.

The new War Minister Terauchi was so emphatic in his expression of distaste for the old parties, and for 'renovation' of government, he was accused in parliament of "foisting a dictatorship upon Japan" by an aging Diet member who stated that he would commit *seppuku* (ritual suicide) if he was proven to be wrong.[124] Not long after this, the cabinet fell.

After some intervening difficulties, General Hayashi Senjuro formed a cabinet, taking a very strong anti-party position and insisting that members of his cabinet distance themselves from any previous party affiliation. Scalapino wrote of him: "his ideas were far more in line with the old 'transcendental' concepts of the Meiji Genro than with the revolutionary concepts of the radical right or ultranationalist concepts of most elements now dominating the army."[125]

There were other differences between the Hayashi and Hirota cabinets. Hayashi and his Foreign Minister Sato Naotake were installed to revive the internationalist view of national survival, focusing on industrialization and engagement with world markets, to solve Japan's economic and population pressures. This policy that resolved to give up military goals in northern China was to have been a first step in the development

---

[124] Ibid P385

[125] Ibid P386

of renewed interdependence and a re-opening of resources to international trade.

The timing of this coincided with a seventeen-nation League committee in Geneva, which worked to assert international trade inter-dependence. Had the Hayashi cabinet been able to survive, it might have enabled Japan's emergence from its growing isolation.

This Cabinet failed only months after being formed, presumably because of resistance from the parties, but also because the forces behind the adoption of autarky and neo-mercantilism were reasserted. The Japanese Tientsin Army in China were alarmed by this attempt to undermine their hold in the north, believing that any sign of peaceful engagement would be seen as a demonstration of weakness.

This brings us to the last election in Japan before the Pacific War. In this election, *Shakai Taishuto* doubled the number of seats it had achieved in 1936 to thirty-six seats, representing a labor vote of one million people, mainly from urban areas. *Minseito* held 179 seats and the *Seiyukai* held 176 seats, perpetuating the status quo but by a closer margin. Once again, a democratic election had supported progressive and moderate parties, and once again, the military were rebuked but not deterred.

Marco Polo Bridge

The situation in China changed substantially when, having suffered major defeats, the communists were forced into the famous Long March and the apparent possibility of political oblivion. But their decision in 1934 to change from a policy of national class struggle against the Nationalist government, to a united effort in defeating the Japanese, appealed to the growing nationalist and anti-foreign sentiment across the country.

The Japanese army was threatened by this attempt at unity and reasoned that either the Nationalists should be helped to finish the destruction of the Communists and then be brought under greater Japanese influence, or some opportunity should be created to crush the Chinese while they were still weak and vulnerable.

Prime Minister Hayashi adopted a conciliatory policy toward China, reasoning that Japan should aid China's efforts in unification with an economic offensive in an attempt to eliminate American and British influence there. An economic mission was dispatched to China, but the cabinet fell before it could achieve its objectives.

With the resignation of the Hayashi cabinet, the role of Prime Minister was once again offered to Konoe Fuminaro who was a favorite of the army, and it was hoped that he could provide a restraining influence. It was anticipated that his noble lineage would ensure that he maintained the balance of power enshrined in the political system since the Meiji restoration. He was widely regarded as a conciliator capable of drawing together the broad range of interests among conservatives of the oligarchy and in the military, but he had been an angry man since Versailles.

Konoe is a difficult figure to assess from a Western perspective. His early experience led him to a cynical view of Western intentions but, in hindsight, we can empathize with many of his observations and the reasons for his inclinations. The Pact of Paris had entrenched the international system in the status quo, and he long held that this was unjust. The difficulty he encountered in this was that the Washington system sought to overcome and move beyond imperialism while power was still entrenched in the hands of the former aggressors, and this allowed economic imperialism to perpetuate and even build upon the advantages that were gained by force in the previous century.

In his book, *The Origins of the Second World War in Asia and the Pacific*,[126] Akira Iriye represents the Konoe appointment as a clear negative, guaranteed to reverse the progress made in China policy, and he bases this on Konoe's stated militant position. However, Konoe was given the task of controlling the military, and his response from this point became increasingly moderate. That his foreign policy was in line with Hirota's rather than that of Hayashi may be seen as an attempt at containment of the army rather than support of it.

His was a poisoned chalice, but that seems to have been an inevitable consequence of pre-war power in Japan. Within a month of being in office, the so-called 'Second China Incident' unfolded. He would have to deal with a crisis that would ultimately bring Japan to its knees.

---

[126] Iriye, A. *The Origins of the Second World War in Asia and the Pacific.* Longman UK, 1987, P39.

13

THE FAILURE OF
POLITICS AND WAR IN CHINA

O N THE NIGHT of July 7, 1937, during a regimental
exercise, several shots were heard and, after a quick
roll call, it was discovered that a Japanese soldier was
missing. The army demanded a search of the city of Wanping
for the missing private but the demand was rejected. Minor
violence erupted, and on the following day, the Japanese
commander demanded the surrender of the city and a brief,
improbable truce followed, but only for a matter of hours.

Having been Premier for just over a month, Konoe
might have struggled to understand exactly the nature of
the incident. Initially, it might have seemed an isolated
skirmish, and War Minister Sugiyama reinforced this
impression. Downplaying the significance of the incident on
one hand, Sugiyama then set about organizing a preliminary
mobilization on the basis that, in order to secure an apology
and some guarantee by the Chinese, the Japanese North China
Army would need reinforcement from its current strength of
only 5,000 men.

His proposal was accepted on the understanding that reinforcements would be used to protect Japanese lives. Konoe might have preferred to avoid this action, but refusing the War Minister might have led to his resignation and the subsequent fall of the Cabinet.

There was a clear delineation between the policies of the War and Foreign Ministries, and this delineation extended to within the Army itself. The Army General Staff Officers opposed an escalation in China, but officers in the War Office were generally in support of it. These intricacies of allegiance amounted to a break in the chain of command that proved crucial in several pivotal incidents. In this case, again, it worked in the War Office's favor with the added dispatch of troops to quell what was already a calm situation, and having the opposite effect.

The leaders of the opposing Chinese forces had been pro-Japanese and had benefited professionally from their favor with the Japanese authorities. Chinese General Sung Che-yuan had been installed as Chairman of the Hopei-Chahar Political Council, but he was not prepared to submit to the intimidation by the Japanese General Kazuki when it was demanded that Sung's troops be evacuated to the south of Peking. Intimidation led to obstinacy, which led to the loss of 5,000 Chinese troops in a single day. Predictably, Sung became firmly aligned with the Nationalists under Chiang Kai-shek, escalating the intensity of the incident further.

Soon after this, another Japanese-sponsored group of the Chinese Peace Preservation Corps killed their Japanese officers and subsequently massacred over two hundred Japanese civilians, providing the tipping point into violence from which there could be no face-saving reversal.

Indeed, reversal was the last thing on the minds of the Japanese forces. Within three days of the completion of their reinforcement on July 27th, they had created new enemy forces from the ranks of their former associates, killed thousands of Chinese troops, and produced a perfect excuse for retribution in the deaths of Japanese officers and civilians. Peking and Tientsin fell on the 29th. Three more divisions were mobilized and a special sitting of the Diet was ordered to approve emergency funding.

Konoe was probably relieved when the Emperor stepped in at this point, ordering the Prime Minister to commence negotiations with the Nationalist Government in Nanking. Even the North China forces in the Japanese Army could not ignore an order from the Emperor, but they were adamant that the Chinese should be seen to sue for peace in order to save face.

Recognizing the pragmatic nature of the relationship between the two governments, a businessman in the China-based Japanese textile industry was chosen by cabinet as emissary to meet with a member of the Chinese Foreign Office, although this was pre-empted by a circumstantial Ambassadorial meeting. The early negotiations seemed far too costly to Japanese interests in the army view and gave no hint of a Chinese request for peace.

The various views about the potential for rapprochement became academic when another incident unfolded, but this time in Shanghai, and so things escalated further, so that by September, the newly created North China Army numbered 200,000 men, and fighting had spread to the Yangtze.

The rapidity and ferocity of this escalation can be attributed not to the various incidents and provocations, but to the belief in the General Staff that if the situation could be brought quickly to a head, a robust victory would result. This could lay the 'China problem' to rest. But it didn't. The army would sink into a quagmire of completely unmanageable proportions, eventually taking Japan's international credibility with it.

That is of course a post-war assessment, but for a little while in 1937, the Japanese position looked quite different. Both the United States and Britain expressed caution and a desire for a peaceful resolution to the conflict. US Secretary of State Cordell Hull implied that he would agree to the modification of existing treaties, as long as it was done in a co-operative spirit. Great Britain offered help in mediation to protect the peace and ensure the safety of its huge financial interests in China.

From the Japanese point of view, Hull's statements gave a strong impression that the United States would remain uninvolved, which meant there would be no threat to the supply of gasoline, oil, and scrap iron to support the Japanese campaign.

When China and the Soviet Union signed a treaty of non-aggression on August 27,' 1937, Japanese propagandists must have felt quite vindicated. Soviet arms and supplies eventually bolstered the Chinese armies, but this played out to be as much at the expense of the Nationalists as it was of the Japanese. But for a short time before October 1937, it may have appeared that the international allegiances could find Japan alongside Britain and the United States against communism in particular, but on the Chinese mainland.

But Roosevelt's position stiffened, and he sought a way around the American electorate's isolationist sentiment, in order to be more open in his opposition to nations perceived to be aggressive. His famous 'quarantine' speech of October 5, 1937, presented his concerns within a metaphor of a healthy world community dealing with the spread of a physical disease.

The speech had an immediate impact within Japan, mostly negative, but it also rallied the more liberal elements within the government circles that felt it was imperative to maintain co-operative and cordial relations with the West, and particularly with the United States. The Foreign Office applied pressure on the War Minister to reassure the West through news conferences, which he duly did.

There was a new situation in China. It became apparent that the Nationalists would fight on, and the Japanese would not back down, but the General Staff became increasingly alarmed at the possibility of a Soviet attack on Manchuria. Given the stretch of its resources against the Chinese, it was felt that such an attack on Manchuria could only be held at bay for the first half of 1938, with a likely defeat following that.

An effective mediator was needed, and while the cabinet would have been more comfortable with the British in that role, the General Staff pushed for German intervention. Germany was in an interesting position with regard to the two combatant countries. In the case of Japan, Germany was a partner in the anti-Comintern pact, being in the hot seat on the opposite side of the Soviet Empire geographically. Its relationship with China also reflected the desire to limit the growth of communism, but was also based on the more fundamental issues of trade and business.

Germany was acceptable to the Chinese because it had relinquished its special rights and the concession in Shantung and was seen to have a less intrusive role than either Britain or the United States. In terms of strategy, Germany had a vested interest in preventing its ally from becoming weakened in a protracted, costly struggle there.

Mediation as a Tool in the Factional Struggle

War Minister Sugiyama had imagined that an escalation of hostilities would provide an opportunity to re-establish control within the Army, furthering the Control Faction (*Tosei ha*) agenda, and he was supported by General Terauchi in this.

We have seen that the General Staff, on the other hand, were more concerned about a possible invasion of Manchuria and were in favor of finding a settlement with China. General

Ishihara, as head of the Division of Strategy in General Staff, stood in opposition to the Control Faction and seems to have won a significant battle within all factions by getting mediation accepted as a worthwhile option. The Prime Minister, Prince Konoe, supported him in this, as it was in both their interests to counteract the dominance of the Control Faction. The acceptance of mediation represented an obvious weakening of the War Minister's political position, and by extension, also that of *Tosei ha,* which he headed.[127]

German Ambassador Trautmann made an offer of mediation to the Chinese and it was well received. Trautmann would meet the Generalissimo, Chiang Kai-shek, at Nanking on December 2nd. The meeting was very cordial, and it is reported that Chiang was quite willing to take the mediation forward. He expressed his hope that Germany would remain as mediator. Chiang was supported in this by his top military aids. The only concern expressed was that the Japanese might demand more than had already been put on the table. To this, Vice Foreign Minister Hsu Mo asserted that there were no other demands. It is reported that Chiang replied, "If this is all they are asking, what are we fighting for?"[128]

We have reached another of those pivotal moments when the will of an individual becomes internationally transforming. But the individual concerned is neither Chiang Kai-shek, nor Roosevelt, nor Prince Konoe, it is Japanese War Minister, General Sugiyama.

By the time Foreign Minister Hirota had been informed of the Trautmann-Chiang talks, Japanese troops were closing on Nanking and its fall seemed imminent. The Japanese response to this critical opportunity for a negotiated settlement was therefore delayed pending news of the victory, which occurred

---

[127] Lu, David J. *From Marco Polo Bridge to Pearl Harbor: Japan's Entry into World War II.* Washington: Public Affairs Press, 1961, P24.

[128] Ibid P24

on the 13th of December. The military success stiffened Sugiyama's position, 'raising the bar' for Chiang in the pursuit of peace. The War Minister now demanded effective recognition of Manchukuo, special administrative areas in North and Central China, and the payment of reparations. Military action had once again strengthened the power base of the War Minister.

On December 14th, the North China Army established a puppet regime in Peking, despite the expressed wishes of the Cabinet and the General Staff.

What followed the Japanese capture of Nanking was an undisciplined frenzy of cruelty brought upon the defeated soldiers and citizens of the city. This involved some of the most unimaginable atrocities of the war, and the incident is generally referred to as the 'Rape of Nanking.'

The withdrawal of the Nanking government to Hankow involved a procession of Chinese officials and foreigners escaping upriver, including three Standard-Vacuum Oil tankers escorted by the American gunboat *Panay*. When this boat was attacked and sunk by Japanese aircraft, the loss included several American lives. The next day, a very angry Roosevelt spoke to his advisors about the possible nature of reprisals. He considered the seizure of Japanese assets to cover the cost of the damage to American property, but later favored a ban on transactions in foreign exchange with the Japanese government. The crisis played itself out with the acceptance of a Japanese apology and payments from the offending nation. But the incident had caused a re-evaluation of American options and a hardening of its position. The incident transformed the Chinese situation into a moral cause for many in America who were more concerned about humanitarian issues than commercial ones, so public sentiment came into line with that of more commercially exploitative agencies through the terrible brutality of the Japanese forces there.

Throughout December and January, competition was fierce for policy ascendancy. The Cabinet grappled with the policy direction forced upon it by the War Minister, details of new demands were communicated to Chinese Premier Kung, and the War Ministry drafted a formula for non-recognition of Chiang Kai-shek's regime, to be followed by negotiations with the puppet regime. Kung predictably and understandably responded to the new Japanese terms as a clear breach of faith. The Japanese General Staff maintained their insistence that direct negotiations should still take place with Chiang Kai-shek, and Konoe must have been wondering about his options. The *Genro*, Prince Salonji, had to face the terrible prospect of the Emperor having to ratify a policy statement with which he had no sympathy when an Imperial Conference was called to confirm the new China Policy.

In maneuvering towards the Imperial Conference, General Sugiyama was bent on achieving the Imperial sanction that would cast his policy in stone. At the conference, the Emperor said nothing, despite his reported inclinations, in keeping with his desire to be seen to remain aloof from the cut and thrust of politics.

Meanwhile, Hirota pressed for a quick response from the Chinese. On one hand, he knew of further military operations planned by the Japanese and, on the other, Japan was aware that Chiang's Ambassador in America was in talks with Roosevelt, attempting to get American support. The German Ambassador became aware that the Control Faction were increasing their pressure and he feared, correctly, that the moderates would give in to this pressure unless a negotiated breakthrough could be achieved. When the Chinese answer came on January 13th, it included a request for clarification of the new terms, which it was claimed, were too broad to be judged conclusively. In response, the Cabinet Conference decided to cease negotiations altogether.

This caused a fatal realignment, leaving the General Staff without support. General Ishihara and Vice Chief of Staff Tada insisted that policy be reversed, but Hirota was able to argue convincingly that there was very little hope of a settlement and therefore efforts should be focused on the successful conclusion of the war. The Foreign Office may have been expected to seek a peaceful solution, but it was "jealous of its own prerogatives and resented any peace moves started by the General Staff."[129] The Navy were also able to be convinced as it was not inclined towards supporting Chiang's regime, especially if the mediation would eventually lead to an emphasis on the Soviet threat and greater budget allocations to the Army. Supreme Command finally gave the Cabinet the authority to conclude negotiations.

Despite some reaffirmation of China's desire for a negotiated peace, the Japanese were adamant. This brought expressions of alarm and concern from Dirksen, the German Ambassador.

Konoe had tried to rule by consensus, but it was clear that government as it stood was not working effectively. He had entertained the idea of altering the constitution so that the Cabinet could be empowered to control defense policy, but he feared the Emperor might veto the idea. He did try to work with a reduced wartime Cabinet but the idea failed. Several other reorganizations and structures were tried but they each created unforeseen complications.

National Mobilization

Konoe's attempts to concentrate power in the Cabinet had little real effect, but there was an incremental concentration of the political power of the Army throughout the period after the Marco Polo Bridge Incident. The twin problems of transforming the economy into one capable of sustained

---

[129] Ibid P27

military action and securing sufficient resources and raw materials for the same task, were addressed soon after the incident. The laws that followed included one to encourage and supervise the production and use of gold, several to control the importation of materials and control foreign exchange, and a licensing system for the control of the sale and prevention of the export of certain goods that were deemed essential for carrying out war. Heavy industry was encouraged to expand through the availability of special finance arrangements.

These and other arrangements, despite being portrayed as essential to national defense, were quite contrary to the spirit and letter of the Meiji Constitution. The Diet was faced with a grave situation.

The dilemma faced by the Diet may be likened to a disagreement amongst a number of people who find themselves below an enormous boulder rolling toward their homes at the bottom of a hill. Do they agree to act together in trying to deflect the boulder from their houses or risk being flattened by trying to stop it? In the event of their continued disagreement and indecision, anything is possible.

On February 19th, Konoe's Cabinet approved a National Mobilization Bill, which sought to control the use of all manpower and national resources for the purpose of national defense. The Army was arrogantly confident that the bill would be passed by the Diet.

The Law was passed, but the Diet managed to have some important qualifications attached to it. The first was that the Government should not automatically use its new power without first resorting to legislation, where possible. The second, interestingly, was that the new law should not be invoked in the current conflict. Several aspects of the bill were dropped, including bans on free assembly, dissemination of news, and the publication of newspapers.

Konoe's Dream Team

Prime Minister Konoe was troubled by self-doubt. He had tried to appease the Army, but they were still uncooperative and belligerent. His Foreign Minister had become entrenched and more powerful. Konoe felt that he had failed to bring about the conditions under which peace could be achieved. He made it known that he intended to step aside as Premier. Senior Army men felt threatened by Konoe's potential departure, fearing a change in the balance of power that might not favor them. Action was taken to force the War Minister's resignation in order to appease Konoe.

This created a possibility for the breakthrough towards which Konoe had been working without success. The man Konoe wanted as his new War Minister was Lieutenant General Seishiro Itagaki, an experienced campaigner in China but regarded as a supporter of a non-expansionist policy there. The Army consented to Konoe's choice and suddenly it seemed possible for the political texture of the Cabinet to change radically.

Itagaki's presence would not only counter-balance the Control Faction (*Tosei-ha*) but would make possible the inclusion in the Cabinet of several influential people who would otherwise have been unavailable. Another significant change happened soon after his inclusion. Foreign Minister Hirota resigned and was replaced by General Ugaki, who was considered a moderate and who had many important connections within the Chinese Nationalist Government. A condition of his taking the post was that Konoe must agree to overturn his earlier decision that Japan would not deal with Chiang Kai-shek. This was agreed, and several other appointments were made that further moved the balance of power away from the *Tosei-ha*.

By the end of May 1938, the new Cabinet became a very effective political instrument, representing a powerful coalition of the court, military, and financial circles. The old factions had slid into irrelevance, and Army groups became more aligned according to their geographical power bases in China. The polar tussle changed from one of ideological agendas to one of defense agendas; that is, the relative importance of either the Russian threat or the 'problem' of Chiang Kai-shek. By this time, 62,000 Japanese troops had been killed in the China Incident and an end was nowhere in sight.

The new situation could have led to a turn-around in China as well as improved relations with Britain and the United States. The Cabinet was the most moderate in Japan for years. It comprised talented, well meaning but tough men.

This was a moment filled with possibility. Britain's new Secretary for Foreign Affairs, Lord Halifax knew it. Chiang Kai-shek knew it. America's Ambassador to Japan, Joseph Grew, knew it. Explaining the failure of the moment is very difficult. The answer lies somewhere in the inter-relationship and the agendas of all of these countries, further complicated by the opportunities and challenges presented by the impending war in Europe. The Japanese weren't the only ones to struggle with foreign policy.

Britain began to look more narrowly to the European balance of power and its own survival with the rebirth of an aggressive Germany, but its Asian colonies represented vital wealth and war materials as well as the gateway to the Indian Sub-continent. In China, Chiang would certainly benefit if the war with Japan caused further American intervention, helping him defeat the communists. America would benefit if Britain won the European War, if in so doing it lost the Empire. American war with Japan would be more easily won if Japan were mired in China. A Japanese war with Britain would enable the American President to join the European War. War with Japan could ultimately redefine Asia at the behest of a strengthened America.

These grand ideas of strategy, like dismissive passes of an imperial hand over a map, make little allowance for notions of self-determination or nationhood. Those issues would have to wait until after 1945.

Undermining Ugaki

Ugaki Kazushige had been a favorite of Prince Salonji and he was widely touted as a future Prime Minister, despite his inability to form a Cabinet in 1936, due to Army interference. The Genro was unhappy that he had been offered the role as Foreign Minister, as he feared that the torturous path through factional politics would leave his reputation too damaged for a future leadership role. He was right, but in a sense this was already true in 1938, despite appearances at the time.

Ugaki's optimistic arrival occurred at the same time as Lord Halifax's appointment in Britain, and the two set about trying to improve relations between the two governments. His first press conference included the declaration that "we have had special relations with Great Britain in our traditional friendship. I will do my best to restore them and make them even closer than in the past." The press in Japan and Britain were enthusiastic about the new attitude and the possibilities it represented. Follow-up discussions with the British Ambassador were also fruitful, with Ambassador Craig being reassured that British interests and rights in China would be respected.

The British point of view expressed at the time was that Japan would ultimately be master of its region, but that it must be patient in its dealings with China. The British offered to mediate in the China conflict, but the Cabinet[130] was hesitant and somewhat non-committal, much to the Genro's disgust. Ugaki did not have a mandate to offer anything more substantial than reassurances about respect for British rights, and for their

---

[130] Or more correctly the Five Minister's Conference, a sub-group within Cabinet.

part, Britain could not countenance any surrender of their enormous influence or control.

Ugaki's engagement with the Chinese Government began in a similar, positive manner, with a plan for a Chinese representative to come to Japan for talks. Some preliminary conditions for peace were drafted. Even this was fraught with difficulty, because if the Chinese negotiator were seen to be pro-Japanese at home, the negotiations would come to nothing. They came to nothing, however, for a more predictable reason.

Changkufeng was a dangerous place at the conjunction of the borders between Manchukuo, Korea, and Russia. While Ugaki was drafting the conditions for a negotiated settlement, an incident took place there that redirected Ugaki's full attention, leaving negotiations permanently on hold. It also demonstrated the grim reality of the Russian threat so very close to Japanese soil.

It seems that the war at Changkufeng was another incident and another reminder that a foreign issue could easily deflect a Tokyo political agenda. This one gave strength to those like Ishiwara Kanji who were adamant that Japan should not be engaged in a 'premature' war with Russia. The eventual success of the Russians in several large-scale operations at Changkufeng appeared to vindicate this position. Elements in the Army who were frustrated at the lack of progress within China had been keen to use this incident as a platform for the build up of arms and men for a strike to the north, but the result was a military debacle, a loss of face, and a loss of thousands of lives.

Ugaki carried political baggage from his previous governmental positions. In particular, he was made to pay for his role in the dispersal of four infantry divisions, even though in so doing he was an unwilling participant in fiscal retrenchments by the Cabinet in 1925. The Army never forgot his involvement and conspired at every opportunity to undermine his position and his policies.

The possibility of fruitful discussions with the British, through Craigie, represented the possible thwarting of army aims in Northern China. Adding Ugaki's potential as a future Premier to these issues saw the Army actively working to preclude his success. Anti-British demonstrations were organized, while forces pushed toward Hankow, and plans were discussed to occupy Canton, which was near the British colony of Hong Kong. An army presence close-by would infringe on British rights and would seriously compromise any softening of the negotiated position between the two countries.

The management of Japan's activities within China had become very difficult, and the Cabinet decided to establish a central body to streamline the process. Konoe could only manage a compromise from the conflicting views expressed on this by the War Ministry and the Foreign Ministry. The former saw this as a logical extension of the Army's semi-autonomous role as defenders of Japanese interests. The latter saw this as a job for one of its specialist bureaus.

Inevitably, the compromise led to a reduction in the importance of the Foreign Office as a separate diplomatic and policy tool. Ugaki was a powerful presence in the Cabinet, but he felt completely cornered and, consequently, in September 1938, he resigned. With him went the particular charisma that had arisen from that combination of statesmen and their unity of purpose. The ramifications for Japan's engagement with the West were even more significant.

Konoe was bitterly disappointed and he sensed that the Cabinet might not survive the change. Privately, he prepared for his own resignation. Vice War Minister Tojo expressed concern about Konoe's intentions because Konoe was a 'known quantity' and his replacement might not be to the army's advantage. His Cabinet continued, but it became split on the issue of a potential alliance with Germany and Italy.

14

THE COMPLEXITIES OF ALLIANCE

THE RUSSIAN BEAR loomed large in Konoe's mind. Russian communism was bulging the northern borders of Japan's backyard, but Konoe's preoccupation with it as a threat left him unprepared for Hitler's devastating duplicity. The Konoe and Ugaki policy of negotiation with Germany to extend the Anti-Comintern agreement was aimed at achieving security against Russia, but they did not wish to achieve this at the expense of the relationships with the United States or Britain. However, the same old divisions within the Japanese power structure, together with a very subtle evolution of global strategy by Germany, achieved all of this despite the stated aims of the Japanese Government. Briefly, this is how it unfolded.

The Anti-Comintern Pact of 1936 had recognized and tried to address the international and anti-national natures of communism. Germany and Japan secretly agreed to inform, consult, and collaborate in the prevention of communist influence generally. They agreed to do nothing to aid Russia in the event of an attack on the other signatory, and they also pledged to conclude no other treaties contrary to the spirit of the agreement without mutual consent. These 1936 pledges were the starting points for further anti-Soviet arrangements sought by Japan in 1938, due to its increased vulnerability caused by the war in China and by continuing threats and engagements with Russia, in northern China.

The 1936 agreement was unusual and threatening to the Foreign Office. It had been negotiated by representatives of the military, bypassing foreign ministries and normal ambassadorial channels. This was a divisive and dangerous precedent, the effects of which were amplified in the subsequent attempts to agree on the way forward with Germany.

By 1938, Japanese Army High Command was very keen to re-direct its forces more effectively against Chinese objectives, but they could do so only if the Soviet threat could be neutralized in some way. Discussions began with von Ribbentrop, eventually leading to the official recognition of Manchukuo by Hitler in February 1938. Hitler then terminated aid to Chiang Kai-shek and recalled his military people from the area. This was seen in Japan as very positive encouragement, and moves began for the negotiation of a new military pact with Germany and Italy.

The Army's proposal to isolate Russia became accepted as Konoe's position by the end of June. The alliance to be negotiated was specific to Russia and did not include any agreement to act against Britain or France.

From the outset, von Ribbentrop made it clear that Germany was not particularly interested in a pact that would be limited merely to consultation, nor was it in favor of limiting the pact to apply only toward the Soviets.

To begin with, the Japanese persisted in pursuing a policy that could enable them to "solve the China Incident." On the basis of proposals by General Ugaki, still Foreign Minister at this stage, the Five Ministers' Conference resolved to work towards a military alliance with Germany against the Soviets and a more subtle neutrality pact between Italy and Japan to restrain Great Britain. In response, the German position was vaguely expressed but obviously very different from that of the Japanese, talking of a three-power alliance offering diplomatic and political support if a threat came from any other power.

Nevertheless, the Japanese situation in China had sufficient heat in it to shift even the Foreign Office to the acceptance of the German terms, with one strong proviso: They insisted that a preamble to the agreement be included, which could express the new alliance as an extension of the original Anti-Comintern Pact. The aim of this was obviously to soften the impact of the agreement on the Western powers, upon which Japan was still considerably dependent.

Some months of diplomatic and political turmoil followed, including the resignation of Ugaki and the replacement of some key ambassadors. Eventually, Konoe appointed Hachiro Arita as Foreign Minister, and negotiations recommenced, but under Arita the stated Japanese position once again referred specifically to the Soviets, rather than a more general potential threat. He was also very keen to obtain German assistance in synthetic fuel production and also that of heavy weapons.

Hiroshi Oshima had been made Ambassador to Berlin at the insistence of the army, and his very pro-German position was backed by a powerful group of young officers at home. When he received Arita's new directive he baulked at the change with regard to the non-inclusion of Britain and the United States. Oshima's powerful backers in the army applied considerable pressure on the Cabinet, while he sought time and clarification before transmitting Arita's wishes to the Germans.

Several key Cabinet members gave support to Arita. Finance Minister Ikeda joined the Foreign and Navy Ministers in trying to prevent the alienation of Britain and the United States, in what they saw as a self-defeating policy that would bring financial and military ruin.

The standoff caused the resignation of Konoe's Cabinet in January 1939, but this time, the Genro was not quick enough to exert his influence on the choice of a replacement. Perhaps by this time, old age limited his ability to exercise or press his customary influence. He died late in 1940. Konoe's replacement was Baron Kichiro Hiranuma.

Hiranuma had a background in the Ministry of Justice and was a vigorous campaigner against corruption in politics, obtaining dozens of convictions. By 1921, he was chief of the Japanese Supreme Court. Later, he was active in the creation of the 'Thought Police' to combat subversive, Western and communistic tendencies. He had a protracted and successful career within politics, and as we have seen, he was also a foundation member of the subversive *Kokuhonsha*.

Forming a workable cabinet required some nimble navigation around the persistent divisions concerning the implications of a German alliance. After some shuffling, Foreign Minister Arita agreed to remain in office, on the strength of Hiranuma's promise not to broaden the terms of the treaty. Against this, War Minister Itagaki submitted a list of seven requirements that would need to be accepted before he would sign on again. Among them was the need to strengthen ties with Germany, but this was expressed in such a way that its real meaning was slightly masked or softened.

Outwardly, the Cabinet appeared to have preserved the position adopted by its predecessor, but there was an important difference. The Navy position had moved, and they were reluctantly prepared to countenance an alliance against Britain and France, but for very obtuse and subtle reasons.

The Navy feared the consequences of a limited alliance more than those of a broader one because of the potential of the former to advance the interests of the Army. This was partly about the traditional rivalry that existed between them but also because of the projected consequences of a combined German and Japanese war against the Soviets if the Germans made war, advancing east. They reasoned that in such circumstances, Britain and France might align with Russia as they had in World War I. The Navy saw that Japan could not survive a war in these circumstances, especially if the United States were to join again, as they had before. This was the chief motivational force within the Yonai faction of the Japanese Navy throughout the period. They did not want war with Britain, France, or the United States. Their strategic aims caused them to shift policy more than once, in response to Army initiatives.

This colossal example of counter-intuitive thinking is a measure of the distrust held in Naval circles, both of the Army and of the German leadership. Their position reflected self-interest, though, too. The broader alliance would allow the Navy to compete more equally for funds and resources, to prepare for a potential war, which would inevitably involve the Pacific Ocean.

Fortified with a new and nuanced power structure in the Cabinet, the Five Ministers' Conference under Hiranuma accepted Itagaki's proposals for an alliance. It was planned that the USA be specifically excluded from the aims of the alliance, but it allowed that, if Germany or Italy became entangled with Britain or France, then Japan might give military aid to its allies. They soon became aware that their agreement still fell short of German expectations; so diplomatic staff were sent to explain the difficulty of their position to an increasingly impatient von Ribbentrop.

For various reasons, the Japanese delegates in Berlin and Rome refused to convey the Japanese policy as dictated by Tokyo. Their inclinations were more in line with the young officers group in the army, which was fully compliant with German expectations.

At this point, in February 1939, the Japanese Government's position was firm. There would be no alliance without the conditional statements. These would make it quite clear that Japan would not render military assistance to Germany or Italy in the event of them being attacked by countries other than the Soviet Union unless the aggressor had become communistic.

Oshima and Shiratori, the Japanese representatives, disobeyed orders and refused to transmit these proposals to the German and Italian governments. Naturally, this caused further mayhem in Tokyo involving anger from Arita directed towards the miscreants, anger from the Army, directed at the Cabinet, and even anger expressed by the Emperor. In the meantime, negotiations in Europe seemed to have a life of their own in heading toward an agreed position contrary to Japanese government expectations.

This unraveling created a stiffening of resolve in Japan. The Navy Minister shifted his position back to that of Arita's, and the Finance Minister joined the resistance to the Army. By April, the negotiations appeared to be running out of steam, and the Emperor reprimanded War Minister Itagaki for supporting the errant Ambassadors. This was done so vehemently that there was talk of the Emperor losing the respect of the army.

By late April, after an unprecedented flurry of all-day meetings, the Five Ministers' Conference came to support the views put forward by Mitsumasa Yonai, the Navy Minister. He had argued very forcibly that there should be no alliance at all if Japanese conditions could not be met. He was determined that his country's relationship with America and Britain should not be placed in jeopardy by seeking to counter the Soviet threat with an unlimited alliance with Germany and Italy. Apart from his desire not to antagonize these nations, he was also aware that Japan would lose a global war.

In the meantime, Germany was busy concluding an alliance with Italy, while also engaging in secret negotiations with the Soviet Union. In Tokyo, Hiranuma was siding increasingly with the Army in the continuing hope that an alliance could be forged to apply pressure against Soviet expansion into the Far East.

Hiranuma was completely unaware that Germany was negotiating with the Soviets and had changed its strategic emphasis from east to west. The unfolding situation intensified amidst a very unstable period in Tokyo. In July, the United States gave notice of the termination of its trade treaty with Japan. Violence broke out with the Soviets on the Manchukuo border with Mongolia. The only good news was the tacit admission by Britain that Japan had special requirements for the maintenance of public order that entitled it to belligerent's rights in China.

The astounding news broke on the 23rd of August. A Soviet-German non-aggression pact was declared in which both parties would "obligate themselves to desist from any act of violence, any aggressive action, and any attack on each other, either individually or in combination with other powers." More alarmingly for the Japanese, the pact also prohibited either party from joining "any grouping of powers whatsoever that is directly or indirectly aimed at the other party." The momentous struggles of the previous months in Tokyo suddenly looked humiliatingly like schoolboy naivety. Having become increasingly isolated from its Western trading partners by its overtures to Germany, Japan now faced the alarming reality of its only possible friend in Europe being allied to its traditional regional enemy. Hiranuma was very angry at what he described as treachery. His Cabinet had been formed specifically for the purpose of increasing Japanese security through an alliance against the Soviets. The Cabinet resigned. Within days, Europe had plunged into a war that would isolate Japan even further.

The Tired Pendulum

The incident at Marco Polo Bridge had created a situation in Japan that demanded unity and focus, and the Diet generally supported government bills with minimum fuss in the face of a growing international crisis. It is quite normal for a government to be granted 'bipartisan support' in a crisis, but in Japan, this became one pressure too many on the party system. While complete harmony was never possible in pre-war Japanese politics, party agendas gave way to the common need to address the new situation. This didn't stop the parties tearing themselves apart, though, as Konoe's talk of a single party gained respectability.

The concepts of state unity and strong control in the Diet eventually found an acceptable leader in Konoe, who formed his second cabinet in July 1940, by which time the old parties had begun to disintegrate. This disintegration was another expression of the near impossibility of achieving a single leadership voice in a system that gave the military the extraordinary power to bring down cabinets.

The major parties had gone by August 15th and were replaced by the inauguration of the Imperial Rule Assistance Association (*Taisai Yokusan kai*) on October 12, 1940. Before this, however, there would be two more Cabinets in a short space of time. One fell as a consequence of the Army's intervention, but the other can be seen as the victim of a last-ditch attempt by the Diet to prevent undue concentration of Cabinet power.

Following the resignation of the Hiranuma Cabinet in 1939, the Emperor made it known in a quite unprecedented way that General Abe had been given an imperial mission in his new task of Premiership, and he spelled out some particular requirements of his time in office. The preferred candidate was former Finance Minister Ikeda, whose appointment would have represented a clear break with Axis-oriented policy, in favor of a more Western-oriented one. The Army blocked his appointment before it could be carried out. There was a very real possibility that political assassinations and general violence would follow his appointment. So when Abe was chosen instead, the Emperor was quite specific in instructing him to co-operate with the Western powers and to select a War Minister who could be relied upon to exercise discipline within the Army. Abe assumed power on August 30, 1939. By September 3rd, Europe was at war, suddenly changing the complexion of international affairs.

Abe still had hopes of an agreement with the Soviets, and he also needed to maintain a trade relationship with the United States, but this became enmeshed in the issue of China. Britain's involvement in Europe caused a fairly sudden withdrawal of influence in China, and this included the British recognition of Japanese belligerent's rights there. If the United States could be convinced to adopt the British attitude, Japan would probably be able to resolve the Sino-Japanese war. From the Japanese perspective, this was an entirely rational idea, which would result in the increase of Japanese influence within its own region.

The American attitude, however, was that the vacuum created by the loss of British influence should logically be filled by them.

The new relationship between the Soviets and Germany seemed to hold within it the promise of a new force, which had the potential to counter the Anglo/American bloc. If this could be harnessed by an improved Sino-Japanese relationship, a way out of the Chinese debacle could be envisaged. This was thought possible because the Soviets were still the major suppliers of material aid to the nationalists.

Togo Shigenori, the Japanese Ambassador in Moscow, was one of a group of civilian leaders who pressed this line of thought. It was argued that this new situation could be used to provide pressure, both on China and the United States, and that it was worth putting anti-communism aside for the time being, in order to create an anti-Anglo and anti-democratic bloc.

The adoption of this view by some civilian and Foreign Office leaders represented a radically different way forward, and it can only really be explained by the cumulative effect of the war in China on Japan's resources, domestic wealth, or lack of it, and morale. Rather than face the fact that Chinese resistance was due to Japanese and other foreign actions, they chose instead to attribute the continued resistance to foreign interference. While this was accurate in the material sense, it was less so with regard to the motivations of the nationalists.

What they chose not to see was that such a way forward made no allowance at all for the real nature of Japanese politics, industry, markets, or economic interdependence on the West. Despite their attempts at creating an autarkic bloc, Japan was still thoroughly dependent on American markets and materials. Politically, Japan had more in common with the West than with the Soviets or the Nazis. Japan's capitalist economy was largely in private hands. As Akira Iriye wrote, "The Japanese fascination and even obsession with distancing themselves from the Anglo-American nations and identifying with Germany or the Soviet Union was an emotional response to the frustration of a long war, and had little to do with a specific program for solidarity with revisionist forces in the world."[131]

Abe, like Konoe after him, was tempted to explore these options, but he realized that such a course would only worsen the already difficult terrain upon which US-Japanese relations rested. His appointment of Admiral Nomura Kichisaburo signaled his intention of healing the relationship and turning Japan back to a more moderate line, but in doing so he faced

---

[131] Iriye, Akira. *The Origins of the Second World War in Asia and the Pacific*, Essex: Longman, 1987, P85.

powerful opposition. His project started with a series of constructive talks with Joseph Grew.[132]

Abe's attempts to streamline domestic power were challenged from within the Diet and the Privy Council. His attempts to strengthen Cabinet power failed to achieve support among the parties. Amid a growing economic crisis, on January 14, 1940, the Cabinet was forced to resign by a majority vote in the Diet.

The appointment of Admiral Yonai was another moderate choice, made with moderate hopes, but the tone and direction of Japanese foreign policy had already been substantially formed. That is not to say that progress toward peace was not possible, but that internal momentum was gathering against moderate voices. At this time, it was still not clear how the European situation would resolve itself, but in the national scheme of things, the army was opposed to Yonai from the outset.

Attempts to Resolve the Issue of China

Given the failure of even moderate cabinets to re-negotiate a commercial treaty with the United States, the need to resolve the war in China seemed even more pressing. The Japanese strength there had grown to over 800,000 troops, with no clear result in sight. Views were divided as to whether it was best to increase the commitment further for a decisive victory, or whether a reduced commitment in a more limited number of areas would be best, to enable preparation for defense in a possible war with the Soviets. The result was a decision for a 'surge,' followed by a troop reduction, in combination with support of Wang, the alternative leader installed in Nanking. Forces would be concentrated in the provinces around Nanking as well as in the north.

---

[132] These issues are discussed further in Chapter 15

Wang Ching-wei had very little real support, but he represented the belief that China would prosper if an accommodation with Japan could be made, to resist what he saw as the increasing domination of China by the Soviet communists. The Japanese aided him by having him establish an alternative Chinese government in opposition to Chiang.[133]

The failure to negotiate a settlement with Chiang stemmed from the same stumbling blocks that prevented one with America, namely the insistence by both parties that Japan disengage, even from Manchuria. At a time when even German supplies of machinery and technology were dwindling due to the war in Europe, the resources of Manchuria became more central to any notion of Japanese industrial and military survival. The nationalist and American demands amounted to a reversal of the Japanese position to the status quo before 1931, and the best political will in the world would not be sufficient to have that accepted in Japan at that time.

It was felt in the United States that there was still a remote hope that the situation in Europe was redeemable before all out war occurred. The American Under-Secretary of State was authorized to explore the notion of disarmament on the basis of resumption of international trade, but only within the bounds of the status quo as it was under the Washington system. This was never going to be supported as an idea in Europe, and it was politically impossible in Japan. The end of the 'phony war' killed the idea before it began, but it also highlighted Japan's isolation by linking American support of China in Asia to its support of Britain in Europe.

Soon after Yonai's appointment, the trade treaty with the United States expired, reinforcing both prevalent views within the government. The pro-Western factions felt that the loss of

---

[133] See Iriye Akira, ibid, P90–91 for a concise account of Wang's relationship to Japan.

trade was the inevitable outcome of Japanese mistakes, while the anti-Western faction had their view reinforced that America was inflexible and arrogant and determined to see Japan on its knees. Whatever disagreement there was about the cause of the new situation, there was growing agreement about the course that must as a consequence be followed. Japan must align more closely with the Italian and German axis.

Meanwhile, towards the end of January and a mere thirty-five miles off the coast of Japan, a relatively minor incident galvanized anti-Western feelings. The Japanese steamship *Asama-maru* was stopped on return from the United States by a British warship. The British apprehended twenty-one German passengers. This caused Media uproar in Japan, and in many quarters, Yonai's continuation of moderate policies was blamed for the deteriorating situation.

Domestically, two further issues added momentum to the militarist agenda. The first was a passionate speech in the Diet, which was critical of the Army and its 'Holy War' in China. Takao Saito caused uproar by claiming, among other things, that the Army was causing unnecessary sacrifice for an unknown cause. The Army demanded that he be expelled from the Diet, and this placed incredible pressure on formerly moderate members to be humiliated and criticized or to support the aggrieved army.

This caused further splits within the main parties and a number of expulsions from the Diet. A further initiative by some remaining Diet members involved the creation of a group called 'The League of Diet Members for the Fulfillment of the Holy War Aims,' which boldly re-asserted the predominance of Army aims.

Until this time, Yuasa, the Keeper of the Privy Seal, had been a conservative and steadying influence, described by some as the last stronghold of the pro-Western group within the Imperial Court. He was replaced in June by Marquis Kido, who brought a new zeal for reform to that esteemed position, in sympathy with Army aims. There was a growing number of factors by this time that made the less moderate approaches to the West seem to be more reasonable.

Re-organization for a Crisis

Europe slid into a series of rolling capitulations and submissions to the Nazi regime. The Dutch had surrendered and the French had signed an armistice. These two events in particular revealed a whole new level of possibility to the Japanese. Yonai faced the reality that, in the absence of trade and particularly fuel from the United States, a new relationship would be necessary with the colonies of the two European nations, and they were subject to German administration.

By the 23rd of May, the British Expeditionary Force had been cornered on the coast of France, and it was entirely possible that it would be wiped out, including its compliment of 250,000 men, their weapons, transport, and artillery. There was no standing army left in Britain capable of replacing it or defending the nation from the anticipated invasion, and Churchill was haunted by the possibility of heading a government in exile from the safety of Canada. Initial prospects of evacuation seemed limited to a possible 45,000 troops. Morale in London was very low as the evacuation began slowly, retrieving only 17,000 troops during the 28th of May. Momentum built into what became a legendary achievement that accounted for the safe evacuation of 224,301 British and 111,172 French and Belgian troops by the 4th of June. Churchill was able to turn an impossible situation into a morale building triumph, but there was no escaping the loss of national prestige.

The humiliation of the evacuation at Dunkirk added urgency to the Japanese desire to negotiate some kind of alliance with Germany before it was too late. Even before that was attempted, however, negotiations were underway to pursue economic concessions in the Dutch East Indies and a neutrality pact with Thailand. Germany was also approached to recognize Japan's special interest in French Indochina. The map of South East Asia suddenly had a different appearance; still colored as European possessions but glowing with new promise.

Mamoru Shigemitsu, the Japanese Ambassador to the United Kingdom at the time, recollected with some passion the impact of the German successes. In his 1958 book, *Japan and Her Destiny: My Struggle for Peace,* he emphasized the power of German propaganda on the sentiment within Japan and the palpable fear that Japan would 'miss the boat' if Germany went on to establish an undiluted influence across the Far East, Africa, Europe, and possibly also within their own sphere of influence.

His recollections gently color Japanese opportunism with a caretaker's concern for world welfare, but they do give us an insight into the urgency and hysteria of the time, and he confronted the gullibility of Japan's contemporary leadership with simple clarity. He wrote: "by now Japan had forsaken the calm, realistic view. She believed that Germany would win and thought only what she could do about it. One might have expected that the Army would prove a good medium for German propaganda but that most Japanese leaders should have fallen into the same frame of mind can be recalled only with a feeling of shame."[134]

In defense of the leadership referred to above, many in the West were also of the opinion that Germany would prevail, until the moment that it invaded the Soviet Union. In late May, Roosevelt suggested that Britain's dominions ought to urge Churchill to send the British fleet to North America, out of harm's way so that it would not be lost in a future capitulation

---

[134] Mamoru Shigemitsu and White, O (ed), *Japan and Her Destiny: My Struggle for Peace,* Dutton, New York: 1958, P189.

by his government. During the same period, serious secret negotiations between Britain and Italy were underway to explore the idea of Italian intervention in a negotiated peace.

At the time, though, the changing European situation meant that, from a Japanese perspective, agreements would be needed with Russia to secure China from further disruption, as well as with Germany to allow Japan to expand its influence down through Asia. Implicit in Japanese thinking was the fear of exclusive German influence being at the expense of Japan. An alliance that included Italy would also make sense because it would spread the benefits of the new world order, diluting the dominance of Germany.

Viewed from the other side of the Pacific, one American fear was that Germany might combine with Japan to crush the Soviets from each side, spreading German and Japanese influence from France to the Pacific, through the heart of Europe. But the Japanese needed raw materials, so the Indies, Malaya, and Indochina became the focus of their thinking.

The Japanese proposal for alliance with Germany still precluded Japan from participation in military support, because they considered the situation in China rendered Japan incapable of further involvement elsewhere. Needless to say, the Germans were not particularly impressed. Neither was the Japanese Army. Yonai's resignation was forced by the Army on July 16th, less than two weeks after the discovery of a plot to assassinate half a dozen government leaders, which included Admiral Yonai. The Army had grown tired of politics and wanted a single party of dependable persuasion. Konoe was once again about to be pressed into service as Premier, but in him they would encounter a different vision again.

During the same month, Shigemitsu was on the spot in London when a very provocative threat was made, concerning material British support for Chiang's forces in China.

The Japanese Army were becoming very frustrated with international influence, both active and passive, which they saw quite accurately as prolonging their campaign in a local war. The Japanese Director of Military Intelligence requested the cessation of British assistance to Chiang by writing,

> "Britain is already beaten and the British Empire faces dissolution. And yet Britain continues to support Chiang and to encourage him to resist Japan. Japan is now strong. The Army has its batteries trained on Hong Kong and it only requires one word of command to them to bombard the island. Britain would do well to cease assistance to Chiang and to control smuggling from Hong Kong. Today in Japan it is the Army that holds the power. The Japanese Foreign Office, on which Britain relies, is powerless and unworthy of trust. Britain would be well-advised to accept this request from the Japanese Army."[135]

The message is bulging with the muscular hubris of a gloating former victim. It also paints a vivid picture of the contempt with which the Army viewed the traditional role of the diplomatic service and politics in general. Shigemitsu was profoundly shocked and threatened by the tone of this threat, writing, "I could not bear to think that the Army would destroy such a valuable relationship. If the words were taken at face value, it meant the severance of diplomatic relations. I felt that it by no means expressed the true sentiments of Japan. Nor should it do so."

The two Foreign Offices worked harder to prevent further deterioration of the relationship between the two governments and, ultimately, Britain did tighten control of Hong Kong's borders and also closed the Burma route for a period of three

---

[135] Ibid, p190

months. Looking back on the developments as they reflected the increasingly militant situation in Japan, Shigemitsu felt that his best efforts, and those of the British, were a "pure waste of time."

At this time, Prince Konoe was trying to complete the groundwork for a single political party that would be capable of overcoming persistent political weakness caused by the divided power structure in Japan. He referred to this as the 'New Order' movement. He had hoped to create the foundation for this party while not in office, to avoid infiltration by the army and the interference of old guard politicians. The removal of Yonai was inconvenient, as Konoe was not ready for the new type of power he envisaged, but he accepted the inevitable when it was offered. Despite appearances, Konoe wanted to prevent a Nazi style of government in Japan by grounding it in a broad spectrum of community representation. Much later, he confided that he felt that he had made a mess of the party and that Prince Saionji had been right to persist in his belief in parliamentary-style representation.

We have seen that Konoe brought with him a history of honest searching for a way to engage properly with the prevailing order. As far back as 1918, he had caused an international sensation when he published a critique of the Versailles conference. In it, he expressed enthusiasm for humanitarian and democratic ideals, but was scathing of the peace terms, seeing them as attempts to perpetuate the current power structure and mask self-interest by burying it in a layer of idealistic rhetoric. Throughout the 1930s, his observations would be proven to be right, particularly with regard to the control of markets.

If the push for an alliance with Germany and Italy was propelled by a fear of missing an international opportunity, the possibility of a single Konoe party within Japan created a similar scramble among Japan's politicians to take their places in the coming juggernaut of domestic power. Putting aside their former parties in the rush to get on board, the process became less than dignified in several instances. This overwhelming race for inclusion caused a shift in Konoe's thinking. Rather than a party, he created a non-party association, incorporating people of all walks of life, including women. Cabinet Ministers became ex-officio members of the core association group.

By broadening the association's base, Konoe had hoped to counter the influence of the Army, but the tendrils of army influence that permeated Japanese society created and perpetuated the very influence that Konoe had attempted to avoid. The *Taisei Yokusankai* (Imperial Rule Assistance Association) was Konoe's Frankenstein.

The one new party was a typically pragmatic solution to the convergence of problems and issues over a decade. The political pendulum had apparently come to rest, but if the solution was pragmatic, it was framed in the typical rhetoric of grand ideas.

The following is an extract from the opening sections of the Provincial Planning Committee:

> "We endeavor to be loyal subjects. That is we believe in our national structure, which is the manifestation of matchless absolute universal truth, faithfully observe the Imperial prescripts of the successive sovereigns, serve the country in our respective posts, and exalt the great Divine Way."[136]

Although the majority of former party leaders joined the new party, the same factionalism persisted along with the contradictions inherent in the system since its inception. The pendulum would swing again.

---

[136] Translation from IMTFE, Document No 451, Exhibit No 67, Regulations of the Provincial Planning Committee of the Imperial Rule Assistance Association, cited in Ibid P389.

Konoe's Second Cabinet

The new Foreign Minister with whom Konoe had to work was Yosuke Matsuoka, a confident speaker and statesman who was known sometimes to be provocative. Shigemitsu's contemporary observation of Matsuoka from his London vantage point gave him hope. Matsuoka had published his views concerning the China question and, in this, he backed the principles of "no indemnities, no annexations, and recognition of sovereignty." Shigemitsu wrote; "That fact alone induced me to think for a while…that now at last, in the association of two liberal thinkers, Konoe and Matsuoka, Japan might keep the militarists in check and get back on the right track again."[137]

Matsuoka was the key figure in overcoming Konoe's fears concerning the possible impact of a tripartite pact on Japanese-United States relations. Matsuoka's view was that the pact would be designed to keep them neutral, for their own benefit. Matsuoka was able to back his judgment by drawing attention to his American Law Degree from Oregon University and Konoe deferred to his forceful confidence.

Konoe's intentions at this point, in regard to the proposed alliance, were still opportunistic and defensive. Japan should make the best of the deteriorating international situation. In so doing, Japan should try to neutralize the impact of Britain and the United States on the war in China, without threatening Japan's relationship with them. From our perspective, the idea is preposterous. From Konoe's contemporary perspective, the driving force in creating the future was Germany, not the United States.

The new Foreign Minister achieved an unprecedented level of independence in his negotiations with Germany. With the backing of the Cabinet, he negotiated directly with German

---

[137] Mamoru, Shigemitsu and White, O. (ed). *Japan and Her Destiny: My Struggle for Peace.* New York: Dutton, 1958, P196.

Ambassador Ott, although from his superior position, the German Ambassador was cool and not altogether responsive.

In the initial meeting, Matsuoka spelled out his desire to avoid a conflict with the United States on the grounds that the new world order would shift its center to the Pacific region, and the two countries could build some understanding along these lines. In a sense, of course, he was right, but it took a war to achieve this understanding, and it occurred completely on the United States' terms.

By August, Germany had signaled its preparedness to embark on a new level of talks by sending General Heinrich Stahmer as von Ribbentrop's personal representative. The Japanese were still bound to a policy of non-aggression towards the United States, largely because of persistent Naval reluctance to risk a naval war. The appearance of Stahmer would require a more sympathetic position.

What happened next was a small, temporary shift in the composition of the Cabinet, to which may be attributed a profound change in the ultimate direction of the nation. On the 4th of September, the Konoe Cabinet met. The Navy Minister was absent, outwardly due to illness, and was represented by the Vice Navy Minister. Until then, the Navy had refused to consider any alliance that could be seen to be aimed against the United States, but the absence of Yoshida and the impending visit by Stahmer combined to allow the possibility of a nuance in the previous position.

On September 4th, they agreed that, unless they were able to discuss a possible military commitment, the alliance with Italy and Germany would be impossible. They rationalized that such an agreement would represent a policy of containment against the United States, to prevent it from interfering in regions other than the Western Hemisphere and its own possessions.

At this meeting, the cabinet group began to plan a vision of the future based upon their expectations of the unfolding world situation. This vision comprised four blocs of regional control and influence. Japan would rule greater Asia, Germany and Italy would control Europe and Africa, Russia would control pretty much what it already had (for the time being), and the Western Hemisphere would be controlled by the United States.

Grasping this global vision created an immediate concern for the Japanese, when it was reported by the Japanese Consul General Yamaji, from his embassy in Vienna, that the Germans were considering the colonization of Sumatra and Java and might even consider a role in French Indo-China as well. It was felt that only engagement with Germany would guarantee the exclusivity of Japanese control in Asia. Given that Japanese foreign policy emerged in, and was fed by, a climate of fear, the importance of this implied threat should not be underestimated.

It does help to explain the extraordinarily expansive list of colonies and countries in the future Japanese-controlled 'Greater East Asia New Order,' designed to impress very firmly on the German command that the region was already allocated to the junior partner.

The exact composition of the Greater East Asia New Order, or Co-Prosperity Sphere, as it became known, is of particular relevance to modern Australians and new Zealanders.

The Invasion, or not, of Australia: a Slight Deviation

Many writers and observers have assumed that the composition of the 'Greater East Asia New Order' included Australia and New Zealand. Evidence suggesting otherwise has become contentious and has produced some emotional debate. The heat in the debate comes in part from the natural assumption that 'the defense of Australia' was simply that, and was part of the resistance by the Allies of global domination by Axis powers, including invasion of Australia.

Australians have long held that their freedoms were preserved by the sacrifices made in the Pacific War and, in a general sense, that is true, but the intentions of the Japanese cannot be simplified to fit all of the particularities implied by that assertion. Admitting this complexity in no way demeans the actions or sacrifices of Australian and Allied soldiers.

In a sense, the real question to be addressed with regard to the Australian situation relates more to what Australians *felt* might happen to them, rather than that which was actually planned by the Japanese. The likelihood of invasion fit well within the experience of being located adjacent to a region that was very quickly being 'overrun'[138] by a non-European enemy. This was happening at a time when the bulk of its forces were in the Northern Hemisphere fighting a somewhat separate war.

By February 1942, the Australian 8th Division were caught up in the disastrous British humiliation at Singapore, and the survivors were prisoners of the Japanese. Australians were very sparsely populated on an isolated continent and they felt particularly vulnerable, especially at the thought that their armed forces were engaged in the preservation of an Empire that could obviously offer very little in return. Many assumptions were made on both sides of Australian politics about the intentions of the Japanese and the need to prepare for the worst.

A significant number of statements and articles since then have built on that feeling and those assumptions. For example, in his farewell message to Australia in August 1945, General MacArthur referred to "a struggle which saw our cause at its lowest ebb as the enemy hordes plunged forward with almost irresistible force to the very threshold of your homeland. There

---

[138] A deliberately emotional word that fits the consistent pattern of fear displayed by an under-populated island with a racially exclusive immigration policy.

you took your stand…"[139] He was stating what felt very real to Australians and was true in that sense, and perhaps even he did not know at that stage that no plans for Japan to invade Australia had been adopted by the Japanese government or by the military. In fact, Tojo said very strongly before he died that "We never had enough troops to do so….actual physical invasion—no, at no time."[140]

This feeling of being invaded has helped many Australians come to terms with the sacrifice of their family members and has been used expansively in nation-building speeches and writings such as that by Paul Keating in 1992, which included the assertion that, "It was only in World War II that this country came under threat of invasion—this was not true in World War I…"[141] Strategic bombing attacks do not automatically lead to invasion. From this type of confusion and these natural, intuitive assumptions grew a general belief that this was the simple truth. Keating's statement may have been more accurate if it had substituted the words "faced the possibility" for the words "came under threat."[142]

Part of the problem of identifying Japanese intentions stems from the many centers of policy feeding into military action. Policy and strategic advice can be sourced from several factions of both the army and the navy. It is possible to find advocates for an alarming number of expansionary ideas, but that doesn't make them policy. Several strategists within the

---

[139] *The Reports of General MacArthur*, Vol 1, The Campaigns of MacArthur in the Pacific: Washington, 1966 P392.

[140] Coulthard-Clark, C. *Action Stations Coral Sea*. North Sydney: Allen & Unwin, 1991 Pxvi.

[141] *Regional Role Demands Mental Revolution*, record of interview with PM Keating, *The Australian*, 21 April 1992 P4.

[142] None of this detracts, incidentally, from the inspirational quality that typified Keating's 'big picture' speeches. As a body they probably did more that any post-war political words to re-orient the Australian view of its place in history, recognizing and addressing some shortcomings in the process.

administration put forward various schemes to neutralize Australia by strikes, and even occupations, and various maps exist that may or may not represent some of these schemes, but an occupation was not an agreed policy.

In addition, Japanese planning struggled to keep pace with the speed of events during the period, so what seemed a good idea in 1940 might have evolved into another idea altogether by 1942. Forward planning therefore was allowed to accommodate a variety of eventualities. This has enabled some very reliable authors to come to conclusions that seem to be in conflict with one another.

For example, in his well-reasoned 1961 book, *From the Marco Polo Bridge to Pearl Harbor: Japan's entry into World War II*,[143] David Lu wrote of the September 4th Cabinet meeting that,

> "The primary objective of the alliance was the establishment of 'Japan's sphere of living for the construction of a Greater East Asia New Order.' The regions were to comprise 'the former German Islands under mandate, French Indo-china and Pacific Islands, Thailand, British Malaya, British Borneo, Dutch East Indies, Burma, Australia, New Zealand, India etc., with Japan, Manchukuo and China as the backbone.'"

The list cited here is indicated as a quotation but no source is given. It is different from several other versions that quote the records of the meeting. According to the International Military Tribunal for the Far East (IMTFE) documents,[144] the countries incorporated into the Co-Prosperity Sphere are "French Indo-China, the Netherlands, East Indies, the Straights Settlements,

---

[143] Lu, D. J. *From the Marco Polo Bridge to Pearl Harbor: Japan's Entry into World War II*. Washington DC: Public Affairs Press, 1961, P108.

[144] IMTFE Judgment Chapter vii, *Japanese Policy 1940*, P848.

British Malaya, Thailand, the Philippines, British Borneo, and Burma."

Australia and New Zealand are absent.

By January of 1942, the successes of the Axis powers enabled the concept to become more fulsome. The references in the 'Draft of Basic Plan For Establishment of Greater East Asia Co-Prosperity Sphere'[145] outline a longer-term plan for the region, which includes in a list of objectives:

> "Next the independence of Australia, India etc. shall be gradually brought about. For this purpose, a recurrence of war with Britain and her allies is expected. This is part of a larger plan to see that 'Aggressive American and British influences in East Asia shall be driven out of the area of Indo-China and the South Seas, and this area shall be brought into our defense sphere.'"

Such optimistic, long-term planning was soon overtaken by the events to which Australian soldiers made a particular contribution, but it does not constitute a policy to invade, or occupy. Of course, this is of little use to the thousands of Australians who were given the task of forward defense in the New Guinea, New Britain, and Timor campaigns and who died or were damaged in the process. A lot of blood was shed demonstrating Australian vulnerability, whether invasion was imminent or not. Even in the absence of a policy to invade, it is difficult to see the sense in leaving a small pro-British dominion free to disrupt Japanese regional security had the war gone to plan, so it is entirely logical that controlling it in some way was included in forward thinking.[146]

---

[145] *Draft Basic Plan*, IMTFE, International Prosecution Section, Document 2402B, Exhibit 1336.

[146] For a more detailed account of this issue see *Invasion 1942? Australia and the Japanese Threat,* Background Paper Number 6, 1992, Parliamentary

The situation in September of 1940, with the imminent appearance of the German secret emissary, encouraged the Konoe Cabinet to establish an elaborate rationalization for the incorporation of the entire region into the Japanese sphere of influence, at least partially to deter the Germans from becoming absolutely global in their hegemony. There is a hint of paranoia in this meeting. The China problem seemed unsolvable, The US was aligning more and more with China and Britain, and Soviet Russia might become more aggressive if Japan became too engaged elsewhere. Surely it should be possible simply to maintain Japanese interests in Manchukuo and China without having to fight a war with all of these? Yet, ominously, Germany was reportedly considering its options in Japan's sphere.

The Signing of the Tripartite Pact

The Soviet threat was perceived to be more manageable from within a German alliance, and Konoe was even persuaded to consider a four-way alliance including the Soviets, but the long-standing mistrust between the two powers caused Konoe to stop short at this point. Instead, it was agreed that the secret agreement contained within the old Anti-Comintern Pact would stand, providing supporting action to a member in the eventuality of conflict between the Soviets and either of the other two members.

By September 5th, Navy Minister Yoshida had resigned, taking with him the last solid opposition to a reasonably unfettered alliance. Two days later, Stahmer arrived in Tokyo, under instructions to negotiate only with the Foreign Minister Matsuoka. Stahmer expressed the German desire to keep the United States out of the European war, encouraging the

Research Service, Brown, G. and Anderson, D. and also *"He's (not) Coming South:" the invasion that wasn't*, Remembering 1942 history conference, Stanley P., Principal Historian, Australian War Memorial, Canberra.

Japanese to reach some sort of understanding. It was felt that Germany could do for Japan, with regard to Russia, what Japan could do for Germany, with regard to the United States. Stahmer also reiterated that his government would not ask for Japanese assistance in acting against the British. Matsuoka resisted the idea of a four-way alliance including Russia despite overtures from Stahmer.

Most historians see Matsuoka's desire to focus the alliance against Russia as evidence of his conviction that the United States would not resort to the use of force to prevent Japanese regional aggression and that a considered alliance might restrict them without offending them. This very dangerous navigation reveals enormous self-belief, since he has been quoted as saying at a meeting on the 19th of September, that the alliance was aimed at America. What Matsuoka would say was apparently dependent upon who was listening. He was genuinely quite fond of things American and held a strong but very naïve view that the future Japanese and American blocs would one day work happily together. They did of course, eventually.

To this end, he held that the wording of the alliance should allow for Japanese withdrawal should the United States enter the war and that it should be explicitly stated that the alliance was purely of a defensive nature. There is evidence that his reservations were as a consequence of the disinclination of the new navy minister for an aggressive alliance, but in any case, the urgency of the situation and the personal power of Stahmer combined to overcome Matsuoka on this. After only three days of negotiation, they had reached an agreement, and, had it occurred some months previously, it might have had an altogether different effect on the war. As it was, the alliance was signed on September 27th, 1940, creating a very negative impact among Allied powers.

If Matsuoka and Konoe were convinced of the wisdom of this alliance, there were certainly many in Japan who weren't.

Ambassador Shigemitsu was certain that the Emperor didn't want it, nor did Konoe's mentor, the Genro. For his part, Shigemitsu had this to say:

"Relations with Britain, the US, and France speedily deteriorated. But Konoe, in defiance of common sense, explained to the Privy Council that the Alliance was consistent with an intention to improve relations with the neighboring countries of Russia and the US. Presumably he expected that Germany would assist a détente with Russia, while the US, as Germany had explained, would be deterred by the might of the three allies from coming into the war. But how could the alliance be other than an obstruction to friendly relations with the British and Americans or even be a means of improving them? If such diplomacy was not sheer bluff, what was it? To those like myself who had consistently opposed the alliance it passed human understanding."[147]

He also wrote of Matsuoka's meeting with the American Ambassador in Moscow in which the former spoke of goodwill and the firm intention of opening negotiations with the United States in the immediate future. Shigemitsu spoke of Konoe's desire to improve relations with Britain but "felt that the alliance had placed Japan in a position from which she could never recover," claiming that he was "plunged into the depths of despair."[148]

Strutting the world's stage, Matsuoka felt able to act expansively in response to what he saw as a new *zeitgeist*

[147] Mamoru, Shigemitsu, Piggot, F., and White, O (ed). *Japan and Her Destiny: My Struggle for Peace.* New York: Dutton, 1958, P204.

[148] Ibid P204

championed by the efficient and apparently unstoppable National Socialists in Germany. Despite his affection for British and American culture, he considered it his most serious task to back the winning side in the coming new world order. The only conceivable alternative was a complete reversal of national policy, which could not be achieved with honor.

Indeed, having come this far, the alternative loss of face was unconscionable for him. We might be tempted to think that this is a very culturally specific issue, but the avoidance of humiliation, or 'saving face' can be attributed to several misguided policies by Western powers, too, even quite recently. For example, a communication written by United States assistant secretary of defense, John McNoughton in January 1966 reveals high-level thinking about the purpose of the Vietnam War. He wrote, "the present US objective in Vietnam is to avoid humiliation. The reasons why we went into Vietnam are largely academic."[149] Similarly, during the 2007 election campaign in Australia, Prime Minister Howard cited potential loss of Western prestige as a fundamental reason to keep troops in Iraq, despite or even because all of the original given reasons for the invasion had been discredited.

Matsuoka had struggled with the idea of re-aligning with Britain and the United States, and said so at a meeting on September 14th. He felt that to do so, however, would mean the loss of the dream of a new order in Asia, loss of face in China on American terms, and more importantly, Japan would become

---

[149] Ham, P. *Vietnam: The Australian War.* Harper Collins, 2007, cited in a review by former Australian Deputy Prime Minister Tim Fisher in *The Australian*, Review P10, October 27 2007. Mr. Fisher also refers to the analogous situation in Iraq. He wrote, in part, "It is gut-wrenching to think that the first Australian taskforce went to Nui Dat only after that admission. It is perhaps equally gut-wrenching to wonder about the present phase of the Iraq War. It is instructive to remember that in order to avoid humiliation in Vietnam, it was acceptable to Washington that acres of Arlington Cemetery be filled with American soldiers." Mr. Fisher is a Vietnam veteran.

dominated by the two powers for another fifty years, should Britain somehow survive the war.

Fear of loss of face partly explains Matsuoka's willingness to compromise his own pre-requisites of the Pact with Germany, but so does his desire to impress his German heroes. This factor led Matsuoka into a radical redesign of Japanese foreign affairs, with the dismissal of most of Japan's diplomats and their replacement by Axis supporters. It was hoped that the enormous gamble on a German victory would also have a significant restraining impact on the United States.

The signing of the Pact certainly had an impact but not the restraint envisaged by Matsuoka. During the period of discussion and negotiation leading up to the signing of the Pact, the situation in Europe began to change.

Churchill's unexpected decision to fight on, regardless of the weakness of the British position, added complications to Hitler's agenda. With a defiant Britain, Hitler could not turn on the Soviets without the persistence of an expensive campaign behind him. The apparently unbeatable German Luftwaffe had failed to break the back or the spirit of the British in the Battle of Britain, and a new sense of optimism was emerging. Churchill knew that, having come this far, he could rely on continued material support from Roosevelt.

Roosevelt won an improbable third term, another event that ran counter to Japanese hopes and expectations. The campaign had been vigorous and heated, with Wendell Wilkie's chance of changing American foreign policy rated highly by the Japanese, despite bi-partisan agreements between the two candidates on several issues. These events received considerable coverage in Japan. It was felt in Tokyo that a firm attitude to the United States at this point would demonstrate to the American public that Roosevelt was in danger of leading them to war. By contrast, a softer policy might act in Roosevelt's favor. In addition, Matsuoka counted on the influence of the twenty million Americans of German descent to influence America's direction.[150]

The new foreign policy rested on the assumption that the South Sea regions were part of Japan's economic and defense sphere so, therefore, the European war should not be extended into that area. As part of the new alliance, Germany had 'generously' surrendered its island possessions to Japan. In fact, this formed part of the leverage applied to Matsuoka by Ambassador Ott. He said, "If Japan refuses to align with Germany, Germany might quickly conclude a peace treaty with Great Britain and take possession of the South Seas regions."[151]

The British and the French had apparently been beaten and had therefore lost their local claim to power, and the United States would never go to war with Japan while it was pre-occupied with the war in Europe, particularly while Japan was backed by Germany.

In so many ways, Matsouka got things horribly wrong. It is hard to imagine ways in which he could have been more terminally, fatally wrong.

Later, in December 1941, Matsuoka was sick and in bed when the attack on Pearl Harbor was announced. He confessed earnest regrets to a visiting friend. "The Tripartite Alliance was my worst mistake. I hoped to prevent the United States from entering the war. I wanted to adjust our relations with Soviet Russia through this alliance. I hoped peace would be maintained and Japan would be placed in a secure position. Instead, we see face-to-face the present calamity which indirectly resulted from the alliance."[152]

---

[150] Lu, David J. *From Marco Polo Bridge to Pearl Harbor: Japan's Entry into World War II*. Washington: Public Affairs Press, 1961, P115.

[151] Ibid P116

[152] Saito, Yoshie. *Azamukareta Rekishi (The Distorted History)*. Published in Japanese, Tokyo: Mainichi Shinbunsha, 1950, P5, cited in Ibid P119.

15

POLITICS STRADDLING THE PACIFIC

L ATER WE WILL see US Ambassador Grew's repeated
pleas with Washington to support Japanese moderates
in their efforts to control the expansionary tendencies
within the army. He understood the need for this because he
could see that the army was not a monolith.

The US Administration continued to evaluate Japanese
intentions in 1930 terms, but the Japanese Army was not in
that same commanding position by the early 1940s. This was
perhaps counter-intuitive, as the situation politically had
become less democratic, but the increase in power of the
bureaucracy was to some extent at the expense of the military.

The plan to advance southward for example became a widely
supported national political policy, because of the growing
tension with the United States and the threat to Japanese oil
and resource needs. It was a plan to replace what the US had
threatened to take away, and while it suited some elements
within the military, it was not simply a military initiative.

In Chicago on October 5, 1937, Roosevelt delivered a speech
that was to change and challenge American isolationism. In

response to Japanese aggression in China, he proposed that aggressor nations be subject to 'quarantine.' Foreign Minister Arita responded by stating that "invoking principles that might have been applicable before the outbreak of the China Incident but that had no relation to the new situation emerging in East Asia would be futile not only for resolving present problems but for establishing lasting peace in that area as well."[153]

This sentiment found wide support in Japan but created a very negative response in Washington. The tide of public opinion there supported the State Department hard-line desire to abrogate the US-Japanese Treaty of Commerce and Navigation. Consequently, in July 1939, the Roosevelt Administration formally notified Japan that it intended to terminate the treaty in six months.

Arita noted shrewdly that he judged the American announcement as substantially political, "first in order to settle the question of its rights and interests in China, and second as a gesture in connection with the coming election in America."[154]

Historians who favor Hull's strategy at this point present the treaty abrogation as a mild, middle-of-the-road policy aimed at the pacification of the hardliners in the State Department. For example, Jonathan Utley in his *Cordell Hull and the Diplomacy of Inflexibility* is careful to point out Hull's strategic failures, but in doing so he understates the effect of the economic weapons used. He wrote, "On the surface, such actions might appear to be a program of economic warfare against Japan. In reality, however, they were only annoyances that carefully avoided any serious pressure."[155]

---

[153] Usui, Katsumi. *Nitchu-senso no Seijitaki Tenkai, Taiheiyo senso e no michi* (1962) P170 cited in Conroy, H., Wray, H. (eds) *Pearl Harbor re-examined: Prologue to the Pacific War.* Honolulu Univ. of Hawaii Press, 1990, P146.

[154] Foreign Relations, 1938, vol III, Pp406–409.

[155] Utley, J. G. *Cordell Hull and the Diplomacy of Inflexibility*, in Conroy, H., Wray, H. (eds) *Pearl Harbor re-examined: Prologue to the Pacific War.*

The Japanese perspective seems from the evidence to have been different. Even seen in isolation, both the imminent threat of the loss of materials for industry and an insecure future in terms of energy supplies struck at the heart of national security. It would be interesting to speculate about the reaction by other nations, including the United States, if they had to face a comparable threat to their energy, resource, and market needs. In any case, a longer historical context for these restrictions must also encompass the trade and other difficulties caused by US tariffs and cartels throughout the 1930s. By any standard, this was serious pressure.

Utley goes on: "From 1937, Hull demonstrated in these and many other ways that Japan could do nothing in China to provoke a war with the United States because there was no vital interest at stake in China." This viewpoint is in stark contrast to Arita's, given above. Clearly, the US did have interests in China, and the Japanese view included this fact in its presentation of the 'new situation in China,' in which American principles would have to accommodate Japanese realities.

By August 30th, the Hiranuma cabinet had been replaced by the Abe cabinet, whose new Foreign Minister was Nomura Kichisaburo. Although his role as Foreign minister did not last very long, he became a very important figure in the final attempts to maintain a working and optimistic dialogue between the two countries. Nomura immediately let it be known that he strongly believed that the relationship with America needed to be normalized "by ensuring respect for foreign rights and interests in China and for the principles of the Open Door."[156]

Several zealous renovationists of the Shiratori group led by Matsumiya Jun criticized Nomura's position very aggressively and worked to undermine it in the belief that his influence

Honolulu: Univ. of Hawaii Press, 1990, P77.
[156] Ibid

could prevent the establishment of their New Order in East Asia. They were members of a committee set up to formulate Japanese policy in response to America's tightening position, so they were at the cutting edge of contemporary influence.

Ambassador Grew was not in accord with Hull's line of thinking, and he did not believe that the Japanese military influence could be neutralized simply through a protracted war in China. Grew understood the concepts of 'blood debt' and 'face.'

Grew was also very concerned that the US would intensify the sanctions. He warned the Japanese leadership that by continuing to expel American interests in China they would eventually find themselves at war.

By referring to American interests rather than Chinese humanitarian concerns, he demonstrated his view about American motivations. He suggested that the Japanese moderates would be well advised to make a substantial conciliatory gesture. They responded with a promise to open part of the Yang-Tze River to commercial traffic for the first time since 1937. It was hoped that a new treaty might follow this, replacing the one that had been abrogated and was about to expire.

Abe was certainly well-intentioned with regard to the American relationship, but he was not only hamstrung in his capacity to offer real concessions, he continued to support the policy of a new order in Asia, which included the southward expansion of Japanese interests. His hopes lay in the unlikely belief that the United States would accept Japan's special position and protracted difficulties in China and re-engage commercially.

Grew put these matters to Hull with some diplomatic emphasis in the hope that Hull would keep the possibility of incremental diplomatic progress alive. If Hull had developed a better appreciation of Grew's grasp of realities at this point, or if Grew had better understood Hull's ironclad adherence to principles, the Japanese offer could have been better targeted, or Hull could have responded with more wisdom. The ideals from America and the practicalities from Japan crossed without recognizing each other, as they each wafted over the Pacific.

The hardliners in the US State Department continued to push the idea that Japan was weakened and should be pressured further. The readjustment of Soviet policy with regard to Japan had the potential to allow an increased American influence in China, and this idea was gaining popular support. Cordell Hull felt unable to raise hopes for a new treaty when his position on China was based on the 'four principles.' He feared that a concession would send the wrong message, offering false, short-term hope instead of a lasting solution to the problems in Asia.

Despite the careful new direction Nomura had embarked upon, Washington made it clear there would not be a new commercial treaty without a fundamental change in Japan's China policy. Nomura's thinking was rejected by America and, as a consequence, his rejection by the renovationists at home was made easier.

Predictably, the Abe cabinet soon fell and was replaced in January 1940. The new Yonai Cabinet included Arita as Foreign Minister once again. With the final abrogation of the commercial treaty taking effect, the renovationists became increasingly insistent in their determination to find non-American sources for war materials in Manchuria and China and a peaceful path into Indochina. This came to pass when the Franco-Japanese Agreement on Joint Defense of Indochina enabled the Japanese Army to enter the northern area of the country.

The potential for Hull's no-compromise policy to be effective was severely reduced by German successes against France and the Netherlands. Together with the threat of invasion of Britain, these factors could undermine British influence in East Asia. Here was a potential for the Japanese to fill a possible power vacuum, particularly if Britain was conquered too. Indochina therefore also became a very strategic frontier.

The apparently random change of cabinets in Japan was in fact a pendular swing between two approaches toward national defense and security in response to American foreign policy. If Washington could not appreciate or accept this it was because they could not see beyond Japanese military action in China, or because the real American purposes were a response to the same opportunities that motivated Japan.

The Nomura approach was to work within the US relationship while the renovationist approach was to persist in the creation of an Asian trading bloc that could replace America's trading relationship with Japan. Each major exchange of initiatives, or failures of initiative, was echoed in the fall of a Japanese Cabinet. Small victories, incremental concessions and, above all, consideration of the American Ambassador's advice may have enabled a stable, moderate Japanese government to survive.

Since the early 1930s, there had been strategists in Japan who had tried to convince governments in America that Japan would one day play a role in China that would also be in the interests of America, for example Admiral Toyoda wrote in 1932:

> "We or our near posterity, will have to decide between Sino-Russian Communism, or the Anglo-Saxon capitalism. If China should fall under the rule of Communism, and if Japan keeps up her present policy… the chance is she will be forced to play the role of…the advance posts of the Anglo-Saxon capitalism."[157]

---

[157] Admiral Teijiro Toyoda to Ambassador Cameron Forbes, Tokyo, March 3, 1932 793.94/4877, cited in Barnes, H. E. *Perpetual War For Perpetual Peace: A Critical Examination of the Foreign Policy of Franklin Delano Roosevelt.* Caldwell ID: Caxton, 1953, P319.

Further, in May 1939, Baron Hiranuma talked to embassy official Dooman in terms of Japan's relationship to the European conflict through the influence of Russia:

"Japan could not ignore the fact that Russia straddled Europe and Asia, and whether Japan liked it or not, Japanese policies and actions form a bridge by which events in the far East and Europe act on each other." As Mr. Dooman had been informed in other quarters, Japan feared involvement with the United States, "not directly across the Pacific but by way of Europe."[158]

Japanese governments had a traditional suspicion of the threat from Russia and an equal abhorrence of Communism. Their sense of 'mission' in China was not just a romantic dream, nor even just about markets. It had a great deal to do with their potential role as gatekeeper to East Asia, and they had a lot of difficulty understanding the complete lack of support for this in the United States.

In America, the hardliners determined, in the words of Hornbeck, to 'tighten the screws.' In contrast to the State Department's position, the American Ambassador in Tokyo showed his awareness of the imperatives on both sides of the Pacific.

John K. Emmerson was a Foreign Service officer working with Ambassador Grew in Tokyo and later in Washington. His view of Grew's grasp of the problems in Japan at the time are given as follows:

"The Ambassador's New England conscience supported wholeheartedly the 'principles' on which [America's] policy stood, but he also recognized the 'realities' that guided Japan: strategic protection against Soviet attack; economic security through control of raw materials

---

[158] Dooman cited in Ibid P321.

in China; and eradication of anti-Japanese and communist activities and propaganda in China."[159]

Emmerson also held Grew's belief that "Japan's determination to gain influence in China would not be deterred by the termination of the treaty or by embargo."[160] He argued that the effect of these would be negative because the spirit of Japanese-determined stoicism would increase the Japanese resolution to maintain national aims.

From first-hand experience of the period in Japan, Emmerson painted a vivid picture of Japanese dependence on the outside world for raw materials. His was a street-side view of the effects of the protracted war in China combined with the Depression and an American embargo on ordinary people in the city. In these things he referred to the 'realities' that Japan had to confront.

Roosevelt also had realities to confront at home. While opinion polls recorded changed public feelings towards Japan, he still felt constrained in carrying out his determination to help Great Britain in the war effort.

The political platform he accepted in 1940 included a commitment to peace, 'except in case of attack.' In campaigning for his third term in Boston on October 30, 1940, he pledged to parents "again and again and again" that "your boys are not going to be sent into any foreign wars."

Roosevelt's speech writer later admitted that, although the pledge was deceitful, "I…urged him to go to the limit on this, feeling as I did that the risk of future embarrassment

---

[159] Emmerson, J. K. *Principles versus Realities: US Prewar Foreign Policy toward Japan*, in Conroy, H., Wray, H. (eds) *Pearl Harbor re-examined: Prologue to the Pacific War.* Honolulu: Univ. of Hawaii Press, 1990, P38.
[160] Ibid

was negligible as compared with the risk of losing the election."[161]

In all human relationships, each partner plays a role in the creation or *realization* of the other. Each person, partner, spouse, or country evolves partly in response to the dynamic context provided by his or her 'other.' We create each other almost as much as we create ourselves.

From a 1940 perspective, had Japan been just another nineteenth century European conquest, America's domination of the Pacific may have eventuated simply as a consequence of the demise of the French, Dutch, and British Empires at the hands of the Nazis, or the Soviets, or both. The strength of Japan dictated that American Pacific hegemony would require the decline of four empires rather than three. On the other hand, the Japanese saw their survival as dependent on the limitation of Soviet and American power as the British Empire faded. In both cases, the Japanese's first preference was for a non-aggression pact, and in the case of the United States, an ongoing trade relationship as well. American expectations at the time were more global and less compromising.

Even if these particular assumptions are debatable, they hover around the reality that Asia and the Pacific would continue under 'white' control in all scenarios except one that allowed for Japanese persistence as a major regional power. In this, the Japanese were to find tacit and sometimes very active support from many Asian people in colonies all over East Asia, South Asia, and the Indian subcontinent. Indeed 'collaboration' became a very difficult, violent, and emotional issue in Japanese-occupied colonies when the Europeans were humiliated and, again, when the allies won the war. Beginning

---

[161] Sherwood, R. E. *Roosevelt and Hopkins.* Harper & Bros, 1948, P201 cited in Barnes, H. E. *Perpetual War For Perpetual Peace: A Critical Examination of the Foreign Policy of Franklin Delano Roosevelt.* Caldwell ID: Caxton, 1953, P319.

with the Japanese success against Russia in 1905, Japan had dislodged the notion that Europeans, and recently, more particularly Anglo-Saxons, were their inevitable masters.

Asian and Pan-Asian nationalism became inevitable consequences of economic domination and exploitation. Seething resentment was an inevitable consequence of racial arrogance—on an individual and a national level.

Later, this surprised the Japanese as much as it had surprised the British, and decades later it would surprise the Americans even more.

16

HARNESSING DISCONTENT
AND THE ISSUE OF FASCISM

Making National Policy from National Discontent

T HE DIVERSE TASKS involved in subverting and harnessing
the widespread feelings of discontent, which fed and
sustained various revolutionary movements, became
a major national project in Japan. The success of the project
provided a relatively stable national platform for industrial
growth and the generation of wealth, but it also created a
military movement that saw its legitimacy as rivaling that of
government, rather than merely being its instrument. This
chapter explores the accumulation and the nature of military
power: the threads that became woven into the mantle of
Japanese militarism.

We have seen that the project began with the young.
Some of the youth movements that evolved in pre-war Japan
combined the expertise of the War and the Education Offices
in their establishment and in their running. Just as men of

influence congregated in groups of common interest to press for change, the youth were encouraged to seek higher purposes both in and out of school.

The Society of the Military Valor of Great Japan had about three million members in 1935. It was supported and supervised by military officers in preparing boys for military life and learning the benefits of obedience and discipline, including "exultation of the Japanese war spirit, and rallying the entire nation, united by Samurai traditions, around the sacred person of the Emperor." The Japanese Youth Association organized by the Home Office maintained sixteen thousand groups with a membership of over two million in the 1930s. There were many others.

Military societies originally founded to support ex-servicemen were expanded to play a larger role in developing and maintaining militaristic traditions. They often distributed huge quantities of propaganda material, and they also organized mass meetings in villages and cities across Japan.

The Ex-Serviceman's Association, or *Zaigo Gunjinkai* became much more aggressive after 1932, and it was this organization that was able to humiliate several leading liberal thinkers over subsequent years including Minobe Tatsukishi.

Many early protagonists for totalitarianism used secret societies as training centers for terrorist activities. Membership of these included many of the younger officers of the army, and these formed an interesting group for several reasons. With senior figures heading these societies, it is no surprise to find ambition and zeal amongst the young, but socio-economic factors played a part as well. Many of the young recruits and conscripts came from backgrounds of rural poverty or the urban working classes. They harbored resentment toward the privileged upper strata that could evade military service by simply continuing their studies. They also resented the corrupt alliances between the parties and the *zaibatsu* and the bribery and scandals among political leaders.

Recruits were exposed to many books of the period, written with their sympathies in mind. The powerful nationalistic rhetoric in them appealed to their resentments and ambitions, filling a need that may otherwise have been satisfied through socialist or communist ideals.

Writing in 1936, Kenneth Colgrove puts their position this way: "their salaries are small, their education is limited. In the large cities, on the crowded Ginza, and in the restaurants, they feel out of place. Their self-respect is preserved only by resort to a preposterous patriotism and anti-foreign prejudice. And they burn with indignation at the thought of the oppression of their father's families."[162] From these groups came the young men who assassinated Premier Inukai and others.

As a mid-1930s assessment of the progress of fascism, Colgrove's book *Militarism in Japan* is a valuable insight into the mood of the country at the time, because without the benefit of hindsight he argued that fascism would not become the significant force in Japan. That he was able to reach this conclusion even as late as 1935 tells us a great deal about the force and speed of events over the subsequent five or six years. He was certainly aware in detail, of the many complex forces at work in Japan and had written comprehensively about the stumbles and frustrations associated with the democratic experiment.

Despite the progress made against parliamentary democracy by assassins and terrorists, Colgrove felt that the militarists had failed to unite the nation or capture control of the state. In arguing this he gave six, slightly overlapping, reasons, and these can be summarized as follows.

---

[162] Colegrove, K.W. *Militarism in Japan*. World Peace Foundation, 1936, P38.

First: he cited the lack of unity among the various groups, each with its own program.

Second: there was no co-ordination or strategy as there was in the Italian and German examples.

Third: They lacked unifying slogans and concepts to mobilize the population. The danger of communism seemed too remote. He felt the 'Great Asia' idea was a hackneyed battle cry. Russia and America did not pose sufficient threat.

Fourth: A movement to take the nation by force needed mass organization. The fascists, he claimed, failed to win the masses, and had in fact alienated millions who would have responded to a more aggressively anti-capitalist stance. Terrorism had lowered the prestige of the movement.

Fifth: In spite of the Manchurian Incident, the bourgeois parties had not entirely lost the battle for parliamentary government. They had succeeded in gaining universal suffrage [for men], and there had never been a complete surrender to the militarists.

Sixth: The Genro, the Emperor, and the circle of high officials surrounding the Emperor had not been in sympathy with the militaristic movements. At that time, he felt the Emperor appeared to favor a constitutional regime.

There is one issue, which, by itself, can address at least the first four of the limiting factors given above. That is to say, it informs them and sheds some light on our understanding that Colgrove's conclusion is still debatable. It points us to the leadership in Japan and its traditional attitudes to the population and to politics.

What German and Italian totalitarianism had in common was a cult of personality, a singular voice and a focused vision, which were thrust energetically upon an audience of individuals who could be motivated to think as a mass. Political leadership was public, noisy, and seldom subtle.

In contrast, Japanese leaders remained aloof and unwilling to be seen to engage with the socially inferior electorate. To explain this it is necessary to look briefly and relatively at the absorption of individualism as a Western concept in Japanese political practice.

In the West, authoritarianism had to develop in societies for which individualism was relatively more entrenched than it was in Japan. Despite its exposure to modernity, Japanese society never found it necessary or possible to consider the individual as an isolated unit. That Japanese modernity had built upon and embraced many traditional values, enabled leadership to gain enormous power, by Western standards, without the need for the mass rallies and stirring speeches used in Europe.

The majority of the Japanese elite appears to have had nothing but abhorrence and fear of mass movements of any type and therefore had no desire to create a personal political relationship between the leader and the led. As Scalapino wrote in 1953, "oratory continued to be considered vulgar, and there was probably no group of modern political leaders who maintained such resolute silence in public as the Japanese statesmen."[163]

The difficulty with oratory was probably that, to engage in speech making or debate, was to admit to the existence of pluralism, and this by implication means it is possible to be wrong. Most other parliamentary traditions had their foundations based in oratory and debating skills. This is part of the Western inheritance of Greco-Roman intellectualism. The difference is also partly directional, in that power and wisdom traditionally flowed downwards in Japan, just as allegiance flowed upwards.

---

[163] Scalapino, Robert. A. *Democracy and the Party Movement In Pre-War Japan: The Failure of the First Attempt.* Berkeley: University of California Press 1953, P304.

Colegrove gave what seemed to be a reasonable assessment from an informed 1936 point of view. Many commentators probably shared his overall assessment at the time, and as we gain distance and moral perspective from the horrors of the Pacific War, scholars may now be more likely than they have been, to accept it again. In the post-war years, the label 'fascist' was to become a very hot potato among scholars and apologists.

Nevertheless, fascism has been described and defined in many ways, and the consensus of most modern scholars of Japan seems to be that Colegrove's assessment was correct. A more thorough exploration of this question follows.

Fear Challenging Pluralism

The extent to which a society can adapt and learn, take risks, and face complexity is dependent upon the safe persistence of pluralism. These things were all prerequisites to Japan's participation in modernity, world industry, and global power. Paradoxically, the very creation of complexity threatens pluralism, and this was the case in Japan, as it was in many countries in the period following World War I and the Depression.

When investigating the disintegration of party politics in Japan we can justifiably regard it as a failure of pluralism. Pluralism in society can be inclusive, energetic, creative, and evolutionary, but it is often also relatively threatening and challenging as people are taken into the unknown and the untested.

Many rural Japanese were happy to have the possibility of a disposable income and perhaps some previously unavailable goods, but many were also unprepared to turn their backs on the traditions and values that had formed the pattern and texture of their collective lives for centuries.

The non-progressive society may appear quaint by modern standards, but it provided reliable parameters and something of a predictable future—with all the positives and negatives that could be entailed in that. Modernity challenged the fundamental relationship between the Japanese people and the natural world, as well as their sense of belonging within a traditional community and their spiritual relationship to both the landscape and their ancestors. Those embracing or demanding modernity regarded all of these as simply irrational and inefficient.

To drag a newly developing industrial economy into the modern world, the fears and conservatism of the largely uneducated labor force needed to be redirected to the national purpose. Our judgment as to whose purpose was the national one will color our view of the various realities in which European and Asian people found themselves in the 1930s.

With Japan under enormous economic and social pressure, the forces that were able to endure and to break through the 'noise' of choices, fear, and confusion were the ones that could most closely become identified with safety, survival, and strength.

The Totalitarian Mindset

In one sense, the Japanese had to deal with a pluralism run riot, as hundreds of societies, groups, and parties, each with its own agenda, vied for support, often from overlapping as well as from competing interest groups. This was a time of kaleidoscopic ideation, a bit map creating too many images to comprehend. A type of fractured pluralism developed that could never be inclusive or even stable in the long term.

The decay of party politics in Japan and the tightening grasp of totalitarian government, involved normal human responses to generalized threats and uncertainties, but it did so within the context of a fragile and immature democracy, which was not able to offer a simple, rational set of choices to the electorate.

The parallel arm of militarism, with its link directly to the national symbol, was able to benefit from these uncertainties and anxieties, as were the arms of bureaucracy. The convergence of industrial and military imperatives around the concept of national survival created the necessary conditions for a kind of totalitarian gestalt.

Before we assess the political transformation that followed, there are some factors that allow the possibility that in differing degrees, the human and social responses to extreme situations are predictable and normal. Cynical leaders, for reasons of wealth, power, and control, are able to intensify the degree of the response. Threatening or emergency situations create a desire to reduce ambiguity and complexity in social systems in favor of simplistic binary thinking typified by choices such as us/them, good/evil, or right/wrong.

This is a form of totalitarian thinking, and it can exist in varying degrees even within outwardly liberal states, or as a tendency that can be harnessed even by a single confusing issue. It does not require very much imagination to see modern occurrences of this type of thinking, as prevalent now as it has ever been.

In Japan, to keep things in perspective, many people were not compliant or involved in totalitarian thinking. Pacifists, people of some religious faiths, elements of the moderate and extreme left, and ordinary people resisted, personally or outwardly.

Some of them were silenced by fear, by gaol, or by assassination. We have seen that by 1935, however, they had become silent or silenced. It should also be remembered that for many, a Western style democracy was never considered appropriate for the traditional Japanese social structure, and indeed many saw goodness in the paternalistic alternative, which was not inevitably linked to rampant militarism or its consequences. That apparent inevitability is a consequence of hindsight.

In traditional Japan, paternalism was familiar, while ambiguity was culturally distasteful. In discussing the influence of ambiguity in the authoritarian mindset, Sampson wrote in 1999:

> "First when confronted by an ambiguous situation, one allowing for a variety of meanings or shades of gray, they feel discomfort. Second, they deal with the discomfort by seeing a quick and easy solution that minimizes the subtleties that exist. In short, they make their world into simple black and simple white. From time to time, all of us show aspects of this intolerance. The mark of high authoritarianism, however, is the tendency to deal uncharitably with ambiguity most of the time."[164]

Uncertain situations, like the disarray of party politics in Japan, a growing trade crisis, and major population shifts from traditional rural centers to the cities, as well as other factors outlined elsewhere, here, were all causes of social stress and anxiety. Perhaps we can establish a direct link between anxiety and the need for order and predictability, in the attempt to avoid potential chaos. As a social phenomenon, this seems almost always to occur at the cost of novelty, originality, and creativity, producing a restrictive, controlling atmosphere, which is intolerant of differences.

Diversity is likened to ambiguity by authoritarian personalities who show a preference for eliminating them in favor of conformity and homogeneity. Under extreme situations of pressure, even individuals who are not normally so inclined

---

[164] Sampson, E. E. *Dealing with Differences, An Introduction to the Social Psychology of Prejudice*. Fort Worth: Harcourt Brace, 1999, P85.

will exhibit authoritarian tendencies to deal with anxiety, and this makes them particularly susceptible to propaganda and prejudicial thinking.

Another indicator in the totalitarian mindset is the creation of an out-group as a potential threat, and therefore an enemy. The well-known Nazi Hermann Goering maintained that this was a key strategy for uniting people and enabling them to set aside internal differences while emphasizing separateness from 'the other.'

Perceived differences may be racial, religious, or ethnic, and leadership will often seek to identify the threat of 'the other' in such a way that people see a polarity—such as, for/against or patriotic/traitor. Emphasis on 'otherness' enables the stereotyping of groups and their consequent dehumanizing. 'Scapegoating' is an easy progression wherein problems can be linked to the actions or qualities of the 'other.'

A fear of imminent threat can also give strength to a leader who can paint a simple picture of the threat and appear to be decisive about its solution. The need for strong leadership associated with the factors mentioned above can also allow a population to make significant personal sacrifices to fund a military effort, for example.

In a journal article, Alfonso Montuori wrote that,

"the literature of social psychology provides us ample research into the dynamics of conformity and conversion. Particularly when there is great anxiety, the forces of conformity come into play and an increasing alignment occurs to what is perceived to be the voice of authority.

"Psycho-dynamically, a process of collective projection occurs, endowing the leader with all the clarity and power individuals seem to lack—and playing into the leader as a father role."[165]

In the case of Japan, this latter point is subtler than it was in either Germany or in Italy during the 1930s. The Emperor embodied a spiritual as well as father role, and while this is arguably also true of Hitler, if it existed, it was a recently invented, superficial affectation. In Japan, the Emperor was very remote from the population and was perhaps more powerful and unchallengeable to the Japanese psyche as a consequence, and the 'spiritual' nature of his position had roots deep in national history.

Some comparison of the Japanese experience to that of Europe is inevitable, despite the obvious fact that Japan shared almost none of the Western historical experiences. The sweep of history uses the same cast of players in creating different dramas, and on the level of the individual, humans tend to respond to situations in ways they always have. Brilliance is the exception.

Japanese Fascism, Corporatism, or Unique Entity?

In 1946, the populations of the allied countries were more than happy to be reassured that Imperial Japan, like Nazi Germany and Fascist Italy, was a criminal nation that had engaged in a conspiracy to take over the world. They had been stopped, but attribution of blame would stem from that premise. In the 21st Century, historians have much more access to research material that can enable a view with more nuances and possibly less bias?

In the late 1920s, 1930s, and 1940s, the Japanese Press was regularly discussing fascism and, also in that period, many

---

[165] Montuori, A. *How to Make Enemies and Influence People: Anatomy of the Anti-Pluralist, Totalitarian Mindset.* Futures, Vol37: 1, 2005 P4.

books were published discussing the merits and disadvantages for Imperial Japan.

In his article on Japanese fascism in 2005[166], Marcus Willensky claims that for the allies there was never any question that Imperial Japan was a fascist nation. He maintains that it was only in the immediate post-trial era that Japanese authors seriously began to discuss the implications for historians, of labeling the pre-war era *fascist*.

The Cold War and the economic miracle of Japanese recovery added strength to the arguments of those who felt that the Japanese experience was somehow different, and that 'fascist' was not an appropriate description of the movement that occurred there. In reconfiguring national policy to include the former enemy as an ally against communism, many American voices were enthusiastic in avoiding 'fascism' as a descriptor in relation to Japan. Study of many sources finds that most Japanese of the period were adamant that what they had was a Japanese phenomenon. Consensus among international scholars in the half-century since has vacillated.

In a recent book, David Williams argues that despite the grievous crimes committed in the name of the Emperor, the regime should not be labeled as fascist. His major interest is in exploring the role of the Kyoto school of philosophers in Japanese thinking and re-examining their contribution as the formulators of the first rational philosophy that could embrace and inform a future in which 'non-white' cultures could be more than mere reproductions of 'whiteness.'

Williams examines a strong Japanese case against Western hegemony, challenging an orthodoxy, which, he claims, "dishonestly insists that we set allied ideals against Japanese

---

[166] Willensky, Marcus. *Japanese Fascism Revisited*. Stanford Journal of East Asian Affairs, vol 5 Number 1, Winter 2005, P59.

moral failure."[167] His main focus is on the Kyoto school of philosophy and the misguided criticism of it since the war. He strongly resists the use of the term fascist as a descriptor, but it is sensible for us to separate the philosophers from the government, with the possibility that one may be fascist and the other not. We will look further at this issue again, but at this point, it is useful to keep to the question of fascism and whether it developed in Japan or not.

In debating the merits of calling the Japanese phenomenon 'Emperor-System fascism,' Herbert Bix draws an interesting distinction between militarism and fascism. He writes:

> "Where militarism denotes a technique of class rule associated with military budgets, the arms race, the development of weapons technology and everything which contributes to the spiritual support for waging war, the discussion of fascism is intended to focus attention on the process of change in the political form itself and the conditions under which such changes persist."[168]

Is it important to have a view on this? Does it matter what we call the system that contributed to the Pacific War? That question raises a further complication in that we have already seen that the reasons for a confrontation between America and Japan may have pre-existed Japanese totalitarian government. In this case, the existence, or not, of fascism may be simply academic, or it might mean that fascism was in part a response to American attempts at hegemony.

---

[167] Williams, *David. Defending Japan's Pacific War: the Kyoto School Philosophers and Post-White Power.* Curzon NY: Routledge, 2004, P16.

[168] Bix, H. P. *Re-Thinking Emperor-System Fascism: Ruptures and Continuities in Modern Japanese History.* Bulletin of Concerned Asian Scholars, Vol14:2 1982 P7.

In recent times, the term *fascism* has been rather loosely applied in conversation and in the media, and it has come to be used in describing almost anything vaguely right wing. It is worth being a little more definitive here. Is fascism a general concept or a specific description, and in either case, is it instructive or accurate to use it as a reference to the final stages of pre-war Japan?

The intention of this book is to explore the roots and meanings of the war, and since debates of this kind can reveal the processes at work from different viewpoints, it is worth delving deeper than a simple chronological outline. We don't need to adopt a position on these questions to benefit from a discussion of the issues involved.

The term "fascism" is used to represent a range of meanings. Beyond its application to Mussolini's Italy, scholarly consensus dissipates as the exact meaning and application become more general. For some scholars, fascism was an Italian movement and even German National Socialism does not fit within their definition. For others, fascism was a general phenomenon in Europe between the wars, and an inevitable outcome of capitalism.

In his essay, "Fascism," Wolfgang Schieder felt that the term applied to "any extremist and nationalist movements with authoritarian and tightly hierarchical structures and anti-democratic, anti-liberal, and anti-socialist ideologies which founded authoritarian or totalitarian regimes, or aimed to do so..."[169] This is a very general description, which for the non-specialist seems quite useful in illuminating the situation in Japan. But is it too general?

The international socialist movement first identified the fascist "movement" as it observed the rise to power of Mussolini. It was seen to have pan-European roots in the "social, economic,

---

[169] Schieder, Wolfgang. "Fascism" in Kernig, C.D. (ed) *Marxism, Communism and Western Society: A Comparative Encyclopedia,* Vol 3 NY P282.

and political upheavals of the immediate post [first] war, which bred a turn against liberalism, democracy and socialism."[170] The early Stalinist view was that fascism represented the final, and necessary, form of bourgeois-capitalist rule, and was therefore welcomed as a sign of the death of European capitalism.

Of the dozens of theories explaining fascism, the work of AKF Organski provides a useful insight into the Japanese case, without referring significantly to it. In discussing fascism as a phenomenon linked to the persistence of an established governing class in the face of accelerated modernization, Organski identifies three patterns that mark the political transformation.

First Organski sees clearly detectable, long range, rapid economic growth. His second observation is of large-scale mobilization with a heavy component of rural to city migration. His third element is vast and rapid political mobilization, particularly acute just before the fascists assume power.[171]

A development of this attention to the role of modernization was made by Barrington Moore, Jr., who maintained that for late industrial developers, "the pre-industrial elites in these societies were not displaced by revolution and thus were cast in the historically anomalous role of directing the process of 'revolution from above' to try to rationalize and modernize their societies, while at the same time ensuring that they retain their social dominance. To this end, mobilization and repression were necessary, and the contradictory nature of the combination in turn necessitated militarism."[172]

---

[170] McCormack, G. *Nineteen-thirties Japan: Fascism?* Bulletin of Concerned Asian Scholars Vol 14; 2 1982 P21.

[171] Organski, A. K. F. *Fascism and Modernization* in Wolf, S. J. (ed) *The Nature of Fascism*. London: Weidenfeld and Nicholson, 1968, P23 cited in McCormack P22/

[172] Moore, B Jr. *Social Origins of Dictatorship and Democracy: Lord and Peasant in the Making of the Modern World*. Boston: Beacon, 1967, P442.

Both of these theories are very general and do not address class issues in a way that would be satisfactory to a Marxist historian but they do inform our search for understanding the Japanese phenomenon. Explaining Marxist dissatisfaction with such views, McCormack claims that "bourgeois scholars are inclined to want to set aside the theoretical problems of definition, partly because they see further research as necessary...but also because of a more fundamental ideological reason; too many of the paths of theoretical enquiry lead to various formulas for the association of fascism with liberalism, middle-class society and capitalism..."[173] There is more than a little truth in that, but we might simply argue that most scholars are more interested in the forces at work behind the events of the period than they are in nomenclature or definition.

The period after World War II saw the politicization of some academic research, as governments encouraged an accommodation of the fact that the former Soviet ally was now the 'enemy' and the former fascist enemies were now allies. Wartime rhetoric suddenly seemed inappropriate. Establishment views of each regime were encouraged through funding, patronage, and appeals to patriotic principles, to recast the popular perception in a more palatable way. The major thrust of the Western agenda quickly shifted from being anti-fascist to anti-communist.

From seeing the Japanese in the 'fascist camp,' the conventional explanation became that they had been taken over by militaristic cliques and ultra-nationalist secret societies.

The extension of this thinking saw a growing emphasis on the importance of constitutional contradictions inherent in the Japanese attempt to place the Diet, the military, and the emperor in a nationally appropriate relationship. It is hard to

---

[173] McCormack, G. *Nineteen-thirties Japan: Fascism?* Bulletin of Concerned Asian Scholars, Vol 14; 2 1982 P25.

ignore these structural factors, though, because they create the entire internal context of national development.

Militarism as a descriptor became a Western orthodoxy in a way that was never applied to the European examples.

The historian Albert Craig asserts that "Japan in this period is better labeled militarist than fascist. The basic state apparatus was not new or revolutionary, but merely the 'establishment' overlaid by controls and permeated by an unchecked spiritual nationalism"[174].

European Comparisons

The Italians and the Germans of the 1930s provide examples to compare with, and contrast to, the Japanese developments. The Italian case is represented best through the words of Mussolini and the writer Alfredo Rocco. The following description gives some insight into the Italian Fascist thinking.

"Fascism never raises the question of methods, using in its political praxis now liberal ways, now democratic means and at times even socialist devices. The indifference to method often exposes fascism to the charge of incoherence on the part of superficial observers, who do not see what counts with us is the end and that therefore even when we employ the same means we act with a radically different spirit and strive for entirely different ends."

In this, Rocco embraces the contradictory and pragmatic nature of fascism. He asserts that, for fascism, the goal and not the path is the key to understanding the term; therefore, fascism will undoubtedly take on different forms in different situations and in different hands.

"The end towards which Rocco was striving was the creation of an all-powerful state that would play the central role in

---

[174] Reischauer, E. O., Firbank. J. K., and Craig, A. *East Asia: The Modern Transformation*. Boston: Houghton Mifflin, 1965, P605.

organizing the lives and livelihoods of its citizens. How this was achieved was less important than its realization." [175] In the Japanese example, a preference for pragmatic action unfettered by political principles represents the right-wing determination to catch up with other imperialist powers as fast as possible, by whatever means, to assert their unique cultural agenda and their spiritual mission.

Writing in 1932, Yoshino Sakuzo explained that,

"To define fascism is an extremely difficult task. We can, however, say in general terms that it implies the rule of the disciplined and resolute few as against that of the undisciplined and irresolute many. It is anti-democratic, and particularly anti-parliamentarian; it is national rather than international; and it tends to dignify the State as against the individual, or any group of individuals, except of course the resolute group in whose hands power is concentrated. These are the ideas which animate the various groups in Japan…and therefore, in spite of their occasional repudiation of the title, they can be reasonably be called Fascists."[176]

Pre-war Japanese politics can be said to have exhibited these particularities: It was intensely nationalistic. It was racialist—expressing a belief that the Japanese were racially superior to Westerners and all other Asians. It was militaristic and imperialistic.[177] The element missing in defining the period

---

[175] Willensky, Marcus. *Japanese Fascism Revisited*. Stanford Journal of East Asian Affairs, vol 5 Number 1, Winter 2005, P62.

[176] Sakuzo, Yoshino. *Fascism in Japan* 1932 vol.1 No 2 P185, cited in Willensky, Marcus. *Japanese Fascism Revisited*, Stanford Journal of East Asian Affairs, vol 5 Number 1, Winter 2005 P63. Yoshino is often referred to as the foremost democratic theorist in the Taisho and Showa eras.

[177] Willensky, Marcus. *Japanese Fascism Revisited*, Stanford Journal of East Asian Affairs, vol 5 Number 1, Winter 2005, P64.

as fascist is "the totalitarian organization of government and society by a single party dictatorship."[178]

It can be argued that this missing element was no longer missing from 1940, following the disbanding of opposition parties. This left the Imperial Rule Assistance Association as the only functioning party, and this, combined with the consolidated powers of the Emperor, was the final link in functionally legitimizing de facto fascist elements and tendencies, which had been evolving on a separate path, politically and in the military.

Most Western writers, including Peter Duus and Mark Peattie, both of whom have been referred to frequently in this book, argue that Imperial Japan was not fascist. Duus and Okimoto, after dissecting the literature and demonstrating several inconsistencies and the unsatisfactory nature of fascism as an analytical concept, suggest a possible alternative paradigm of 'corporatism.' They argue that the 1930s were a period of "general impulse toward managed economies that was on the rise all over the world," and in the Japanese case it saw "the formative period of a managerial state or polity, in which a dirigiste bureaucracy became the central element in the formation and execution of national policy."[179]

Willensky takes a different view. His main emphasis involves the role of social, rather than economic, factors. He points out that "the Imperial Japanese Military and bureaucracy placed great emphasis on collective belonging and a shared past." He goes on:

---

[178] Ebenstein, William. *To-day's ISMS: Communism, Fascism, Capitalism, Socialism*. NJ: Prentice Hall, 1967, P105, cited in Willensky, Marcus. *Japanese Fascism Revisited*, Stanford Journal of East Asian Affairs, vol 5 Number 1, Winter 2005, P65.

[179] Duus, P. and Okimoto, D. I. *Fascism and the History of Pre-War Japan: The Failure of a Concept*, in JAS 39:1 Nov 1979 Pp65-76, cited in McCormack P30.

"Starting in the Meiji, Taisho and certainly in the Showa era there was no lack of government-sponsored propaganda designed to help the average citizen to see his place in terms of the family, the household, and the nation, and their relationship to the Emperor in an unbroken line through history. This process stressed the sacred importance of Japanese language, culture and history. Part of this indoctrination was an emphasis on the importance of the *Kokutai*, literally the 'body of the State' in which the concept of the individual must be subsumed."[180]

It is fair to argue that most of the concepts of Mussolini's fascism existed, at least as tendencies, in Japan from the beginnings of the Meiji period. The Meiji vision projected Japan forward as a nation built upon its past and not as a diluted European democracy, nor a nation of individuals.

The Emperor remained central to the Japanese concept of State, despite several contradictions in his actual relationship and role with regard to the oligarchs in the Meiji period and the Military in the pre-war period, for example. In Willensky's words, "Imperial Japan was fascist not because it successfully copied what was happening in Italy and Germany but because that is what the Meiji oligarchs intended it to be, though at the time they lacked the words to describe it as such."[181]

In this, Willensky implies that the various expressions of fascism in the 20th Century were manifestations of pre-existing phenomena which, when combined, can be labeled as fascist. This is an important difference from the view of Japanese fascism as a version of an Italian theory or concept. Carl Cohen puts it this way:

---

[180] Willensky, Marcus. *Japanese Fascism Revisited*. Stanford Journal of East Asian Affairs, vol 5 Number 1, Winter 2005, P65.

[181] Ibid P67

"For Fascism, Society is the end, individuals the means, and its whole life consists in using individuals as instruments for its social ends. The State therefore guards and protects the welfare and development of individuals not for their exclusive interest, but because of the identity of the needs of individuals with those of society as a whole."[182]

The Japanese expression of these elements was called *Kodo*, and this included a quasi-religious relationship to the Emperor, who represented the link with cultural roots and the very birth of the State. In this, the highest achievement of individuals was the sublimation of their wills to that of the Emperor, regardless of the sources of his policy.

In 1932, Hiranuma Kiichiro made a speech in which, among other elaborations of national militarism, Kodo claimed, "The individual Japanese never hesitates to sacrifice his life for the maintenance of that great national life…" He adds, to clarify the Japanese position, "Fascism, which has become important of late, is the product of a foreign country resulting from national circumstances in that country. Our country has its [own] independent object and its [own] independent mission."[183]

Our comprehension of Japanese totalitarianism depends greatly on our understanding of the democratic movements in Japan, which developed in the period following the Washington Conference in 1922. The liberal and democratic elements that grew in this period should not be seen as forces that could have prevented totalitarianism but as those that were necessary for totalitarianism to move to center stage. This seemingly counter-intuitive argument was well explained by Ebenstein when he

---

[182] Cohen, Carl. *Communism, Fascism and Democracy: The Theoretical Foundation*. New York: Random House, 1972, P323, cited in Willensky, Marcus, *Japanese Fascism Revisited*. Stanford Journal of East Asian Affairs, vol 5 Number 1, Winter 2005, P67.

[183] Kiichiro, Hiranuma. April 28 1932 in The Trans-Pacific P12 cited in Willensky, Marcus. *Japanese Fascism Revisited*. Stanford Journal of East Asian Affairs, vol 5 Number 1, Winter 2005, P69.

wrote, "No fascist system can arise in a country without some democratic experience (as in Germany and Japan), there is not much likelihood of fascist success in countries that have experienced democracy over a long period."[184]

In Japan, a level of democracy enabled a literate society exposure to a pluralist media, which produced a diversity of opinions and a level of discontent and confusion. The democratic movement lacked a singular sense of purpose.

Although the party system gave hope and a voice to some elements, there was a backlash against it because of confusion and bitterness within others, undermining the sense of security that modernization had set out to achieve. Seen from this perspective, democracy was a gamble with which the nation was unable or unwilling to persist.

The growth in power and prestige of party politics during the late Meiji and Taisho eras was largely eradicated by changes in the composition of the Justice and Home Ministries and the death of the last of the Genros,[185] or elder statesmen of the Meiji restoration. The result was a return to a power structure more in keeping with the authoritarian and bureaucratic inclinations first outlined by the Meiji architects.[186]

The National General Mobilization Law, passed in 1938, gave the government much greater power than it ever had in previous eras. Among other things, it gave authority to move people anywhere the state needed them. In practice, this created a mobile slave force of Koreans and others.

---

[184] Ebenstein, William. *To-day's ISMS: Communism, Fascism, Capitalism, Socialism*. NJ: Prentice Hall, 1967, P105, cited in Willensky, Marcus. *Japanese Fascism Revisited*, Stanford Journal of East Asian Affairs, vol 5 Number 1, Winter 2005, P72.

[185] *The last Genro* was a book published in 1938, focusing on the last member of a distinguished group called genros—elder statesmen—who were responsible for drawing up the Imperial Constitution.

[186] Willensky, Marcus. *Japanese Fascism Revisited*, Stanford Journal of East Asian Affairs, vol 5 Number 1, Winter 2005, P74.

By 1939, government power was stronger still, but almost as an instrument of the military, in the form of the Ministry for the Army. The following example demonstrates its confident power; it is part of a statement by the Army Minister quoted in the *Trans-Pacific*.[187]

"The basic policy regarding the disposal of the China incident has been established with Imperial approval. It is immutable and will not be affected by Cabinet change. It is the intention of the Army to pursue its fixed course and concentrate on containment of the objectives in the holy war."

In this, the Minister refers to direct access to the Emperor as being the unquestionable justification for the initiation of government policy at a domestic level as well as foreign policy, beyond the jurisdiction of constitutional government. Note also the jingoistic reference to the pseudo- religious 'holy war' in defining national goals. The transformation to totalitarianism is complete.

Is this representative of a breakdown of the governmental processes that evolved from the Meiji restoration? Or does it represent a system returning to its truer roots, those implicit in the initial authoritarian and bureaucratic restoration of the Meiji era?

At the heart of the Meiji restoration was an ancient, exquisite culture that was fiercely conservative and non-progressive. Faced with a modern world that would no longer be ignored, it embraced change and modernity but in doing so it grasped even more firmly the central qualities by which the people could define themselves.

Security and freedom from fear—as opposed to freedom— could only be achieved by making even more precious the core identity values that had become the national 'story.' The pressures for economic and technical change served to intensify

---

[187] Ibid PP74, quoted from *The Trans-Pacific* Jan 12 1939, P8.

and concentrate conservative forces in direct proportion to the insecurity that came with change.

The kind of change faced by Japan was not the gradual, incremental change mostly experienced in the West; it was explosive and confronting, changing roles that had been constant for centuries. It produced the type of anxiety and stress discussed at the start of this chapter, which made the people even more susceptible to the authoritarian mindset.

These factors allow a view of the transition to totalitarianism "as a manifestation of cultural continuity."[188] Ebenstein goes further, saying, "In Germany and Japan [in that period] the authoritarian tradition has been predominant and democracy is still a very frail plant. As a result, a German or Japanese with fascist tendencies is no outcast and may be considered perfectly well-adjusted to his society."[189]

In fact, in the case of Germany, the liberal cultural tradition that existed outside the Prussian field of influence may well mean that the German fascist experience does not sit well in that example. In Germany and in Italy, separate states with strong, independent cultural traditions and identities were unified into nations, and this may have been a more central issue for them.

The need to find a common national identity in these cases involved a good deal more invention than in the case of Japan. For example, the people of Bavaria continue to embrace an independent self-image, despite their 19th-Century domination by Prussia and unification into Germany.

In summary, those who believe that Japan became a fascist state might use the following seven events to indicate the unfolding of such a development.

---

[188] Duus, Peter and Okimoto, Daniel. *Journal of Asian Studies.* Nov 1979 P68.

[189] Ebenstein, William. *To-day's ISMS: Communism, Fascism, Capitalism, Socialism*. NJ: Prentice Hall, 1967, P111.

The first would most probably be either the Manchurian Incident of 1931 or the Japanese withdrawal from the League of Nations in 1933. Then, the 'Emperor as Organ Theory' controversy of 1935 cemented the Emperor as Supreme Commander. Following this, the commitment to the Ant-Comintern Pact of 1936 committed the Japanese to an international anti-socialist allegiance.

In 1938, the National General Mobilization Law placed the country effectively in the hands of a military dictatorship capable of over-ruling the legislature, followed by the dissolution of Political Parties in May 1940.

The sixth event was the signing of the Tripartite Pact with Germany and Italy in September 1940. The final point of transition is possibly the inauguration of the Imperial Rule Assistance Association as the only political force in October of the same year.

These events moved Japan into a pattern of behavior that fits many definitions of fascism, despite Japanese denials at the time, wherein Kodo is explained as a Japanese phenomenon free of Western inspiration. As we have seen, this latter point may well be true, and their path to the pattern we call fascism may have occurred, even in the absence of a European model.

A lingering doubt arises from the fact that in Japan, so many moderate and flexible minds were still able to stay within the political process, even after the installation of Major General Tojo.

When we examine the final negotiations to stave off a war with America in a later chapter, it becomes evident that Japanese politics oscillated from extreme positions, but centered on a persistent fear for national survival. Among all this, there remained a core of people of significant humanity whose grip on power was only taken from them when it was finally believed that America's intentions amounted to starvation of resources and probably war.

Even when Tojo was given the Imperial sanction to govern, he did not become a dictator in the conventional sense but the instrument of mobilization for the national task. Seen from the point of view of those charged with national survival, this was an entirely rational process—even if Premier Tojo acted in an irrational manner in carrying out his task.

It can also be argued that 'fascism' as a descriptor is only useful as a polemical concept in the context of Marxist orthodoxy, which is no longer particularly relevant.

In any case, we can revel in the marvelous irony that a political and social phenomenon, which sought to address fear and disorder by a reduction of them to simple dichotomies, without shades of gray or expressions of doubt or uncertainty, can be so difficult for scholars to agree upon in its definition.

17

THE KYOTO SCHOOL OF PHILOSOPHY

"*T*O BECOME GLOBAL *Oriental culture must not stop at its own specificity but rather it must shed a new light on Western culture and a new world culture must be created.*" Nishida Kitaro

The Japanese struggle to modernize detonated a powerful tension between two apparently irreconcilable realities. It was impossible for Japan to avoid the technological challenge inherent in the Euro/American appearance on their horizon. This appearance was set uncomfortably against the need to maintain a national cultural identity in order not to be subsumed. Decades of political contradictions followed, and yet these finally focused on the single issue of control within the armies that were created to defend Japan.

Modern Japan evolved in a Western colonial context, responding to Western actions and the failure of Western ideals. The Japanese people of the time had to take responsibility for the actions of its government and its armies, but the cumulative effect of frustrated engagement with the West in commerce and politics ran almost parallel to the cumulative growth in power of the ultranationalists within the Japanese armies.

However, the Japanese mission was not intended to be just military and defensive. Those reactions were born of an understandable paranoia. The challenge to reconcile national identity with modernity required the creation of an intellectual framework more than a military one. The first step in this process was to understand modernity.

For those of us who were raised in the West, it is difficult to see modernity as anything other than a normal consequence of the passage of time, leading to the undisputable present. Modernity, though, is an attitude as much as a location in recent time. It has a huge collection of roots that are invisible to most people in their everyday lives. A Protestant context in Scotland produced the 'founder' of capitalism. Western philosophy retains its Greek rationalism. The technology of the industrial revolution, also emerging from Scotland, redefined workforces and cities and the countryside, and so on.

The consequence was an amalgam of concepts and structures that placed Britain and Europe at the center of progress, technology, and wealth. This was an unseen by-product of the capacity of the individual to reshape culture through invention and creative thought. While always present as a tendency, throughout the ages, this creative energy was generally considered to be culturally very dangerous if uncontrolled in the individual. Some progressive societies emerged gradually into 'The Age of Reason' partly as a consequence of allowing the freedom to reject Myth on an individual level. Importantly, though, they maintained the right to embrace Myth collectively. This is an expression of pluralism. Few collective human changes have offered more promise or created so many problems since the first use of language.

Cultural domination was implicit in this transition, despite the enormous sophistication of many subjugated cultures, and it was assumed as a consequence, that the rest of the world would provide cheap labor and raw materials. In the European mind, Western rational materialism became the measure of value and progress, and it seemed universal and inevitable. To many, it still does, but materialism tends to undermine cultural meaning, personally and collectively. Modernity in the Western sense is not the inevitable form for a progressive society. Imagining that, and constructing an alternative from within a pre-modern society was, and is still, a huge task.

The 'Post-Perry' Japanese nation found themselves on the wrong side of a bi-polar world: East/West, progressive/backward, traditional/scientific. Western/Other.

The East/West view of the world (*toyo vs. seiyo*) became ingrained as the framework for Japanese people to understand their path to progress and the sometimes radical changes this brought to their lives.

Many romantic reinventions of Japanese tradition followed as reactions against change, but this split view also had the effect of politicians, military men, and intellectuals becoming more receptive to philosophical ideas and theories than would have been normal in the West. The Japanese had embraced the challenge of creating the ideal nation state with enormous enthusiasm, and they were receptive to those who could provide the language and the terms in which this could all be expressed. A similar motivation occurred in America when revolutionaries rejected colonial rule and turned to the language and ideas of the European Enlightenment to give shape to the new democratic dream. By comparison, though, this was a minor paradigm adjustment because it represented cultural extension or adaption, rather than reinvention.

Japanese philosophy came to be most representative and influential at Kyoto State University, mainly under the guidance of Nishida Kitaro around 1913. Several generations of scholars followed. It was never a 'school' as such, but a loose aggregation of independent thinkers. The scope of the work done under this banner is huge, touching on developments from Greek, French, German, and English philosophers, Theism, Christianity, and Buddhism.

What is particularly interesting for the purposes of this book is the self-positioning of Japanese philosophy relative to a Euro-centric world, which expressed itself through what is often called Western universalism. As it represented the center of progress, the West had no need to define its achievements in relation to the rest of the world. But thinking or action elsewhere occurred in an inevitable Euro-American frame of reference, and it hadn't been very long since America itself had become part of that frame of reference.

Third–world, or even First World, *colonial* intellectuals felt compelled to reference European examples while their European counterparts felt no need to reciprocate. Eastern intellectuals often felt compelled to write for an unseen Western reader, but no Eastern equivalent exists for the Western writer. Of course, this is not a 'racial' phenomenon; it is a cultural one, to varying degrees applicable to everyone on a periphery, and it applied in Sydney as it did in Tokyo. The difference between these two in degree can be expressed in terms of the relative capacity to apply the general concept of 'us' to the relationship.

By emerging into a confident and optimistic position in the new century, it was felt that Japan could provide its own version of 'universality,' drawing upon its own traditions, but speaking in a philosophical language that would not only be understood by Western scholars but also be recognized for its own truth and universal relevance. Nishida expressed this idea in many ways and the following is from his collected works:

"Up to now Westerners thought that their culture was superior to all others, and that human culture advances toward their own form. Other peoples, such as Easterners, are said to be behind and if they advance, they too will acquire the same form. There are even some Japanese who think like this. However... I believe there is something fundamentally different about the East. They [East and West] must compliment each other and...achieve the eventual realization of a complete humanity. It is the task of Japanese culture to find such a principle."[190]

This seems unremarkable at first reading, but it contains the kernel of an idea that challenges the West's 'ownership' of universal culture, hinting that history can no longer claim to culminate in European civilization. This required that history would need to recognize multiple centers.[191]

Whatever meaning we ultimately attach to the causes or outcomes of the Pacific War, and how ever repulsed we are by the conduct of the war, this emerging philosophy was the first serious intellectual challenge to Euro-centrism. Given that the vast majority of people in the world are not Western or Euro/American, this is hugely significant in modern history. It is destined to become more so.

Our examination of the Kyoto school will be quite superficial. Philosophy makes for demanding reading, and this school in particular has been the subject of a huge body of writing and debate. The reason is that Japanese philosophy has been both blamed for, and absolved of, guilt and complicity in

---

[190] *Nishida Kitaro Zenshu*, vol 14 Pp404–405, cited in Yoko Arisaka. *Beyond "East and West": Nishida's Universalism and Postcolonial Critique*, in The Review of Politics 59:3 Summer 97.

[191] Yoko Arisaka. *Beyond "East and West": Nishida's Universalism and Postcolonial Critique*, in The Review of Politics 59:3 Summer 97, P3.

the development of imperialist and ultranationalist tendencies in Japan before and during the war. Several difficulties apply in particular.

First, nearly all the philosophers produced contradictory statements over the course of their careers. This should not seem surprising when dealing with subtle human minds, particularly when the analysis of a pure idea can often relate opposites to each other by virtue of their extreme difference. This is further complicated by the application of the Zen notion of absolute *nothingness* to an entity that in the West is seen as an absolute *something*. These things are compounded by the political climate of the time, the subtle but all pervading censorship as well as the potential consequences of challenging the prevailing view.

Second, the Japanese language and the presentation of its concepts do not lend themselves to simple translation into English. Huge differences in meaning can arise from a culturally insensitive choice of a word. Where possible, it is helpful to work from texts by Japanese nationals who learned English, or scholars who have lived for significant periods in Japan and have studied there.

Further, the method of debate and the presentation of argument in Japanese culture cannot be appreciated from a simple Western perspective. Language use in forming an argument in Sinitic cultures is different from the Western, linear, polemic methods. Opposing arguments may be approached in a more circular manner, converging on points of similarity or difference, somewhat like an insect spiraling down to land on a flower, considering its object throughout several passes. The consideration of the 'object' may be likened to recognition of status and the preservation of 'face.'

Nishida began a national, intellectual project that involved the very rigorous study of Western sources synthesized with core Zen Buddhist concepts. But by the early 1930s, the wider national discussion focused increasingly on nationalism, causing the critique of Euro-centrism to become more emphatically nationalist, rather than universal.

Unless you are prepared for an enormous research task (and possibly even then), your view of the position of Kyoto thinkers within this debate will depend on your choice of reading and your view of history. It is still debated, but it does seem that the most compelling and consistent writings by the leading philosophers, notably Nishida and Tanabe, emphatically rise above extreme nationalism, expressing abhorrence for any abuse of people for national purposes. Their support for a national agenda was perhaps no more nationalistic or imperialistic than that which was considered moderate in Britain, America, or Australia at the time. The difficulty is that there are exceptions.

What Kyoto intellectuals were searching for was a particular form of modernity, which could address a persistent aspect of Euro-centrism that sought to dominate other cultures. Some would argue that in addressing it they became it, but that is to confuse the idea with the reality. One inhabits the realm of the philosopher and, the other, the realm of the soldier. The issue came to a head during a series of discussions, or symposia, held immediately before Pearl Harbor and not concluding until 1942 but published in 1943. The realities that needed to be dealt with were very different from those at the beginning of their intellectual journey, and they took place in a very different atmosphere and context.

The language of the wartime debates became more expansive in a way that, to modern eyes, might sometimes seem imperialistic. But since Japan's struggle in China, Taiwan, and Korea had been both imperialistic and in competition with other imperialistic powers, this is not surprising. A China of the 1930s without Japanese interference would have been a China under either Soviet, British, or American influence or control, or any combination of those. But they spoke in terms of freeing Asia from foreign domination by unifying these and other Asian nations in a new world order. In doing so, they unwittingly provided the rationalization for aggression. However, the kind of mind capable of imagining the transformation of the Asian peoples into co-operative, post-colonial nations was not the kind of mind that had been trained by the Army and placed into politically ambiguous frontiers.

In fact, semi-autonomous sub-imperialists whose military conditioning was based on the mythological and the quasi-religious staffed the Japanese overseas project. Many were agents for all that was irrational, self-serving, and chauvinistic, and their semi-autonomy was the basis for all of the 'incidents' that undermined Japanese intellectual life, politics, and foreign policy.

From the Kyoto School point of view, Ultra-nationalism and Fascism were manifestations of a Romantic exuberance, born of, and fed by, suffering, poverty, fear, and frustration, and they were destined to fail. Despite the debates about the meaning of the School, this much is clear: They understood that Tojo's aggressive policies would fail and they acted, as best they could, to undermine them. They stood instead for rational self-mastery.

The Japanese experience understood in these terms can inform our understanding of current struggles against imperialism and the subjugation of peoples, as well as the futility of resorting to emotional and irrational means in the pursuit of self-realization.

We are not really naive enough to believe that the West's interest in the Middle East is about the altruistic desire to export freedom and democracy. Modernity demands fuel and raw materials, and the actions of America, Britain, and Australia in the early 21st Century have parallels in those of Japan of the late 1930s: If not to own the supply, then to make sure the supplier is of a co-operative or compliant frame of mind. The Kyoto struggle to find a non-dominating form of modernity has to be our struggle, if the West is to earn its unlikely claim on continued hegemony. Further, the facile attempts to transplant democracy into countries that cannot embrace intellectual pluralism represent a shameful ignorance or disregard of the Japanese experience. First, rational pluralism, then, gradually, democracy. Democracy is potentially dangerous and very superficial until *certainty* is widely superseded as a national paradigm.

What was the thrust of Kyoto thinking as it developed into the 1930s? A very good place to start is with Tanabe and his thoughts on subjectivity, arguably his central concept.

Subjectivity (*shutaisei*) is the essence of this rational self-mastery, a complex set of values, practices, and institutions without which the planet cannot be properly managed, or in the language of the Kyoto School, history cannot be made.[192]

But self-mastery is also that quality that equips a people to become dominant over other peoples. By itself and without a rational foundation, self-mastery is not only potentially destructive, it is also ultimately self-defeating. The North American democratic adventure that seemed so pure an example of Enlightenment thinking still managed to enslave thousands of Africans and almost purge the entire continent of its First People and is a perfect example of the dangerous paradox within the concept of subjectivity.[193] Huge power harbors huge temptations. To illustrate this point, compare our understanding of the actions of the Japanese Army to the words of one of Japan's leading philosophers, Hajime Tanabe.

---

[192] Williams, David. *Defending Japan's Pacific War, Philosophers and post-White power*. London & NY: Routledge Curzon, 2004, P11.

[193] Ibid, P 139 Read Williams' on 'European origins of the Kyoto School crisis' for an excellent and very thorough account.

The following extract is from *The Philosophy of Crisis or a Crisis in Philosophy, Reflections on Heidegger's Rectoral Address*, 1933. The translation from the Japanese is by David Williams.

"To reject philosophy and acknowledge only the rule of political necessity as a standard for state conduct exposes the state to the judgment of history, a judgment that in the end it cannot endure. No state can long survive, let alone flourish, if it turns its back on reason.

"When Athens rejected the philosophy of Socrates and Plato, Athenians proceeded down a one-way street to their destruction. In the same way, when philosophy disregards the historical necessities that press on states in a self-satisfied manner, philosophy invites its own ruin. The fate of late Greek philosophy is one of the best known examples of such a failure.

"Abandoning the struggle, each side should recognize that the realist moment and idealist moment form an absolute identity. This holds out the promise that a concrete unity of these two moments is achievable. This is what Hegel's expression 'What is rational is actual, and what is actual is rational' means."

This is a very grounded perspective from the period before war with China, but what does Tanabe have to say after Pearl Harbor, when Nazism appears to be all conquering in Europe, and the Pacific appears to have been recast as a Japanese possession? The following are extracts from Tanabe's article "On the Logic of Co-prosperity Spheres," again translated by David Williams, and dated September 1942.

Noting that the British concept of equality as expressed by Missionaries stood in marked contrast to the reality of the situation in which the developed country relentlessly exploited the undeveloped one, Tanabe typifies this as vertical hegemony dominating horizontal equality. He adds the observation that "Western colonialism attempts to hide the realities of economic exploitation behind this pretended commitment to equality." He wanted Japan to do better, by openly facing the gap between developed and developing nations and managing the imbalance to the advantage of both. He wrote:

> "The link between the persistence of power and order as well as the hierarchy of power between states that results from this relationship—need to be acknowledged clearly by both leader and follower states. But it also implies that this imbalance of power must not result in the imperialistic exploitation of one side by the other. The autonomy of the developing states needs to be advanced and their sovereignty recognized. Effective integration between the member states is vital to the success of any great project such as that of building a co-prosperity sphere."

David Williams provides the first port of call for the reader who needs to explore the topic in some depth. He demonstrates an intimate knowledge and understanding of Tanabe's work and the challenges it poses for the orthodox view of Pacific War history. In explaining the relevance of the Kyoto philosophers he writes, in part,

> "[the Kyoto philosophers] were rational thinkers in a sense that any educated European will find plausible. This is what makes the Kyoto thinker so formidable and therefore so disturbing to any proponent of Pacific War orthodoxy.
> "This brings us to the greatest failure of the Western critic of the Wartime Kyoto School. In the eyes of the

Kyoto philosopher, the war against Anglo-American hegemony had to be fought with rational means for rational ends; otherwise, it was wrong metaphysically and would not succeed practically. But because the Tojo regime pursued the war for other than rational ends and insisted on fighting it with less than rational means, the assessment of the war effort by the Kyoto School may qualify as among the most important expressions of public criticism (admittedly oblique) of the government's military strategy to appear in print in Japan between 1941 and 1945."[194]

Tanabe was involved in secret discussions with the Yonai Faction of the Imperial Navy to bring down the Tojo Cabinet. The writings and actions quoted here are not those of a person we can justifiably call fascist. By seeking to apply universal standards to national behavior, the Kyoto group threatened the very basis of the ultranationalist appeal. As Williams put it, "Like the American exceptionalist, the Japanese chauvinist believed that his country was in the world but not of it."[195]

The Kyoto group were not interested in a national narrative but in the Japanese role in world history as conceived by Hegel and judged by universal standards. Tanabe was loathed by the nationalists, in the same way that Minobe had been in the controversy surrounding his 'Emperor as Organ Theory.' Minobe and Tanabe both tried to subject Japanese institutions to rational analysis, challenging the distribution and the application of power. Their persistence, despite criticism from the left and from the right, from Japanese Government and Allied Occupation Forces alike, can explain in part the success of post-war Japan, the 'economic miracle' that became the exemplar for post-colonial Asian subjectivity.

---

[194] Ibid P20

[195] Ibid P68

A neo-Marxist will take issue with this line of thinking, and with the arguments omitted from this very brief and somewhat shallow outline but will do so because history from that position must follow a predictable path. This book has been an attempt to avoid a rigid starting position to let the events lead us to a rational, satisfying view. The dissatisfied reader can do no better than refer to David Williams' thorough dissection of these issues. His analysis is extensive, rigorous, and incisive.

18

VIEWS OF AMERICA'S ROLE

"*THE SIMPLE FACT is that we are here dealing not with a unified Japan but with a Japanese Government which is endeavoring courageously, even with only gradual success, to fight against a recalcitrant Japanese Army, a battle which happens to be our own battle...If we now rebuff the Government we shall not be serving to discredit the Japanese Army but rather to furnish the Army with powerful arguments to be used in its own support. I am convinced that we are in a position either to direct American-Japanese relations into a progressively healthy channel or to accelerate their movement straight down hill.*"

US Ambassador to Japan, Joseph Grew, December 18th Telegram to Washington, 1939[196]

Over the years, many histories have been written and many opinions voiced about the role played by America in the years leading up to World War II. Most people who have grown up

---

[196] Foreign Relations Papers, 1939, vol III, Pp620–622.

during or since the war have been exposed to accounts that support the idea that America went reluctantly to war against an aggressive Japan, responding to an unprovoked attack. American actions before this had been to protect China from Japanese aggression. In this view, the US is regarded as an isolated, neutral, and militarily limited nation whose actions were generated from a sense of morality and duty.

This has been a particularly comforting view in the post-Vietnam era, because the Pacific War is often regarded warmly as a clear-cut conflict between the forces of good and the evil forces of a militarist nation. It was seen as un-corrupted by the politics and failures of the wars that have happened since.

Those of us in Australia who lost family in that war have taken some solace in the belief that a way of life, not only in Australia, was under attack and that the human cost of its defense was justified. Australia declared war on Japan as a consequence of the Japanese attacks on American, British, and Dutch possessions and bases.

While Australians feared the invasion of their own country, both Japan and America saw the significance of Australia in very different terms. To American interests, Australia provided the fallback position when the Philippines under Macarthur were defeated and they needed to maintain a strategic supply base in the region. This was a surprise to the Japanese, who expected the US forces to fall back to Hawaii.

To Japan, Australia represented an under-utilized space in so far as population and resources were concerned. While there were those who, flushed with early military success, wished to push the Japanese advantage further, most recognized that they did not have adequate supply lines to sustain such an action. Australia simply represented a strategic threat to their main objectives. This situation would no doubt have been re-examined had the battles in the Pacific continued to favor them.

The Japanese command suffered from a de facto decentralization in that new strategies sometimes appeared out of perceived opportunity. The battle for Kokoda, for example, was an initiative made "on the spot," rather than in Tokyo, and was very costly to them and to Australia. Lines of supply were the limiting factors in that example, but enthusiasm overcame caution.

In any case, as our concern is more with causes than conjectures, we are justified in looking more deeply at the differing establishment and revisionist views of the events that led to war. In this chapter, we will examine historical views of America's role in general terms, and in a later chapter we will look at the contemporary views held by the American individuals who contributed to policy.

In the years following World War I, there was a view that America's position had been one of cynical self-interest in the role it played before the war and the timing of its entry. The power of this argument was underlined when the US Senate Nye Committee explored the relationship between Anglo-American capitalists and the decision of the Wilson Administration to become involved when it did. Several historians supported and expanded this dark view of America's war.

One of these was Charles Beard, who presented a strong case that President Wilson had led the American people into World War I to avoid an economic crash and that similar conditions existed in the mid-1930s. In his 1934 book, *The Idea of the National Interest*,[197] Beard established that American leaders since Hamilton had pursued national economic advantage beyond its own borders, making the US into an aggressive, imperialistic sea power. According to Thomas Breslin,198 Beard was one of a powerful group of scholars,

---

[197] Beard, Charles A. *The Idea of the National Interest*. New York: Macmillan, 1934.

[198] Breslin, T. A. *Mystifying the Past: Establishment Historians and the*

including Sidney B. Fay and Charles Tansill who "united the vast majority of Americans in contempt for the 'merchants of death' and in determination to avoid another war."

These and other writings had a profound effect on the Roosevelt Administration in that the public sentiment against war stayed his hand in openly supporting the British, as an active participant at the outbreak of war.

Breslin maintained that the "powerful and influential Americans of that era knew that they were again leading the nation to war,"[199] and that the public face to represent their views was the Council on Foreign Relations (CFR). It was to be through the CFR and its membership that they would "later develop histories of the Pacific War which would meet the needs of the established order." To begin with, this involved the immediate post-war need to defend the actions of the Roosevelt Administration from criticism of the type that was leveled at Wilson in the 1920s.

Breslin cites Dr. Troyer S. Anderson, who was to become special consultant to the Secretary of War in 1946, in his memo to the Secretary of War of January 24, 1946:

> "While you have been away I received a telephone call from Allan Nevins. He said he had been devoting a good deal of thought to the subject of my letter and had formulated a general plan for one project which might be undertaken very soon. He thinks it would be wise, promptly after the conclusion of the Pearl Harbor inquiry, to have a small group of historians with established reputations go over the testimony of the hearing and prepare an analysis of it which would serve to dispel the notion that this country was pushed

Origins of the Pacific War. Bulletin of Concerned Asian Scholars, Vol 8: 4, 1976 P18.

[199] Ibid P19

or tricked into war by its government. This would, of course, be a strictly private venture, but Professor Nevins thinks he can get two or three outstanding scholars to join in the task…"[200]

But the revisionists were already rallying as serious questions were being raised about America's role. Had Roosevelt lied to his electorate? Had he goaded or provoked a war? Charles Beard published his *American Foreign Policy in the Making, 1932–1940,* in 1946, and it demonstrated not only that there had been significant questions about what Roosevelt had been telling the American people concerning his intentions, but also that Roosevelt had "knowingly broken undertakings to the people that he would not involve the United States in war."[201]

Early efforts in opposing this view were successful in presenting Roosevelt well, but they did so by painting the Japanese in a very negative way, and this became embarrassing to an administration that had decided to re-create Japan as an ally in the global (cold) war against communism.

The next stage was reached in the works of several authors,[202] which allowed the American establishment finally to acquire a "scientific political analysis and histories purporting to show that most, but not all, of the blame for the Pacific war fell on Japan, and the extent to which the United States was to blame, it was the people, not Franklin D Roosevelt or an imperial presidency, that was at fault."

The arguments put forward by Paul Schroeder, for example, in *The Axis Alliance and Japanese-American Relations, 1941,*[203]

---

[200] Ibid P20

[201] Ibid P21

[202] Morgenthau, Langer, Gleeson, and Kennon cited in Ibid P19

[203] Schroeder, P. *The Axis Alliance and Japanese-American Relations.* Ithaca: Cornell University Press, 1958, cited in Ibid.

were along the lines that there was nothing between the two nations that made war inevitable. He maintained that the war in Europe caused America to adopt a tougher attitude toward Japanese operations in China, and, on the other hand, Japanese leaders made sincere efforts to avoid the conflict, but these were rejected by the American leadership that was responding to popular pressure, despite the likelihood of a diplomatic breakthrough.

The Japanese had moderated their mobilization toward Western colonies, but President Roosevelt, needing to avoid being seen as an appeaser, responded to a public moral outrage at Japanese actions against the Chinese. The result was the economic freeze of Japanese assets. In short, the culprit in America was seen to be the public and its inflexible moralism.

The thrust of this line of argument is that, far from exercising colossal Presidential power and leading the nation to war, Roosevelt's role as Chief Executive was compromised by the power of public opinion.

This view and variations of it have been put forward by several 'establishment' historians in response to the suggestion that the President lied his people into a war they didn't want. In this it is an elaboration of the popularly-held view that the war in the Pacific originated from an unexpected and unprovoked attack by the militarists in Japan against an isolationist, neutral America.

In his 1959 work, *The Tragedy of American Diplomacy*, W.A. Williams[204] analyzed American foreign policy in the light of Beard's earlier work. His view repudiated that of the establishment historians, arguing that America had been so successful in absorbing much of Asia into its economic system and doing so at the expense of the Japanese, that the latter were forced to find a way to break American domination in a sphere of influence they regarded as theirs. He felt that American

---

[204] Williams, William A. *The Tragedy of American Diplomacy.* New York: World Publishing Co., 1959.

leaders behaved as if their system could not adapt to the loss of the China market to Japan.

All of these beliefs have been examined over the decades since; and we will attempt to explore some of the implications of several versions of the story.

Effects of the Tripartite Pact

When Japan signed the Tripartite Pact of Berlin in September 1940, the three countries vowed to "assist with all political, economic and military means when one of the three contracting parties is attacked by a power at present not involved in the European War or the Sino-Japanese conflict."

At the time, Germany was committed to the pragmatic and brittle nonaggression pact with the Soviet Union, so the Tripartite Pact had the flavor of an arrangement made with America as its object.

A cynical view would see in this the convergence of Germany's desires and Roosevelt's needs. As we shall see, Hitler eventually became more than a little supportive of a Japanese attack on the United States, or its interests. For his part, Roosevelt saw the Tripartite Pact as a way into the European War, by means sometimes referred to as the 'back door.' Even though he was inclined for the moment to follow the moderate line advocated by Hull, he knew that an incident with Japan would automatically mean war with Germany and Italy.

The establishment view of this represented by Gleason and Langer in *The Undeclared War, 1940–1941* (1953) emphasized Roosevelt's passivity at this point. Rather than seeing an opportunity for entering the war through the actions of others, they point to his indecision in the face of provocation:

> "Yet no drastic measures were adopted by the Administration. From the records presently available it is impossible to trace the reasons for the President's

indecision. It may be safely assumed, however, that he was swayed by the arguments of his military advisers. Furthermore, Secretary Hull probably relapsed into his customary caution and used his influence to head off risky moves."[205]

The picture changed somewhat in July 1941 when Germany put aside her pact with Russia simply by attacking deep into Soviet territory. America's Ambassador Grew felt that Germany was pressing Japan to divert American attention from Europe, in preference to Japan becoming involved against Russia in support of the Axis.

The Japanese diplomatic relationship with America, outlined elsewhere, continued to offer hopes for peace right up to the point when America's position was reduced to a choice for Japan between total capitulation or war. Capitulation involving complete withdrawal from China became the American demand, but it was never going to be an option for the Japanese. Apart from anything else, it was felt that such an action would invite the Soviets into territory adjacent to Japan, with consequential strategic threats as well as the loss of markets and raw materials. Notably, this would not have suited the Americans either, and this may be a clue to their real intentions.

Roosevelt's alleged provocation of Japan was probably encouraged by Britain and certainly aided by Germany. Protracted pressure on Japan for action against America peaked in November when Joachim von Ribbentrop the Nazi Foreign Minister conveyed to the Japanese Ambassador in Berlin, Major General Oshima, the following:

"It is essential that Japan effect the new order in East Asia without losing this opportunity. There never

---

[205] Langer, W. L., and Gleason, S. *The Undeclared War 1940–41*. New York: Harper and Bros, 1953, P36.

has been and never will be a time when closer co-operation under the tripartite pact is so important. If Japan hesitates at this time, and Germany goes ahead and establishes her European new order, all the military might of Britain and the United States will be concentrated against Japan…If Japan reaches a decision to fight Britain and the Unites States, I am confident that that will not only be in the interest of Germany and Japan jointly, but would bring about favorable results for Japan herself."[206]

At this time, Nazism looked well placed to dominate Europe utterly. Oshima was being asked to imagine Japan's potential role as an underachiever in the new order. The psychological insight implicit in this statement is quite remarkable. In a most subtle way, it *suggests* the shame of failure from weakness and indecision, the very things most abhorred by the warrior class. Nothing would motivate the Major General more effectively.

The verbal persuasion was part of a larger ploy.

On December 6th, Berlin was pointedly celebrating the imminent fall of Moscow. It seemed inevitable that the Soviets would be chased from their own capital. On December 8th, the day after Pearl Harbor was attacked, committing the Americans to war, Hitler's armies in Russia were in full retreat to predetermined positions for the winter.[207]

The bait had been taken, but whose bait was it?

Of all these nations, Japan had the least to gain from its military attack, but it was convinced that it had everything to lose by resisting it. The United States was committed to a war with its third best trading partner. Trade with Japan at the time was more than twice the combined trade with China

---

[206] Intercepts Pp200-212, cited in Morgenstern, G. *Pearl Harbor: The Story of the Secret War*. New York: Devin-Adair, 1947, P97.

[207] New York Times Dec 9 1941 1:7

and Hong Kong. Japan had lost its best trading partner as 6.5% of America's imports had been from Japan. In 1938, Japan imported $240 million in commodities from the United States, three-quarters of which were in petroleum products, heavy capital goods, metals, aircraft and parts, automobiles, parts and accessories, semi-manufactured iron and steel, and pig iron. Almost one sixth of the total was in raw cotton for Japanese manufacture into exportable goods.

This escalation of the situation came after fifty-three months of war between China and Japan. The urgency in the situation certainly didn't come from there. In understanding the Japanese and American arrival at this point we will look at several causal factors.

The Issue of Race

As an issue, 'race' pervades many aspects of the pre-war story. Difficult issues confront us in looking at fast-changing times, and it is not the intention of this book to be overly judgmental of people who express what were the prevalent attitudes in the period. However, these issues deserve not to be shirked or understated. If there was hypocrisy or duplicity in the politics of the time it should be known.

Prior to World War I, many millions of people had no experience beyond their own villages. One could say that many belonged to families that had never been exposed to any form of racial or cultural variation. Attitudes were generally unchanging and embedded in social traditions in which any noticeable sense of 'difference' attracted fear and judgment. There have been dynamic forces for equality and social inclusiveness since the early Nineteenth Century, notably in Britain, but popular sentiment has always tended to retreat from those values under pressure or fear.

World War I took village boys to places all over the world, and traditional insularity was broken down for the first time to a degree, but first contact with other cultures often served to emphasize differences. Population pressures, poverty, and the fear of immigrant labor reinforced insularity, and democratic leaders of the period tended to represent the fears of their electorates in their words and deeds on the world stage.

The 'new idealism' represented by President Wilson after the war was intended to supersede neo-Darwinism and primitive notions of racial purity. The battle was far from over, as the following quotation will show. It is from a United States State Department Memo relating to the Manchurian crisis of 1931–1932

> "Should Japan succeed in getting her way over the protests of the League of Nations and the united States and despite the admitted interests of the Soviet Union, white prestige throughout Asia would be dangerously shaken; the 'Asia for Asiatics' movement would be intensified; and the difficult position of the British in India would be rendered still more difficult of solution."

At this time, it was Britain whose trade with Asia was the most pressing colonial imperative. The above memo foretells the potential calamity of Japan overtaking Britain in this, using Manchurian resources and Chinese and Korean labor to develop trade in India and elsewhere in Asia. The race issues raised in this are shocking to a modern reader; they were typical of the time but are in marked in contrast to the Wilsonian idealism expressed at the founding of the League of Nations, and they illustrate the confusion that must have been felt by the Japanese who responded to idealistic rhetoric and advances, only to be insulted by racist attitudes. The following is a final note in the same group of memoranda:

"Finally, the British are conscious of the need for maintaining the solidarity of the White race to a degree shared by few other countries. The United States, the Dominions, and the British ruling classes are alike race-conscious, and the underlying instinct of the Anglo-Saxons is to preserve the Anglo-Saxon breed intact against the rising tide of color. Despite emotional appeals and jingo talk, the common British and American attitude towards people of other colors is a fundamental factor in the present situation."[208]

The 'rising tide of color' refers in part to the Japanese, who in Western eyes had been ascendant since defeating Russia early in the century. But the reference is subtler than that. It portrays, not so much a threat of being over-run by a 'different' people, as a sense of Western territorial possessions 'falling' under the control of their own indigenous people. Bluntly, the worry was the end of the colonial way of life, in which the wealth generated went predominantly to Britain and Europe. This racial stratification was quite similar to that being developed in Japan.

China. A Moral Cause or an Excuse?

Did the US move to protect its trade with China, protect China from Japanese aggression, or maintain its own regional power base? The wars in China pop up throughout this story, always on the edges, but fundamental to the creation of the Pacific War.

China certainly suffered throughout the years of war with Japan. Exact estimates of the costs are incalculable, but the Nationalist Chinese representative to the Far Eastern

---

[208] Memorandum. *British and American Interests in the Far East* in 'Trade' file Box 414, Hornbeck papers cited in Breslin P33.

Commission gave an estimate of losses at eleven million persons killed, sixty million homeless, and property damage of perhaps sixty billion dollars.[209]

This is destruction on an unimaginable scale for most people. It is the context in which American public opinion can be judged and within which the American government had to find a balance between humanitarian concerns, strategic objectives, and economic imperatives. However, the violence in China was not just caused by imperialist aggression but also by internal, very violent competition for power and unity. It was not clear who would best represent the Chinese, as their interests were represented by many discordant voices.

To be 'for' the Chinese, America might need to be 'against' the Japanese, and that would mean war. This course would enable Roosevelt to support Britain openly and support the American bankers and business interests in China. But Roosevelt had promised his people that he would not take them to war.

Most historians describe America's economic interests in China as being too small to risk war with Japan. It is difficult to know how to quantify that, but how ever much the US had invested in China, there was untold room for growth, if it could be kept from being part of a Japanese trading bloc. Ultimately, this was what caused American action and why action became more intensive after Japan joined the Axis. It became even more emphatic when the Japanese moved south.

It wasn't Japanese actions that were intolerable, it was what an Axis trading bloc could do in dominating the trade in East Asia, at the expense of future American market growth. While Japan was isolated and dependent on US materials and trade,

---

[209] US Department of State. *The Far Eastern Commission: A Study in International Cooperation. 1945–1952*, Publication 5138, Far Eastern Series 60, Washington, 1953, P145.

tariffs could be manipulated and markets controlled to suit American needs.

Further, given the early, dramatic success of the German forces, which included an imminent threat of the invasion of Britain, Southeast Asia became the strategic link not only for British resources but also in potentially linking Axis forces in Europe and Asia. If the Germans were to take the Suez Canal, the British would be cut off from India, Australia, and New Zealand, as well as the resources of Southeast Asia.

In this situation, a potential autarkic trading bloc involving the Axis and excluding Britain and America was capable of turning world trade on its head. Roosevelt and Hull and most American leaders looked upon the world as an economic unit, believing that prosperity was based on freedom of trade. The theory is very egalitarian, but the practice was fairly one-sided and was based on high-value goods being produced by controlling powers and cheap labor being provided by developing ones. Japan needed to join the club.

There is an argument that Japanese expansion into China as a strategy was inadvertently abetted by protectionist tariffs, imposed by Western economies, which clearly discriminated against Japan in the 1930s. The tariffs made it impossible for Japan to sell products that would enable her to buy the resources she so desperately needed. This strengthened the ultranationalist view that, if Japan could not sell, she could not develop the industries to employ and feed her growing population.

Japan's problems stemmed, as we have seen, from an excess of people and high, value-added goods and products. In addition, there was a shortage of resources for her industries and markets for her goods. America had made it plain that there would be no great movement of people onto her continent by the application of immigration quotas and legislation aimed at Japan.

In 1913, California passed a law restricting land ownership intending to prevent the Japanese "from driving the root of their civilization into California soil" as Governor H. Johnson explained it.

The Smoot-Hawley Tariff Act of 1930 placed trade barriers limiting the Japanese capacity to trade high, value-added goods for materials and resources. They also prevented Japan from earning the capital to invest in the US, having operated a trade surplus to acquire viable US assets.

Hoover imposed a 100% duty on silk imports, even though America was not a silk producer. The reason for the tariff was that Reed Smoot, Chairman of the Senate Finance Committee, was trying to influence the Senators from the textile producing States who were already benefiting from very high levels of protection.

The high rates on silk apparently did the trick, but it did so at significant expense to the huge rural-based 'cottage industry' in Japan that employed many Japanese farmers' wives in tending their silk worms, keeping them above the bread-line. In 1930, silk cocoon prices fell to about half of those from the previous year. The amount of silk exported to the United States fell by 44.6% as a result of the depression, tariffs, and competition from rayon produced there.[210]

At the start of the depression, about 40% of farm households raised silk, and for many it was their only cash income.

So in 1930, Japan faced blocking on emigration plans to deal with population pressures, higher tariffs on its manufactured goods, and a reducing capacity to invest offshore. Yet over the water, Western interests were pursuing the Chinese markets, seemingly only to suit themselves. In Japan, there must have been a very real sense that, in order to survive,

[210] Wilson, S. *The Manchurian Crisis and Japanese Society, 1931–33* London: Routledge, 2002, P127.

they had to expand industrially, because the alternative was unconscionable.

The consequence of all this was a choice between giving up her industrial ambitions, effectively reversing modernization, or seizing her share of the resources on the continent. It was a difficult argument for moderates to counter and it won many converts. It also neutralized advocates for internationalism and peace, whose criticism of the Kwantung army's seizure of Manchuria lacked impact.

In an article called "Japanese-American Relations and Perceptions, 1900-1940," Harry Wray explains that there was a tendency in Japan to believe that Japan must achieve autarky or economic self-sufficiency to merit real power status:

> "Japan might be a member of the Big Five in the League of Nations, but to a sensitive and proud Japanese people the record seemed clear. They were taken for granted and regarded as inferior: their complaints against the status quo were not being heard. They believed there would be no change in that attitude by the West. Little by little the Japanese developed a sense of being surrounded by enemies. Paranoia increased. Increasingly the ultranationalists gained the upper hand in the government."[211]

Rather than being forced to beg for markets, they could create their own trading bloc. The huge population over the water was politically unstable, a power vacuum, a danger to Japan, and a potential hotbed of Communist unrest. It was being exploited and increasingly controlled by foreign interests. In addition, it was a controllable market, if a brief, explosive

---

[211] Wray, H. *Japanese-American Relations and Perceptions, 1900–1940,* in Conroy, H., Wray, H. (eds) *Pearl Harbor re-examined: Prologue to the Pacific War.* Honolulu: Univ. of Hawaii Press, 1990, P11.

Japanese incursion could quickly establish local governments there, which would act and trade favorably with Japan.

In the first few months of the China Incident (a wonderful piece of understatement), it seemed that the Japanese would defeat the Chinese armies. It even seemed likely that within the year, Japan would control five northern Chinese provinces and have sympathetic governments set up in them. Experience earlier in the century must have given them confidence that it would all go to plan.

Many in Washington, although unhappy about the likely outcome, did accept the inevitability of it. Hull went so far as to encourage China to negotiate a peace with Japan to prevent the war from spreading into Shanghai.[212]

Despite fast early progress and the occupation of vast territories, the Chinese surrender was not forthcoming.

The Japanese had under-estimated nationalist resistance and found themselves in a war from which they could not be extricated without massive loss of face. Some regard this as Japan's Vietnam. Wray describes the domestic situation for moderates at the time rather beautifully (using the words of Thomas Payne, the American revolutionary): "The voice of reason became the voice of treason."[213]

The nationalists in China boycotted Japanese goods and moved against Japanese concessions and investments. The Ultranationalists urged punitive action, which in turn escalated anti-Japanese feeling within China and in the United States. Humiliation led to reprisals that fueled nationalism and guerrilla resistance, which escalated military operations, and so the cycle went. This cycle has many echoes in recent times.

The actions of the Japanese at this point set the tone in the State Department of the United States for the following

---

[212] Utley, G. *Going to War with Japan 1937–1941*. Knoxville: University of Tennessee Press, 1985, P4.

[213] Ibid P12

decade. The bombing of the railway in Manchuria confirmed suspicions that the militarists were prepared to act summarily and aggressively.

The establishment of the puppet state there contradicted Japanese denials that they would enforce their interests. Wray expressed it in these terms: "Japan's successful annexation of Manchuria through armed aggression was a direct challenge to the rule of international law, the peace system, and the multilateral diplomacy established by the Anglo-American-dominated world in the post-Versailles era."[214]

In assessing the developments in China, the American administration faced conflicting advice. The embassy in Tokyo cautioned against too much pressure in the fear that moderates who opposed expansionary policies would be undermined in their efforts to dampen ultranationalist patriotic emotionalism.

On the other hand, Stanley Hornbeck advocated economic pressure and limited support for the Chinese nationalists. He believed that the militarists in Japan were not a separate aberration from a rational political system, but an expression of a broadly-based popular expansionary agenda.

President Hoover and Secretary of State Henry Stimson, who opted for American non-recognition of Japan's conquest, rejected his ideas. Hornbeck was a man of strong opinions and he described his country's response as 'flabby and impotent.'[215] Most historians would agree with his judgment on this.

There is a view that strong action at this point might have prevented the need for stronger action later, even war. We will see that in the final build up to war, Hornbeck's protracted

---

[214] Ibid P13

[215] Barnhart, M. "Hornbeck was right: The Realist Approach to American Policy Toward Japan," in Conroy, H., Wray, H. (eds) *Pearl Harbor re-examined: Prologue to the Pacific War*. Honolulu: Univ. of Hawaii Press, 1990, P66.

anti-Japanese, pro-Chinese stance appeared immoderate and counter-productive in the light of later Japanese efforts to negotiate a way to avoid war.

Michael Barnhart makes a strong case for Hornbeck's early position in his article, "Hornbeck Was Right: The Realist Approach to American Policy Toward Japan." The invasion of Manchuria in 1931 was initiated by a group of junior officers, with, as we have seen, the tacit but reluctant support of their superiors, who had advised delay in the fear that the international reaction would be severe. Barnhart wrote, "If the United States had announced its determination to shut off exports, Japan would have been in an impossible position. The Imperial Army of 1931 had virtually no stockpiles of oil or other strategic materials." [216]

Action at the beginning of the Japanese campaign might well have given them pause, and it is true that by the time embargoes were applied, the Japanese had invested too much in terms of life, resources, and national prestige for sanctions to work as effectively.

Hornbeck had in mind a program of punitive restraints, which could achieve two complementary objectives. First, Japan could be weakened in preparation for an inevitable clash with America, and second, it could be crippled by the increasing human and material costs of being bogged-down in China. Barnhart points out that, "had the United States, for example, limited its exports of scrap iron and oil from 1938 to 1941 to 'normal, peacetime' amounts, as Hornbeck advocated, Japan would have found it impossible to support two massive campaigns in China…while simultaneously constructing the navy that would deal such sharp defeats to the West in 1941–1942."[217]

---

[216] Ibid P70

[217] Ibid P70

For the five years following this, Hornbeck held his views but said little.

The following memo is by Hornbeck from a series of memoranda after the second Sino-Japanese War in 1937. It portrays foreign policy at its most cynical and manipulative level, but it does represent a mid path in balancing the issues of concern. He wrote:

> "It would seem desirable that: 1. China be not decisively defeated. 2. Japan should not reach a point of internal explosion accompanied and followed by economic collapse, and 3. That neither China nor Japan come under a controlling influence of the Soviet Union. The best ending that could be given the present hostilities would be one in which there has been for neither side a 'military' victory.
>
> "It would probably be good political strategy on the part of the powers to avoid stepping in with any vigorous effort to bring the hostilities to a definite end until one or other or both of the parties has reached a point obviously near to exhaustion."[218]

Hornbeck went on later to advise his superior that as long as the Japanese were tied up with the Chinese, they wouldn't be in a position to engage in any 'new adventures' that would risk war with the US.

These memos suggest helping the Chinese to a limited degree, sufficient only to exhaust both parties to the advantage of the US. The strategy is, therefore, containment of the Japanese by means of a third party, which happens to be an ally of the US. However, the US fear of communist influence in

---

[218] Hornbeck, S. K. *Memorandum, Oct 10, 1937, China-Japan Situation Reflections, IX: A 'Nine Powers' Conference, Box 83, Hornbeck Papers,* cited in Breslin Pp31–32.

the region prevented them from going too far in destabilizing the Japanese.

This is delicate and subtle planning, but it is hardly the isolationist or flaccid policy portrayed by some historians who attempt to portray America as a sleeping giant preoccupied with its own internal machinations. The Roosevelt Administration actively worked toward the non-resolution of the Sino-Japanese War by giving material support to both sides in an attempt to prevent the creation of a competitive rival power in Asia.

For Japan, China became a quagmire, absorbing money, men, and materials completely out of proportion to any immediate economic gain. It was a military project, despite the fact that Japan's greatest potential threats were seen to be the Soviets and the United States. The Japanese could not find a way to end the war in China as long as American support enabled Chiang Kai-shek to continue his resistance.

Evaluating the Naval race

Given an expenditure of US$339,000,000 (Depression Dollars) per year during the great Depression to maintain an American Presence in the Pacific, we should not be surprised that the region was considered part of America's 'interests.' As early as the mid 1930s, it was apparent that the US plan in the Pacific was to engage Japan in a naval arms race, relying on the American ability to outspend the Japanese. The progress being made in China by the Japanese was seen to be a danger in that it would increase Japanese capacity to mobilize resources, human and material.

According to some writers, the Roosevelt Administration's naval building program in 1933 reversed the global, post World War I decline in naval construction, and it was seen both in Europe and Japan as the beginning of a naval arms race.

In a view contrary to this, most establishment historians argued that the Japanese position at the London Naval

Conference in 1934-1935 was the driving force in the revival of British, American, and Japanese naval expansion, the Japanese attitude being responsible for creating a problem where none previously existed.[219]

The building statistics, however, do seem to indicate that America's program began before the Conference and Japan responded to it. It should be noted that all three naval powers portrayed the build up as 'defensive,' but in each case, the proposed defense was not of their own territory, but of their 'possessions' or economic interests.

Stanley Hornbeck was at the time the head of the State Department's Far East Division, and he apparently had the confidence of the Secretary of State, Hull. A series of documents by him outline the development of America's thinking, Asian Policy, and strategy. His April 1934 outline states in part:

> "[In replying to Japan's challenge] our reply should take the form of…going ahead rapidly and effectively (and perhaps ostentatiously) with the building and equipping of our naval and air forces—with a fixed objective of making the navy invincible as a defensive weapon and incidentally of compelling Japan so to expend herself in a naval race that she will not have sufficient energy to proceed effectively with her program of expelling and extracting from China our interests and those of other countries."[220]

In expressing this, Hornbeck is not announcing a new response to a qualitatively different Japanese threat. The

---

[219] Neumann, W. L. "How American Policy Contributed to the War in the Pacific," in Barnes H. E. (ed) *Perpetual War For Perpetual Peace*, Caldwell, Idaho: Caxton Printers Ltd, 1953 P245.

[220] Hornbeck memorandum handed to the Under Secretary and the Secretary of State April 20, or 21, 1934, in *Japan –No Trespass II file, Box 243, Hornbeck Papers*, Hoover Institution cited Breslin P29.

evidence suggests that the long-term expansionary program in Japan pre-dates the slide into a totalitarian-style government, just as American aims at regional hegemony date back to a period before World War I. Both sides were adjusting their courses for strategic advantage in a possible war that they had been rehearsing since the 1920s.

Whatever Roosevelt told his electorate, there is evidence that the US was always going to support Great Britain in the European theatre at some point, beyond aid and material assistance. It really became a question of how and when, and their great advantage was that, as in the previous war, they could choose the timing and the nature of their entry.

Of course, a pre-emptive strike by Japan at Pearl Harbor suggests something different, but not if it is seen to represent the only possible outcome of the failure of negotiation combined with a policy of embargo. It is likely that the US was theoretically already at war with Japan and, by extension, Germany, before the attack on Pearl Harbor, so the issue of provocation is impossible to represent in simple terms, especially since the United States' priority was to deal with Hitler first. We will briefly explore how this could all be possible.

The Issue of Provocation

For many reasons, Britain and America faced a possible future in which they could be isolated in a world governed by loosely allied totalitarian regimes. At home, Roosevelt was limited in his capacity to be active in his support for Britain, by a population whose strong inclination was to remain aloof from the carnage.

One should never assume that a nation should be desirous of war when the absence of it makes more domestic sense. People want work, safety, and food on the table. Leaders are required to see the broad sweep of events on a much larger scale, and whatever his faults, Roosevelt was a 'big picture' leader whose ambitions for his people encompassed a vision beyond immediate threats and domestic concerns to a visionary sense of the historical potential of America's position.

Like the Japanese leadership, he faced pressure from many directions to protect various national interests. Like the Japanese, his agenda included a controlling interest in Asia and the Pacific, and together, the two nations were prepared to play a game of brinkmanship in maintaining or developing those interests. For Japan, this was seen to be a matter of survival, while for the United States the mission was ultimately to replace Britain as the dominant force in Asia. But he was also quite sincere and transparent in his conviction that Nazi Germany was the major threat to the persistence of democracy and indeed to America. He was committed to supporting Britain.

Roosevelt was not able, directly, to go to war in Europe. The forces of non-intervention in the US at the time were vast and very popular. They ranged from pacifists—some being very public figures—at one end, through to groups who have been labeled pro-fascist at the other.[221] In the years since, there has been some heat in the debate about the agendas of those who opposed Roosevelt on the entry into the war. The operative word in understanding them is the plural 'agendas.' It would be wrong to paint them all with one brush.

Accusations have been made that the non-interventionist movement was anti-Semitic, but this certainly did not apply generally. It has even been argued that the McCarthy trials were a form of retribution leveled against the left as a consequence of the pre-war debate. There is no doubt, though, that the groundswell of resistance to intervention came from

---

[221] The most vociferous was the famous aviator Charles Lindbergh, but other well-known names included EE Cummings, WH Auden, Henry Miller, Frank Lloyd Wright, and Charles Beard. Collectively they claimed to represent a significant majority of popular opinion.

people who simply didn't want America to become embroiled once again in other people's war. Many felt that American lives should not be spent keeping the Dutch as masters of the East Indies and the British as masters of Malaya and Singapore. How far was Roosevelt prepared to go to create a situation in which his population would support such an action?

The very close relationship with Britain had the capacity to threaten Roosevelt at home, as it implied a solidarity that would take the country once more to war. To mask this, the American leadership maintained a level of secrecy about its plans and dealings with Japan and Britain. We saw in Chapter 11 that, during 1934, the State Department encouraged US oil representatives to threaten Japan's oil supplies rather than submit to a loss of increased profits.

Later, in 1938 and 1941, high-level secret military discussions were held, exploring the possibility of collaboration with the British against Japan in the event of war. Another conference in Singapore also included Dutch military representatives in further planning.

These conferences gave rise to a plan called 'Rainbow 5,' but as far as the author is aware, it is still not proven that the US was bound to act in support of the Dutch or the British in the event of an act of war. Establishment historians generally admit the importance of these conferences and the subsequent plan, but pull back from the idea of America's commitment to them.

This question of America's obligation or otherwise to fight is very important in our ultimate assessment of Roosevelt and his Administration. It appears that the Dutch implemented Rainbow 5 on the 5th of December 1941, therefore committing America to war some days before the attack on Pearl Harbor on the 7th of December. If this is true, and it seems likely that it is, then Roosevelt knew of a theoretical state of war with the Japanese—and by extension, with Germany and Italy—in good time to warn those at the base in Hawaii.

The following is a diary entry from the Secretary of War Stimson, US Administration, November 25, 1941:

"The question was how we shall maneuver them [the Japanese] into the position of firing the first shot without allowing too much danger to ourselves. It was a difficult proposition."[222]

The meaning of the above entry is magnified by the following telegram allegedly received at Manilla by the Commander of the Asiatic Fleet, Admiral Hart, December 6, 1941, from the US Naval attaché at Singapore. It informed Hart that,

"The British Commander–In-Chief, Far East, Brooke-Popham, had received a message from the War Department in London relaying news of American assurances of armed support in the event the British fought to assist the Dutch or attempted to repel a Japanese invasion of Thailand."[223]

There has been a great deal of speculation concerning the timing, the nature, and the transparency of events immediately prior to the attack on Pearl Harbor.

The Japanese advance into Indochina and toward Thailand represented a threat to the colonies of several European countries toward which the American public had no reason to feel any loyalties. The US Administration saw these colonies differently. They saw the potential of the material and human resources that could give strength to the Japanese advance and security to her war-making machine, especially rubber and fuel.

Public opinion in America was cold, and the US Navy wanted more time to build and prepare, but in the larger picture, Roosevelt could sense the convergence of opportunity and danger.

---

[222] Langer, W. L. and Gleason, S. *The Undeclared War 1940-41*, New York: Harper and Bros, 1953, P886.

[223] Ibid P921. The author has not been able to verify the existence of the telegram, beyond citation given.

A very significant 'strictly confidential' memo written by Hornbeck to Hull on December 1, 1941, explains his view of the situation. In part it reads:

"There has never been a more favorable moment for us to fight than the present (i.e., beginning in the next few weeks). And, if Japan is permitted now to move forward in the Indochina-Thailand-Yunnan area without resistance from us and/or the British, time will henceforth operate in Japan's favor rather than in ours."[224]

Those in the inner circle of government in America must certainly have known that they were approaching the sharp end of the relationship with Japan. On the night of the above memo, Hull attended meetings until he went to bed exhausted. Meanwhile, Under Secretary of State Welles met with Roosevelt and then with the British Ambassador, Lord Halifax, and then with Roosevelt again.

Later still, Roosevelt met with Admiral Stark, ordering him to arrange, in very short order, the deployment of three small naval vessels. These were quickly to form a 'defensive Information Patrol' to operate in the path of the southward moving Japanese fleet. The president's urgency was such that only one of the vessels made it to sea in time, and the Japanese ignored it.

When the ship arrived back at Manila, Hart is reported to have told the Commander that he hadn't expected to see him alive again.[225]

Thomas Breslin makes the point that for convenient and fast reconnaissance, scout planes would have been much quicker and more efficient in tracking the progress of the Japanese.

---

[224] Hornbeck, S. K. Memorandum, Dec 1 1941, in 'Japan-United States' file, Box 253, Hornbeck Papers, cited in Breslin P34.

[225] Herzog, H. *Closing the Open Door: American-Japanese Diplomatic Negotiations, 1936–1941*, Annapolis, Md: Naval Institute Press, 1973, P251, cited in Breslin P34.

He then makes the alarming conclusion that has an aura of truth about it, that "the President wanted an incident which could furnish a pretext for war."[226]

At this point, despite the breaking of Japanese diplomatic codes, no one knew of the planned attack on Hawaii.[227] In fact, it was not generally believed that the Japanese would be naive enough to contemplate an action that would so galvanize American popular opinion behind Roosevelt and against the Japanese Imperialist dream. The Philippines were considered to be a certain target, but Western attention was focused on the colonial objects of Japanese desire.

The alleged attempt to goad the Japanese into 'an incident' was an echo of the previous attempt to achieve the same result with the German Navy. This took place about a month after the Atlantic Charter meeting between Roosevelt and Churchill in August 1941. Churchill told his cabinet that the President had confided that, "he would wage war, but not declare it, and that he would become more and more provocative…Everything was to be done to force an incident." [228]

Later, a German U-boat fired two torpedoes at the United States destroyer *Greer*, causing Roosevelt to broadcast on radio that henceforth the Navy would repel the piratical acts of these seagoing 'rattlesnakes' defending freedom of the seas by firing first. This created a very positive and aggressive shift in popular opinion, as measured by a Gallup Poll that people overwhelmingly supported the concept of shoot-at-sight.

---

[226] Breslin, T. A. *Mystifying the Past: Establishment Historians and the Origins of the Pacific War*. Bulletin of Concerned Asian Scholars, Vol 8: 4, 1976, P34.

[227] Although there are researchers who claim the military codes were broken and that FDR knew in advance of the attack on Pearl Harbor. Debate continues. See Stinnett R. B. *Day of Deceit: The truth about FDR and Pearl Harbor* or the Independent.org web site.

[228] Doenecke, J. *Storm on the Horizon: The Challenge to American Intervention, 1939–1941*. Lanham, Md: Rowan & Littlefield, 2000, Pp 239–40.

More than a month later, it became known that *Greer* had been trailing the U-boat for three and a half hours, reporting and broadcasting the latter's position to British destroyers when the submarine came about and fired. Thomas A. Bailey, in *The Man in the Street: The Impact of American Public Opinion on Foreign Policy*, said of this event, "Roosevelt either knew of these facts or he did not know them. If he knew them, he deliberately deceived the American people; if he did not, he handled a critical situation with inexcusable precipitancy."[229]

Bailey, in fact, then goes on to justify Roosevelt's deception. He wrote, in part:

> "A President who cannot entrust the people with the truth betrays a certain lack of faith in the basic tenets of democracy. But because the masses are notoriously short sighted, and generally cannot see their danger until it is at their throats, our statesmen are forced to deceive them into an awareness of their own long-run interests. This is clearly what Roosevelt had to do, and who shall say that posterity will not thank him for it?"[230]

Our first response to this view is to notice how, as a 1948 viewpoint, it fits the pattern of paternalism so prevalent at the time. Can a 'father knows best' attitude still have currency? Granted, being held accountable to an electorate inhibits long-term thinking. Granted also, people are often motivated first by self-interest.

However, if deceit is acceptable because of the self-interest of the electorate, who is to judge whether the government is acting in the interests of the nation? If they are above judgment,

---

[229] Bailey, T. A. *The Man in the Street: The Impact of American Public Opinion on Foreign Policy.* New York: Macmillan, 1948 P13.

[230] Ibid

then what is the purpose of elections? The argument is seldom spoken aloud.

This deceit or that lie may be proven to be for the 'greater good,' but as a principle of operation, deceit can only remove the future option and benefits of adopting an ethical position. The extent to which deceit persists as an on-going reality is a marker of the pragmatic use of government for political and commercial ends that lurk *behind* the public facade of politics.

Can we genuinely regard the US at this point as a neutral, isolated, pacifist nation? The labels don't fit the facts. They were going to war and Roosevelt knew it. The European campaign was to be given first priority but policy was ambiguous as to the circumstances under which Japan would be engaged. America had temporarily occupied Greenland and Iceland, had troops in China and the Philippines, a fleet in the Pacific, and naval patrols in the Caribbean and in China. This included Army, Navy, and Marine flyers fighting as 'American Volunteer Groups.'

American engineers worked to improve the passage of goods and supplies to China over the Burma Road, threatening Japanese forces that were being supplied with American fuel, powering machines made by American and Australian iron. Owen Lattimore, an American recommended by Roosevelt, was General Chiang Kai-shek's political adviser.

The US Navy was the second largest navy in the world at the time, and the administration had been talking in terms of supporting Britain for years. These are the military factors. The economic ones are just as compelling and could be seen as the foundations for the world's first energy war.

How can we reconcile these realities with the aim of 'Europe first,' which was the essential element of 'Plan Dog,' or 'Plan D,' approved by Roosevelt in mid-January 1941? The plan called for a defensive posture in the Asia-Pacific region to allow the European theater to be brought under control before the inevitable war with Japan was undertaken. This, on the face of it, makes the alleged provocation of Japan seem unlikely at best.

The answer may lie somewhere in the conflicting views of Roosevelt's various advisors, combined with an under-estimation of the impact of economic pressure brought to bear on Japan, and most importantly, Germany's astute psychological pressure on Japan to act quickly to dissipate America's efforts. We also need to separate in our minds those actions designed by Roosevelt to gain domestic support for war in general, from those which were aimed at restraining or provoking Japan.[231]

The case against provocation rests substantially on the view that, although Roosevelt knew that the war was inevitable, he recognized that it would take all of his country's resources just to win the war in Europe and that this was his first priority. This does not allow the counter claim that Roosevelt was becoming increasingly impatient with the powerful isolationist lobby that claimed vast popular support and that he was prepared to act in any way possible, to rally his nation for support of Britain. It has been shown that he was prepared to lie to his electorate.

Plan D had at its heart an impossible contradiction that was never openly resolved. It suggested that if the Japanese were to press on through Asia, America would have to accept the loss of the entire region west of Hawaii until Europe had been stabilized. This was incompatible with the aim of resisting Japanese aggression in support of China. It also guaranteed an

---

[231] Robert Stinnett, for example, has pursued the subject of provocation for many years and has been able to access many previously unseen official documents under Freedom of Information. His work has that unsettling quality, though, which comes from research that is assembled selectively, purely to reinforce a singular view. It is not clear from a great deal of data that anything new, of substance, has been raised to back his claims. If interested see: Stinnett, R. B. *Day of Deceit The Truth about FDR and Pearl Harbor.* New York: Touchstone, 2000.

expansionary Japan access to fuel and resources in Southeast Asia, in the potential context of a powerful autarkic trading bloc.

When negotiations with Japan finally came down to the wire, it was the inability of both nations to back away from their position on China that led to the great unraveling. That brings us back to the notion that it was for access to China's markets and resources that Roosevelt was willing to take Japan to the brink of war. In itself this doesn't quite seem enough. Behind that, American intransigence with regard to China would allow them to act in support of the European colonies of Southeast Asia, thereby automatically committing the Americans to the European war.

It may therefore have been the threat of Japan's Southeast Asian access at America's future expense, combined with America's potential loss of access to China that were worth the risk of a premature war in Asia in order to enter the one in Europe. The actions of the United States were provocative, and Japan's attack on the West was a consequence of them. The question is not whether Roosevelt provoked Japan but whether he meant to. On balance, it seems that he did, but some would argue that his policy was simply more successful than he had anticipated it would be.

Europe first? Well, as it panned out, America was able to carry that priority into the double-pronged war as an ongoing policy. Japan provided the angry American electorate at Hitler's ultimate cost as well as their own. The mere *possibility* that all of the lives lost in the Pacific War could have been spared if America had been able to support Britain without the subterfuge is unconscionable, but it continues to haunt us. Let's hope that Roosevelt and Churchill are found to have been trying to restrain, rather than provoke, Japan and that Pearl Harbor represents their failure rather than their success.

History is very cruel. Just as post-war Arabs can be seen to have become indirect victims of pre-war European anti-Semitism, a good case can be argued that Japan became an unwitting tool in overcoming American peace-loving non-interventionists, enabling America to engage in Europe. Both of these instances originate in the works of German Nazism, which was arguably the illegitimate child of the Treaty of Versailles. Wilson's critics have a lot to say about that, but that is another story.

19

EMBARGO OR ENERGY WAR

I N THE PERIOD before the war, the world's largest exporter of oil was the United States of America. At that time Japan sourced 85% of its oil from them.

By world standards, Japan was not a big user of oil, consuming about thirty-two million barrels annually by 1941. As a comparison, Japan now consumes about three billion barrels annually.

As the American responses to Japanese actions in China became more severe, Roosevelt was able to use supply of resources as a bargaining tool. In 1940, the Export Control Act empowered him to impose an embargo on the export of scrap iron and steel by citing US defense needs under the Act. Soon after, he prohibited the sale of aviation fuel and lubricants, selectively, to exclude supply to Japan, but oil and regular petrol were not affected.

Japanese diplomatic responses were menacing. On October 5th, Matsuoka pleaded with Ambassador Grew to urge his government to refrain from further trade restrictions, actions that would "intensely anger the Japanese people."

Three days later, Hull was handed Tokyo's formal statement, which claimed that, "In view of the high feeling in Japan, it is apprehended that, in the event of the continuation by the United States of the present attitude toward Japan in matters of trade restriction, future relations between Japan and the United States will be unpredictable." The embargo was declared to be an unfriendly act.

In his memoirs, Hull recalled his reply to the ambassador that…"it was unheard of for one country engaged in aggression and seizure of another country, contrary to all law and treaty provisions, to turn to a third peacefully disposed nation and seriously insist that it would be guilty of an unfriendly act if it should not cheerfully provide some of the necessary implements of war to aid the aggressor nation in carrying its policy of invasion."[232] It is difficult to fault Hull's line of thought, but only if we allow his clear distinction between economic and military aggression.

When the Japanese installed Prince Konoe as Premier in 1940 the situation had became more complex. The Prince was unable or unwilling to prevent further military aggression on the Asian mainland, but the civilian arm of government actively pursued accommodation with the US. The advent of further movement into French Indochina and the signing of the Tripartite Pact made it very difficult for the US Administration to find points of negotiation with the Japanese, without opening themselves to criticism at home for appeasing them.

The Dutch East Indies[233] had been the supplier of the balance of Japanese oil requirements. With the occupation of the Netherlands by the Germans, the Japanese view of the

---

[232] *Foreign Relations of the United States: Japan*, 223 ff.; Hull: Memoirs, 1912 ff, cited in Langer, W. L, and Gleason, S. *The Undeclared War 1940–41*. New York: Harper and Bros, 1953, P37.

[233] Now 'Indonesia,' then, also sometimes referred to as Netherlands East Indies.

East Indies changed, as they now felt more able to press for favorable treatment from the colony. This shift of view was similar to that which arose from the occupation of France and the new Japanese relationship with French Indochina[234] under the Vichy French regime.

To begin with, Japan sought reassurance that the Dutch authorities in Batavia would continue to supply oil to Japan at pre-war levels. Soon the Japanese demanded much more. From a basis of 4.5 million barrels per annum, they put the case that they wanted to buy twenty-two million barrels, a figure just enough to replace their dependence on America. In response to this, the Dutch played tough in negotiations and were able to avoid committing themselves to the total increase while also managing to stall the process considerably. This was achieved in consultation with American personnel stationed there, who were in regular contact with Washington. The stated Japanese aim of a preferably peaceful advance into Asia to ensure supply of essentials was therefore blocked and prevented. From the Dutch perspective of course, the potential loss of their colony was a very real concern, and their desire for American intervention was desperate and very urgent. They must have sensed a dual danger: that the supply of enough fuel could enable further Japanese aggression, while withholding it could force the Japanese into a desperate strike.

A new Japanese ambassador, Admiral Kichisaburo Nomura, was sent to Washington with a new set of proposals to discuss, including significant concessions. As we have seen, on behalf of his government, he offered a freeze on Japanese military operations in China involving negotiations with Chiang Kai-shek. In return for these concessions, Japan sought the lifting of embargoes on critical materials and resumption of normal trade with the US.

---

[234] French Indochina became known as Vietnam.

At this point, almost anything was possible. Japan could have struck into the Soviet Union, making Hitler's task much easier. Japan could have withdrawn from the Axis and turned to join the Soviets in a super alliance against the Germans and the Italians. America could have accepted the situation in China and found a negotiated settlement that allowed the Japanese to back down from the brink with honor. Japan could have moved steadily through South East Asia unhampered by US sanctions. There were other possibilities. Some of them were much less likely than others, but the way forward for Japan, at least, did not rest upon ideology. They were prepared to discuss all options, examining each possibility to find security.

Secretary Hull attended fifty secret meetings with Nomura but refused to agree to specifics until Japan agreed to four points of principle. Japan should pledge respect for the territorial integrity of all nations, non-interference in other nations' internal affairs, equality of commercial opportunity, and a commitment to peaceful change of the status quo.

These four points were powerful inhibitors to progress, especially as they demanded that Japan agree to act in a manner the US has often had difficulty in adopting in its own actions. It is difficult to imagine any ambassador being able to accept these on behalf of his government without it being considered as a defeat and a humiliation. The talks, which began with the offer of concessions, ended in stalemate.

If the Japanese goal appeared to be the resources of the Indies and Malaya, a means to that goal increasingly appeared to be from China, into and through French Indochina.

The Japanese in Indochina

Occupied France was under the Vichy government and allied to Germany, but Gaullist French forces continued to oppose German occupation at home and in French colonies. As a consequence of the Tripartite Pact in 1940, the Japanese felt able to pursue a new relationship with Indochina. This was perceived in the West as aggressive, reinforcing the view of Japan as a belligerent, expansive nation. In Japan, the move was represented as protective, inclusive, and embracing.

The following is part of an address by the Japanese Foreign Minister, Yosuke Matsuoka, at the opening of the Thai-French Indochina border dispute Mediation Conference, Tokyo February 7th 1941:

> "It is my firm belief that the establishment of a sphere of common prosperity throughout Greater East Asia is not only Japan's policy, but indeed a historical necessity in the event of world history. And those countries which exist in that sphere can contribute to the peace of Asia as well as to the world by their procuring each its own place and enjoying common prosperity amongst them. For that purpose I need hardly say that it is of vital importance that there should be security and stability in this part of East Asia. Therefore, when there arose a dispute concerning the boundary between Thailand and French Indochina last year, I sincerely wished that the dispute would be amicably settled. Unfortunately, however, hostilities began between the two countries. The Japanese government considered that it would be undesirable in the interests of the whole East Asia if this state of affairs were allowed to last long, and therefore we have decided to mediate between the two countries..."[235]

By July 21, 1941, after a series of diplomatic exchanges, France and Japan concluded an agreement "pledging military co-operation in defense of Indochina." The Matsuoka-Henry agreement of August 1940 was a real negotiation, not just a

---

[235] *Tokyo Gazette* Vol. IV, No. 9, P384-5.

French rollover. In fact, the final agreement was closer to the French counter-proposal than to the original Japanese one, and the French were very skillful in pressing their needs.

This indicates that the Japanese position in Indochina was not ultimately an example of the army overriding the government, although their initial move into northern Indochina involved unauthorized and typically aggressive enthusiasm by the South China Army under Major General Tominanga, despite opposition from most of the high command.

This confusion of command created a border confrontation with French forces in September, at the very time when French Governor General Decoux was conceding an agreement to allow the peaceful entry of Japanese troops to monitor supply routes for Chinese forces. This resulted in an apology by the Japanese Emperor to the French and a declaration of Japanese respect for French sovereignty.

At the same time, a crucial event occurred that hardened attitudes in Japan and in America. The invasion of Soviet Russia by German forces effectively neutralized the perceived northern threat to Japanese interests in Manchuria. Even while Matsuoka was in Moscow negotiating with the Soviets, the German-Soviet relationship appeared to be crumbling.

Stalin was therefore quite happy to engage in a neutrality treaty with Japan to take the heat from his southern concerns, and it appeared to Matsuoka to be mutually advantageous. The April treaty went so far as to recognize Japanese rights in Manchukuo, which of course was seen by the Chinese as a colossal betrayal, who relied so heavily on Soviet support. What Matsuoka didn't know was that the Soviets had by then begun talks with the Anglo-American nations, in a bid to restrain Hitler. This effectively meant that Japan would be further isolated rather than better protected.

There had been debate in Japan for decades over the relative importance of north/south threats and interests. One view held that, having settled the northern question, the south could be attended to, but this was an oversimplification of a complex web of threats. The Germans for their part felt they had cause to be suspicious of Japanese intentions in the light of the Washington talks, but also in view of the Japanese refusal to instigate an attack on Britain in Singapore. They were right to be suspicious.

Konoe felt strongly that German actions had driven the Soviets into the Allied camp, and that the Axis arrangement had failed to deliver. He felt that the time had come to re-adjust Japan's position once again, to be in line with the United States. He understood that such a return to an old arrangement would require a resolution of some sort in China. But Konoe had never given up hope of a settlement with Chiang, so this didn't seem to be an insurmountable obstacle.

At this point, it is common for analysts to reiterate Konoe's weakness and his inability to take the military with him in his thinking. Matsuoka would not sanction a reversal of policy that would effectively unwind his international efforts. The military chiefs of staff would not accept the idea of admitting failure in China, nor would they sanction the demise of the co-prosperity sphere. Despite Konoe's reasoning that Hitler's attack on the Soviets was one of a number of events that required an adjustment in national direction, his opponents argued that it was simply too late to alter course. In fact, all options were up for debate. Konoe's inability to stamp his ideas on policy at this point was not an expression of his weakness but the weakness of his position—not just his position at that time but the inherent limitations on the position of Prime Minister. The chiefs of staff could force a cabinet resignation at any time.

Matsuoka moved to a new position designed to gain advantage but without risk of offending the Americans. In his view, a southward strategy would bring war with America. He advocated a quick strike on the Soviets, since Germany would have them on their knees by the end of the year anyway. Two of the three assumptions in this thinking were wrong.

Most other strategists preferred caution, to see how 'the persimmon ripened' with regard to German progress. The navy maintained its line that a southern advance would make most sense. Among these discussions there grew a consensus that the world could face a truly global war and that the current deliberations were crucial. This brought them to the policy statement of July 2nd that is referred to later as the 'Outlines of Fundamental National Policy.' In this, the group confirmed the national aim of establishing the East Asian Co-Prosperity Sphere whatever happened internationally.

In effect, this meeting established the need to prepare for both northern and southern strategies simultaneously, but their execution was to be in response to situations as they arose, and there was a greater urgency attached to the southern advance in order to secure energy and materials for war. They had hoped to avoid war with all of these potential enemies but felt compelled to brace themselves for the worst.

Finally, the way forward was almost clear, but not without potholes. Japan's negotiations with France created heightened debate in America, creating greater pressure to increase sanctions. Even before this in October 1940, there were those for whom supplying Japan with anything was an anathema, as shown in the following portion of a letter from Secretary Ickes to Roosevelt:

> "We didn't keep Japan out of Indochina by continuing to ship scrap iron, nor will we keep Japan out of the Dutch East Indies by selling it our oil. When Japan thinks that it can safely move against the Dutch East Indies, and is ready to do so, it will go in, regardless. It

will make it all the more difficult for it to go in if it is short on oil and gasoline."[236]

On July 26, 1941, after Japanese forces moved into French Southern Indochina, the sentiment expressed above became policy, with the freezing of all Japanese assets in the United States and placing all exports of petroleum to Japan under embargo subject to license. Dutch and British authorities made similar provisions soon after.

This licensing arrangement became a much more potent tool than had been envisioned by Roosevelt. The assistant secretary of state is claimed to have administered it very aggressively, with the result that oil was in very short supply from July 25th. Roosevelt was unaware of its potency until September, although even this is debatable. Several historians, such as Akira Iyiye, claim that no petroleum was available from that time,[237] whereas Robert Stinnett provides a scan of a US Navy Department Document that makes it clear that millions of barrels were being supplied to the Japanese from Associated Oil in San Francisco in 1940, with license to sell a further two million barrels in 1941.

The salient part of the document is the assurance that the Japanese had been informed by this source that there would be "no difficulty in a continued supply."[238] Stinnett maintains that this was a deliberate policy known to Roosevelt, to keep the Japanese war machine in business. On the contrary, it may

---

[236] Letter of Secretary Ickes to the President, Oct 17, 1940, Roosevelt papers: Secretary's file box 58, cited in Langer ,W. L. and Gleason, S. *The Undeclared War 1940–41*. New York: Harper and Bros, 1953, P35.

[237] Iriye, Akira. *The Origins of the Second War in Asia and the Pacific*. London: Longman, 1987, P150, apparently citing Utely, Jonathan G. *Going to War with Japan 1937-41*. Knoxville, 1985, Pp154-155.

[238] Stinnett, R..B. *Day of Deceit, the Truth About FDR and Pearl Harbor*. New York: Touchstone, 2000, P304.

simply illustrate that business was not always the handmaiden of government.

Churchill met with Roosevelt between the 9th and the 14th of August to formalize what has become known as the Atlantic Charter, a set of eight principles upon which they agreed to move forward together. For a Westerner of liberal or democratic inclination, the words and the intentions of this agreement must have represented a beacon of decency and profound hope at a time of extreme danger. The language and the sentiment seemed inclusive and balanced: a brown paper bag for a hyperventilating world. Why then do I feel uncomfortable reading it in 2007?

The Charter was an expression of the same idealism that lay at the heart of the Washington system, but projected into a slightly more modern world. Several of its principles therefore represented the promise of a continuation of decency, but still using the wealth generated by the status quo to maintain the status quo. So when it spoke of "access [for all states], on equal terms, to the trade and to the raw materials of the world, which are needed for their economic prosperity," many nations would have been justified in feeling a little cynical.

Equality was seen as an ideal, but the playing field was not level. This was to some extent addressed in another stated principle, which committed the two nations to "the fullest collaboration between all nations in the economic field, with the objective of securing for all, improved labor standards, economic advancement, and social security." This was to address the rapacious degeneration of internationalism during the 1930s.

The area of greatest sensitivity lay in the statement that "The Anglo-American powers respect the right of all peoples to choose the form of government under which they will live; and they wish to see Sovereign rights and self-government restored to those who have been forcibly deprived of them." The good intentions at the heart of the statement could not prevent the Japanese and nationalists in many areas of Asia from wondering why the same principle did not apply to European colonies.

The Charter was covered vigorously in the Japanese Press. Most coverage represented the agreement as warlike expression of the determination to maintain world dominance "on the basis of Anglo-American world views."[239]

By August, then, it was apparent in Tokyo that they must prepare for a war against the combined strength of an alliance in the Pacific. To this end, the army and the navy developed parallel strategies: the army concentrating on a land-based assault through Malaya and Singapore to the Indies and the navy concentrating on the United States and the Philippines. The US fleet in Hawaii became the central target in the plan to neutralize American force temporarily while the Western and Southern Pacific were secured.

These strategies held quite different meanings for the two Japanese services. The navy held that war was not inevitable and could be averted through negotiation, particularly if the embargo on fuel could be lifted. This had after all been considered as an act of aggression by Japan. The army regarded the situation more gravely, maintaining that their gains to this point could not be negotiated away and that diplomacy would only postpone the inevitable.

The hardliners in the US Administration, Secretary of War Stimson, Secretary of the Treasury Morgenthau, and Secretary of the Interior Ickes held sway in a policy designed to bring Japan to its diplomatic knees. They took this attitude despite the fact that the United States had just signed treaties with Denmark to establish a base in Greenland and with Iceland to establish a base there.

---

[239] Tokyo, Asahi as cited in Iriye, A. *The Origins of the Second World War in Asia and the Pacific*. London: Longman, 1987, P156.

The Japanese move into Indochina was explained in the following terms in the *Tokyo Gazette* in August 1941. Parts of the article read:

> "The international situation has undergone radical changes in such a way as to aggravate the situation in which French Indochina is placed. The French colony has come to find itself in an embarrassing situation, as was Syria in the current European War. In view of this situation, additional Japanese forces have been dispatched to this part of the Asiatic continent in accordance with the provisions of the Protocol for Joint Defense of French Indochina, concluded between Japan and France on July 29…
>
> "The Political situation…has for some time remained complicated and chaotic with Governor General Vice Admiral Jean Decoux and the leading officials of the Hanoi Government favoring co-operation with Japan under instructions from the Vichy Government; while in Southern French Indochina, a group of Gaullists has apparently been endeavoring to defend its ground in league with certain financiers and Chinese residents, with support of third powers.
>
> "During the recent negotiations between Thailand and French Indochina concerning the border dispute and also during the Japanese-French Indochina economic negotiations, the de Gaullists' machinations are known to have stood considerably in the way of progress and said parleys…
>
> "Further, according to later information, there are indications of a significantly closer relationship being effected between Great Britain and the Chiang Kai-shek regime, while the charges of some form of co-operation between Great Britain, the United States,

China and the Netherlands, which form what is known as a democratic front are being substantiated. Thus, French Indochina, which is a member of the East Asia co-prosperity bloc, has vital economic relations with Japan, has now come to sense a direct danger from the Chunking regime, British Malaya, Burma and the Dutch East Indies, which now constitute a ring of hostile nations around the French colony, jeopardizing its self-preservation and defense..."[240]

Given that this was published and therefore cleared as an official government statement of position, the primary purposes of the statement are quite clear. The population was to feel incrementally isolated by external forces of aggression, acting in the face of transparent Japanese good will and in support of an ally.

But far from being bombastic or xenophobic, it is calm and well reasoned. The Japanese were trying desperately to be respected in the region for being a 'steadying influence.' Looking at this article through Western eyes, knowing what is now known about the war, it is too easy simply to be dismissive of the Japanese intentions in Indochina.

It is very important to see examples like this, to understand how it felt to be Japanese, with due consideration to the information available to them, but also, it is helpful to know that American leaders were not alone in manipulating the perception of events to gain public support in advance of action.

In any case, the point of view is Japanese, encapsulating their contemporary worldview of an Asia governed by Asians, in which the only leaders capable of getting the job done were the Japanese. As a worldview it is chauvinistic and quite threatening but it really is no more radical than one in which

[240] *Tokyo Gazette,* Vol IV, no 9, P384-5.

people from Europe should govern Asia. Neither view would outlast the century.

For all that, it is evident that the Japanese government was respectful of French sovereignty, even at the expense of local nationalist groups, which the Japanese may have seen as destabilizing at that time.

A hardening in Churchill's position followed the American sanctions. Whereas in July he had been willing to close the Burma Road to supplies for Chiang's regime, by September his view of the future was bolstered by a new confidence in Roosevelt's support. By October, the route was once again open in defiance of Japanese expectations. This was a very significant boost for the material concerns and the morale of Chiang's forces.

There is still speculation as to whether Roosevelt believed the embargoes and freezes would lead directly to war. This is dealt with in greater depth elsewhere, outlining strong cases that have been made both ways. Some observers argue that he believed that the Japanese would capitulate, and if not, that a short, easy war would neutralize their threats. But they did leave almost no room for the Japanese to negotiate without losing face.

The view of the 'easy war' seems difficult to grasp in retrospect, but according to some observers, such a view was prevalent among various American officials. George Morgenstern quotes a Dr. E. Stanley Jones, "a widely known missionary of long experience in the Orient" who acted as an unofficial moderator between the Japanese and the White House.

"The attitude of some of our officials seemed to be: 'Well, we have Japan by the throat by this oil embargo and we'll strangle her. If she kicks and there is war, well, we'll send a few planes over from Vladivostok, burn up her inflammable cities, and it will be over in a few weeks.'

"They felt that Japan was mired in China, that she was at the end of her resources, and that this anxiety for peace on the part of her Washington representatives was because she was weak and helpless in our hands. As Ambassador Nomura said to me one day, 'Everything I propose is suspected as weakness.'"[241]

Consider the last quote: "Everything I propose is suspected of weakness." To offer hope of compromise is weakness. To offer no hope of compromise is regarded as bellicosity. Apparently, the plan amounted to dealing with toughness by being tough, and dealing with weakness by bringing Japan to its knees.

Despite emphatic advice from his inner circle for aggressive blocking of Japan, Roosevelt still had to deal with US Naval pressure, seeking more time to prepare. The navy stressed its inferiority in the Pacific and also expressed displeasure at having the fleet exposed provocatively at Pearl Harbor. Roosevelt may have believed that a Japanese response would occur against the Dutch, or the British in Malaya, either instance being far enough away to buy time for his forces, but even these possibilities brought their own pressures. Since the Atlantic conference, Roosevelt had shown signs of a hardening attitude in response to Churchill's formidable powers of persuasion. Churchill needed a lever with which Roosevelt could be committed to the European war, and he used every means possible, including the 'back door' option, to convince the American of his responsibility to the Anglo-Saxon way of life.

Prince Konoe in his Own Words

Prince Konoe was an early casualty of the embargo in his apparently genuine attempt to find a diplomatic way through the quagmire of conflicting demands. The following extract is

---

[241] cited in Morgenstern, G. *Pearl Harbor: The Story of the Secret War.* New York: Devin-Adair, 1947, Pp100-101.

from his own account of the times, taken from International Military Tribunal for the Far East, Prosecution Document 499, Pp10:

"The 3rd Konoe Cabinet started off with the great mission of readjusting the Japanese-American relations. For this reason, the retirement of Foreign Minister Matsuoka was brought about and as only that was done, it can be said that all efforts were solely exerted toward the accomplishment of this great mission ever since the formation of the Cabinet. However, America's attitude was by no means definite. There were various opinions as to why her attitude was not definite, but the opinion of the War Minister was that since America's basic policy is to advance into Asia, the reasons for America's indefinite attitude is fundamental and consequently she lacks sincerity even in her negotiation. However, we continued our negotiation with the view that a temporary compromise and conciliation may be possible in regard to the current situation, even if our basic traditional policies may have been different.

"Recently the negotiation reached a state of temporary deadlock due to the occupation of French Indochina by our troops, but as it became known that we wouldn't go any further, the situation eased somewhat and the negotiation was again resumed. Hence a message was sent to President Roosevelt on August 28 proposing a conference. Nevertheless, since President Roosevelt, in reply to this stated that he was willing to hold a conference, but would like to have a general agreement reached in regard to the important matters, at least, as a premise, an Imperial Conference was held on September 6 to determine the basis of the counter-measure for this.

"As a result of the Imperial Conference it was decided to direct all our efforts toward the diplomatic negotiation to the end, but to resolutely assume a war policy in the event no means for the conclusion of the negotiation is reached by early October."[242]

We will see that, in his efforts, Prince Konoe went on to gain the trust and confidence of Ambassador Grew, and a surprising platform of support throughout the Japanese circles of power.

The Convergence of Opportunity and Danger, August-October

Throughout the Japanese community, the American sanctions were received with genuine shock and dismay. By August, they had only the fuel previously stockpiled to fall back upon. This amounted to a supply for twelve months of fuel for the army and eighteen months for the navy.

In examining events through this period, we will give particular attention to documents and meetings. In these we can 'hear' the voices of the time and perhaps gain a sense of the personal efforts involved in the rough and tumble of trying to negotiate a peace.

The August 28th meeting between the American Secretary and Ambassador Nomura found the Ambassador "much encouraged from his interview with the President," and he had telegraphed his Prime Minister a full account of that interview.

The Ambassador expressed his personal opinion that the suggestion of the President of a meeting between the Japanese Prime Minister and the President being held at Juneau would

---

[242] Document 499, IMTFE, Pp10, cited in Treffousse, H. L. (ed). *What Happened at Pearl Harbor? Documents pertaining to the Japanese attack of December 7, 1941*. New York: Twain, 1958, P246–247.

be "agreeable to his Government and that the Prime Minister would probably proceed thither by Japanese warship, making the journey in about ten days."[243]

The Secretary pointed out the desirability of there "being reached in advance of the proposed meeting an agreement in principle on the principle questions which were involved in a settlement of Pacific questions between the two nations." He emphasized that serious consequences would ensue if there were a failure of agreement.

The Ambassador then reviewed the sticking points between the two countries, and these were: 1. Japan's relations to the Axis, 2. The issue of Japan's retention of troops in North China and Inner Mongolia, and 3. The question of the application of the principle of non-discrimination in international commercial relations. He noted that the issue of China might be a difficulty.

He felt that the relationship with the Axis would not present problems as his people regarded their adherence as 'nominal,' and that the Japanese would not want to go to war with the US for the sake of Germany. The only difficulty he saw was "to ask that Japan give a blank check for action that the United States might take against Germany in the name of self-defense was equivalent to asking for a nullification of the Tripartite Pact."

The Secretary then made the point that the Japanese had entered the Pact at "a most critical moment in our efforts to extend aid to England, and Japan's action, therefore, was given particular emphasis in this country."[244]

In discussing the Chinese question, and the US loyalty and commitment to them, the memorandum reads:

> "The Secretary explained further that we could not now afford to have the Chinese think that we were ignoring

---

[243] Foreign Relations, Japan, II, 576–579 [Washington] Aug 28 1941, cited in Treffousse, P281.

[244] Ibid P282

their interests in going ahead with any arrangements and that it was our idea to help the Japanese achieve the purpose of establishing friendship with China on a solid basis. In this way the Secretary said we could work together, Japan and the United States, in order to make the most of the potentialities of the 500,000,000 people of China as a trading nation."[245]

His reference to China as a potential trading nation reveals something of the values at the core of the US support of China.

Another memorandum by the Secretary of State was made of a further meeting on September 3, 1941 when the President requested that the Japanese Ambassador call at the White House. At this meeting, the President read a written statement (becoming an oral statement), which he had prepared in response to a recent communication from the Japanese Prime Minister.

In this, he particularly emphasized the fact that he appreciated the difficulties of Prince Konoe in connection with the Japanese internal situation but added that he had difficulties there, which he hoped Prince Konoe and his Government would also appreciate. The President was in part referring to the conversations he had had with Churchill.

The President also emphasized the need to discuss matters with the British, the Chinese, and the Dutch since any settlement "must be on a basis that will restore confidence and friendliness among the nations concerned."

The Ambassador said that Prince Konoe, while preferring to go to Hawaii to meet the President for discussion, would be "disposed to go to any place in the Pacific where there was suitable anchorage."

---

[245] Ibid P283

He then went on to emphasize how his government was determined to overcome internal opposition in Tokyo. He felt that a meeting with the President would be very helpful in overcoming such elements.

Very significantly, Nomura said that Prince Konoe thought that he and the President could discuss the three questions, "which were left untouched when the Japanese went into Indochina in July, mainly the question relating to the complete evacuation of Japanese troops from China, the question of non-discrimination in commerce, etcetera, etcetera, and the Tripartite Pact." [246]

While these very positive discussions were happening on one level, pressure was mounting on Roosevelt and in Japan for a different outcome. The following is a summarized account of a memorandum from the Advisor on Political Relations, Hornbeck, headed "Comment on the question of holding a conference":[247]

"The chief danger upon the holding of a meeting between the President and the Japanese Prime Minister is that if such a meeting is held there must emanate from it an agreement...

"Each of the parties would be motivated in large part by political *fears* and *hopes*; each would be playing for time and hoping for miracles to come; each would be expecting that a make-shift and make delay agreement would be advantageous for his side; each would be expecting to tell his own people far less than the whole truth about the meeting and the agreement...

"[It would be] a gesture born of lack of confidence in the present position (actual military capacity) of the

---

[246] Ibid P286

[247] Foreign Relations, 1941, Far East, Pp425-428, cited in Trefousse, H. L. (ed). *What Happened at Pearl Harbor? Documents pertaining to the Japanese attack of December 7, 1941*. New York: Twain, 1958, P286.

United States. It would be utterly unlike the meeting between the President and the British Prime Minister. It would more clearly resemble meetings that were held between Mr. Chamberlain and Mr. Hitler…"

"It would not put a stop to Japanese aggression. It would not bring to an end Japan's effort to conquer China; It would on the contrary tend to facilitate that effort…"

"To wean Japan away at this time—on paper or in appearance—from the Axis would be an achievement spectacular in aspect but of no substantial political or military value. For, Japan is not helping Germany except in a negative way (which she is doing only because the United States overestimates Japan's capacity to injure us) and Japan will not be helping Germany in any positive way unless and until the United States goes to war with Germany (at which time, if and when, it is problematical what Japan would do)."

"The amount of 'tension' between the United States and Japan is exaggerated. The facts of the situation that now exist are working real hardship to Japan (as a nation at war) but are not working any real hardship to the United States. This condition of 'tension' can continue for an indefinite period without our suffering much… We are not 'in a hole' and do not need helping out. Japan is 'in a hole,' she needs helping out, and she is trying to get us to be her helper. (But at the same time she is neither willing nor able to give up her position in the Axis Alliance.) She is half whipped in her war with China…"

This is not half-hearted advice from Hornbeck, and we get a sense that it was not only in Japan that policy development happened in a context of an almost binary pair of contributing values. In a sense, this is an obvious point, but we have come to expect contradictions in the Japanese situation of the time, generated by the dual form of government, including the independent military arm. The contrasting views in Roosevelt's ear were just as contradictory, but from different sources within government circles.

At the Japanese Throne Conference of September 6, 1941, the current events were assessed in the context of previously agreed policies of July 1941. It is worth noting some of the points that had been agreed to since that time.

Three points of policy were decided in the presence of the Emperor on July 2nd:

1. The Imperial Government is determined to follow a policy that will result in the establishment of the Greater East Asia C-Prosperity Sphere and world peace, no matter what international developments take place.
2. The Imperial Government will continue its effort to effect a settlement of the China Incident and seek to establish a solid basis for the security and preservation of the nation. This will involve an advance into the Southern Regions and, depending on future developments, a settlement of the Soviet question as well.
3. The Imperial Government will carry out the above program no matter what obstacles may be encountered.[248]

These three points were expanded to discuss methods and possible complications; so, for example, in the case of the breakdown of diplomatic negotiations, "preparations for a war with England and America will also be carried forward. First of all, the plans which have been laid with reference to

[248] Imperial Conference, July 2, cited in Trefousse, H. L. (ed). *What Happened at Pearl Harbor? Documents pertaining to the Japanese attack of December 7, 1941*. New York: Twain, 1958, P241–242.

French Indochina and Thai will be prosecuted, with a view to consolidating our position in the southern territories."

The following Imperial Throne Conference of September 6, 1941, built upon the above policy in the light of the dangers in the diplomatic situation. This date is only days after the very positive exchange of September 3rd in Washington, outlined above, and one day after the private note from Hornbeck also outlined immediately above.

At this Throne conference, a decision was made to proceed with war plans in an effort to have them ready toward the end of October, in case negotiations failed.

At the same time, they would "endeavor by every possible diplomatic means" to have their demands agreed to by America and England. To this end, they stipulated their minimum demands and maximum concessions in an attached document. The thrust of these concessions and demands become evident from the diplomatic efforts that continued through to November.

From Tokyo, US Ambassador Grew wrote to Roosevelt on September 22, 1941, a personal letter, rather than a telegram, to 'paint an accurate picture' of the events as they occurred.[249] In this letter he says that he is in close touch with Prince Konoe who "in the face of bitter antagonism from extremist and pro-Axis elements in the country is courageously working for an improvement in Japan's relations with the United States."

Grew wrote that Konoe believed that the Japanese had "nothing to hope from the Tripartite Pact and must shift her orientation of policy if she is to avoid disaster," and Grew wrote that he was convinced of the sincerity of these beliefs, adding that Konoe would go as far as possible, "without incurring open rebellion in Japan," to reach a reasonable understanding with the US.

---

[249] *Foreign Relations*, 1941, Far East, Pp 468–469, cited in Trefousse, H. L. (ed). *What Happened at Pearl Harbor? Documents pertaining to the Japanese attack of December 7, 1941.* New York: Twain, 1958, P 290.

The Ambassador then added that, in his belief, the incumbent government had a better chance of implementing any commitments undertaken than had been the case in recent years. He added that "it seems to me highly unlikely that this chance will come again," or that "any Japanese statesman other than Konoe could succeed in controlling the military extremists which that, in their ignorance of international affairs and economic laws, resent and oppose."

Grew concluded, noting that failure to reach a settlement now with Konoe would greatly increase the probability of war, and while the US would likely prevail in such a situation, it was not in her interest to see an impoverished Japan "reduced to the position of a third-rate Power."

On October 1, 1941, Ambassador Grew wrote a note from Tokyo "for the Secretary and Under Secretary only." In this note he reveals that he had information from sources inside the Black Dragon Society who maintained that the proposed meeting of leaders was widely known of in Tokyo and was generally applauded, even in military circles.

A general sentiment was that a political settlement was essential because of the economic situation in Japan. It was further claimed that Konoe had been in receipt of messages from many important political groups, assuring him that the country as a whole would support him in his endeavors to reach an agreement.

These people were under the impression that the Japanese Government had already agreed to meet American concerns and accept that the Japanese Prime Minister would be obliged to accept American conditions "because it would be unthinkable for him to return to Japan having failed in his mission."

The contacts also took very seriously the fact that Prince Konoe deliberately avoided Tokyo on the anniversary of the conclusion of the Tripartite Pact. They claimed the celebration was greatly downplayed and that "German elements in Japan are now under close surveillance by the police."[250]

The American Ambassador to Japan at this time was expressing his view assertively that all indications pointed to a Japanese determination to resolve all difficulties for the proposed conference between the two leaders.

The memorandum by Grew of October 25, 1941, should have been the tipping point. It is difficult to imagine a more significant message in the convergence of peaceful opportunity with the danger of war. But before attending to it, we need to look at the pivotal meeting in Tokyo on the 12th of October, in the words of Konoe himself:

> "Since there was a time limit [to achieve settlement with the US] by early October, the negotiation was carried on hurriedly and as it didn't progress as expected, September passed and October came with the negotiation still not going smoothly. About that time, the supreme command group became boisterous and stated that they will wait until October 15, but won't go beyond that. Therefore I requested the assembly of the War Minister, the Foreign Minister, the Navy Minister and the President of the Planning Board at Ogigaiso for a final conference on October 12.

"However, on the day before the conference, Chief Oka of the Naval Affairs Bureau came and in talking with him, he stated that with the exception of the Naval General Staff, the brains of the Navy don't want a Japanese-American War, but since the Navy, herself, cannot say 'she can't do it' in view of her approval of the decision of the Imperial Headquarters, the

---

[250] Foreign Relations, 1941, Far East, 492, cited in Trefousse, H. L. (ed). *What Happened at Pearl Harbor? Documents pertaining to the Japanese attack of December 7, 1941.* New York: Twain, 1958, P 292.

Navy Minister will propose to leave it in the hands of the Prime Minister at tomorrow's conference; so we would like you to decide on continuing the diplomatic negotiation."[251]

The Prince then went on to detail how Tojo expressed the Army's point of view that "There is absolutely no hope for a successful conclusion of the diplomatic negotiation." The Navy Minister went on to suggest that the Prime Minister should decide if indeed there was any hope, but War Minister Tojo spelled out emphatically the obstacles to success.

In a passionate and animated speech in a cabinet meeting on the 14th of October, Tojo then put the case against a negotiated withdrawal from China. He argued that if Japan submitted to American pressure all their efforts in China would be for nothing, Manchukuo would be jeopardized, and Korea would become vulnerable. The nation would have to revert to its situation in the 1920s, with all of the same problems, and none of its present opportunities. This 'little Japan' is what America wants us to revert to, he said. He also reminded the cabinet of the decisions made on the 6th of September, which made the decision for war predicated on failure to negotiate a settlement by early October. The Cabinet had been responsible for those guidelines and if they were not to be carried out, then the cabinet must resign. In other words, if negotiation were to continue it would have to be through a different cabinet.

The Prince was convinced that Japan could not win a war with America and could not understand Tojo's insistence on risking it, especially considering Japan's isolation and the lack of any material support for its cause.

Prince Konoe telephoned Marquis Kido at 4 p.m. on the 16th of October, to inform him that the cabinet was going to

---

[251] Document 499, IMTFE, Pp10, cited in Treffousse, H. L. (ed). *What Happened at Pearl Harbor? Documents pertaining to the Japanese attack of December 7, 1941.* New York: Twain, 1958, P246–247.

ROBERT DITTERICH   355

resign en bloc. Marquis Kido was shocked at the suddenness of the announcement but conveyed the news to the Emperor, suggesting that a Tojo Cabinet was the way forward.

Grew's Information about The Emperor's Order

Grew's memorandum of the 25th of October concerned information given to the Ambassador by a 'reliable Japanese informant' who "was in contact with the highest circles" in Japan. It was basically an account of the meeting mentioned above by Konoe but from another perspective.

The informant called on the Ambassador on his own initiative. He told Grew of a conference that was held just prior to the fall of the Konoe Cabinet.

Present were the leading members of the Privy Council and the Japanese armed forces, all having been summoned by the Emperor, who "enquired if they were prepared to pursue a policy which would guarantee that there would be no war with the United States."

The representatives of the Army and Navy offered no reply to the Emperor's direct question. The action of the Emperor at this point was unprecedented, revealing his desire to intervene in the interests of peace. He then, "with a reference to the progressive policy pursued by the Emperor Meiji, his Grandfather, ordered the armed forces to obey his wishes."[252]

Grew's informant then wrote that, having taken an immutable position, the Emperor needed to appoint a Prime minister who would be in a position "effectively to control the army, ensuring the resignation of Prince Konoe, and the appointment of General Tojo who, while remaining in the Army active list, is committed to a policy of attempting to conclude successfully the current Japanese-American conversations."[253]

---

[252] Foreign relations, Japan, II, 697-698, cited in Ibid P293-294.
[253] Ibid

The informant, while downplaying the importance of anti-American Press articles at the time, emphasized the desire by Japanese of all classes to improve relations with the US. He added that the new Foreign Minister had accepted his appointment with the specific aim of "endeavoring to pursue the current conversations to a successful end, and it had been understood that should he fail in this he would resign his post."

With regard to the previous impediments to progress, the informant claimed that the leaders were confident that "provided Japan is not placed in an impossible position by the insistence on the part of the United States that all Japanese troops in these areas be withdrawn at once, such a removal can and will be successfully effected." Finally, he added that "for the first time in ten years the situation…and the existing political set-up in Japan offer a possibility of a reorientation of Japanese policy and action."[254]

This must have been a period of terrible frustration for Konoe, who had every reason to believe that he was on course to meet face-to-face with Roosevelt, with the backing of his Emperor and an unprecedented degree of support from military figures in Japan. That the man whose intransigence was the cause of his downfall should replace him, and that Tojo had been directed to conclude the work started by his own protracted efforts must have been personally crushing.

Returning from his post at the Tokyo Embassy to Washington in October 1941, John Emmerson paid a courtesy call on Mr. Hornbeck. He recalled the conversation that followed:

"He asked me rhetorically, since he had read the stream of telegrams and dispatches we had sent from Tokyo, 'What do you people in the Embassy think about a war

[254] Ibid

with Japan?' I replied without hesitation: 'We think Japan wants to dominate East Asia and hopes to do so without war. But if this looks impossible, Japan will go to war in desperation.' Hornbeck looked at me with derision, 'Name one country which has ever gone to war in desperation.' No apt example came to mind, and the conversation ended quickly."[255]

Hornbeck publicly predicted that there would be no war with Japan. He continued to believe that American sanctions would render the Japanese incapable of anything but submission. He under-estimated either the power of the sanctions or the determination of the Japanese to act in accordance with perceived national honor, or both.

---

[255] Emmerson, J. K. "Principles versus Realities: US Prewar Foreign Policy toward Japan," in Conroy, H., Wray, H. (eds). *Pearl Harbor re-examined: Prologue to the Pacific War.* Honolulu: Univ. of Hawaii Press, 1990, P43.

20

THE NEGOTIATORS
AND THE STRATEGISTS

THE ESTABLISHMENT VIEW of the negotiations that took place between Japan and the United States was that, from start to finish, the US position remained unchanged. The fundamental policy rested upon Secretary Hull's 'Four Points': "The principles set forth in our November 26th proposal were in all important respects essentially the same principles we had been proposing to the Japanese right along."[256]

This view has been used to support the idea that, as the Japanese pursued an expansionist foreign policy, it was Japan's actions that made resolution between the two countries impossible, not a hardening of the American position. Japan, in this view, had a single purpose in the negotiations and that was to persuade America to allow her to control the entire Pacific Rim as well as Hawaii and India.[257]

---

[256] Pearl Harbor Attack. *Hearings Before the Joint Committee on the Investigations of the Pearl Harbor Attack, 79th Congress, 2nd Session, 39 parts* (Washington 1946), XI, 5369.

[257] Testimony by Hull, November 27, 1945, Ibid, cited in Schroeder. *Axis*

We have seen that such complex interactions are open to a variety of interpretations and that a simple, chronological list of events does not necessarily clarify the complexities at work behind people's responses.

We will look at the negotiations first from the establishment view, then from others, before looking behind the negotiations at some of the personalities at work behind the public face of each administration.

Hull's View of an Unchanging Policy

From 1937, Cordell Hull worked tirelessly to find a path through the polarized advice he was getting. He tempered the most severe suggestions of the hardliners, resisted the isolationists, and held at arm's length the Americans at the scene in Japan.

If this pragmatism bought some time or caused a change in Japanese politics, then his obvious commitment to work was a worthy effort. By 1940, however, he was unable to respond to incremental shifts in Japanese attitudes and actions that could have prevented a war in the Pacific.

Hull was indeed a principled man of considerable dedication and persistence. There were failures at many levels on both sides of the Pacific in this period. In Hull's case, there are those who consider that he was too idealistic, others who see his approach as too inflexible, and yet others who believe that his failure was due to "his determination that Japanese-American difficulties be resolved rather than papered over."[258]

When confronted with base human actions and crimes, whether on an individual or national level, the former Judge

---

Alliance and Japanese-American Relations, in Offner, A. A. (ed). *America and the Origins of World War II, 1933-1941: New Perspectives in History.* Boston: Houghton Mifflin, 1971, P144.

[258] Utley, J. G. "Cordell Hull and the Diplomacy of Inflexibility," in Conroy, H., Wray H. (eds) *Pearl Harbor re-examined: Prologue to the Pacific War.* Honolulu: Univ. of Hawaii Press, 1990, P75.

was accustomed to being able to bring justice to the issue. He must have found it difficult to read departmental briefings about aggressive, even brutal, acts in China and still be expected to undertake civil diplomacy with the government representing the participants. But he would be aware that the nationalist struggle was also very brutal and that chaotic violence provided the flash-point context in which Japan needed to continue to do business.

The point is, this public official had an incredibly difficult task, and it must have taken its toll on him personally. We can assess his work in the light of these circumstances.

Secretary Hull stressed the peaceful nature of American foreign policy compared to the tradition of aggression pursued by Japan. His view was that the American position did not change on the basic issues at stake.

The noted and respected historian Herbert Feis ran with this argument in general, contending that the two sides maintained their original positions throughout the negotiations, although he recognized the importance of the Japanese offer to renounce further south-western advances and accept some compromise in China.[259]

In the period up to mid-July 1941, the Japanese still expected a German victory in Europe, and this outlook certainly colored their own expectations of the possibilities for expansion against isolated and humbled European powers. In this period, Japan's attitude can be summarized as aggressive and expansionist, but with some doubts and apprehensions about offending its American trading partner. At this time, the Japanese were still adamant that they wanted to resolve the conflict in China on their own terms. The fulfillment of plans for a move into southern French Indochina, Thailand, and possibly beyond seemed likely, and desirable.

---

[259] Feis, H. *The Road to Pearl Harbor*, Princeton, 1950, Pp171–172.

Their expectation of the Tripartite Pact was that it would to some extent isolate the US, and in this belief, the July 2nd Throne Conference resolved to press on with their policies, even if it meant war with America.

Defensive American Policy

What of the US position during the same period? Paul Schroeder typifies it as defensive at this point, determined to hold the line in Asia, while building up their own capacities and aiding Great Britain. Roosevelt's eye was very much on the European war at this time. In this, he was also aiming to stop Japan from menacing British and Dutch possessions and threatening the lines of supply to Britain.

American diplomacy at this time was therefore geared to encourage Japan to withdraw from the Axis alliance, even if incrementally. Regarding the Japanese problems in China, American policy was tentative. We have seen that the hardliners regarded the Japanese situation in China to be such that there was no advantage to America in either side gaining a convincing victory.

The thrust of US policy was therefore against Japan's southern expansion, and, even as late as November, there was discussion to that effect. The following memo was written by Grew in November 1940:

> "We need not aim to drive Japan out of China now. That can be taken care of, perhaps, if and after Britain wins the war with Germany. But stopping Japan's proposed far-flung southward advance and driving her out of China are two different matters. We can tolerate her occupation of China for the time being, just as we have tolerated it for the past three years. I doubt if we should tolerate any great extension of the southward advance."[260]

---

[260] Grew. "Turbulent Era," II, 1232–1233, cited in Schroeder, P149.

In the first half of 1941, America wanted to be of assistance to China within certain limits but did not intend to go to war for China's sake. The initial move to freeze and embargo the Japanese can be seen as Hornbeck and Hull's pursuit of this cautious, defensive policy. It was Schroeder's view that "the embargo produced precisely the result intended. Japan, faced with the consequences of her move, began to recoil. The struggle within Japan for control of policy took a decided turn for the better (from an American point of view), with the initiative passing into the hands of moderates such as Konoe and Toyoda."[261]

Softening the Japanese Position

The immediate impact of the embargoes saw Japan looking for relief from economic pressure and willing to act accordingly. This is a point of debate amongst historians. Langer and Gleason, in *Undeclared War*,[262] advance the view that following the German invasion of the Soviet Union on June 22, 1941, Japan's military course was set irretrievably. Yet we see Japan willing to make two significant concessions in her newfound position.

Japan demonstrably moved away from Germany in its rhetoric and in its actions, and it expressed a willingness to withdraw from its most recent acquisition, southern Indochina.

Withdrawals from China in general, and northern China in particular, were still not options for military, economic, and political reasons. Despite this, Konoe acted with resolve to accommodate the Americans and was in a position to invite

[261] Schroeder. "Axis Alliance and Japanese-American Relations," in Offner, A. A. (ed) *America and the Origins of World War II, 1933–1941: New Perspectives in History.* Boston: Houghton Mifflin, 1971, P149.

[262] Langer, W. L. and Gleason, S. *The Undeclared War 1940–41.* New York: Harper and Bros, 1953.

Roosevelt to meet at a proposed summit, apparently with the assent of the army and the backing of the Emperor.

How then do we regard the position after the fall of Konoe? Some would argue that the installation of Tojo constituted the most significant change in policy imaginable, the final acceptance of the dominance of the military over civil government.

But one can take another, more subtle, view. Konoe's fall increased the likelihood of war because, without the occurrence of the direct negotiation with Roosevelt, Konoe could not appease the army. Tojo's appointment was not representative of a hardening of policy, but a last, desperate attempt by the Emperor to have a premier who, in the absence of the much-expected summit, could control the military while still attempting to negotiate.

Perceptions of US Policy From July

Paul Schroeder argued that the American position changed after July 1941 when its aims were no longer just to hold the Japanese expansion and tempt it away from its alliances. The chief objective now, he argued, was to push Japan back, to withdraw from its conquests. China became the central issue at this point. The complete withdrawal and evacuation of troops became an essential condition of agreement. The weapon of choice to achieve this perceived hardening was the same economic pressure used in the earlier defensive diplomacy.

Was this a hardening of policy, or had policy remained constant while Japanese concessions were serving to exaggerate the importance of China from which they would not move?

Secretary Hull presented the 'Four Principles' in April 1941. In his article "The Hull-Nomura Conversations A Fundamental Misconception," Robert Butow explains that the Japanese government in Tokyo radically misunderstood

Hull's intent for months because of miscommunication and diplomatic amateurism.

The process from March to June produced what was seen as a hardening of the US attitude, when there had arguably been no change in the US position at all, only miscommunication between Nomura and Tokyo about the progress of the talks. This situation did not become clear until after the war. How this could come about will be discussed elsewhere.

Nomura was possessed of good intentions and the right background, in the sense that it was favorable to the Japanese Navy, but he was not a career diplomat. Even so, his good connections and general fine qualities could not mask his inability to handle complex problems of diplomacy, which were exacerbated by difficulties of language and conceptual expression.

Butow wrote:

> "From incorrectly assuming in Spring of 1941 that the American attitude was more favorable than it was, Japan's leaders moved toward the argument some two months later, that the American mood was stiffening and that the terms then being offered by Washington were harsher than those originally proposed."[263]

The Japanese response to this perceived hardening of the American attitude was to harden its own position, after seeing the American draft plan of June 21st, which apparently confirmed their fears.

Whether the two positions were based on a real or only a perceived shift in the American position, China became

---

[263] Butow, R. "The Hull Nomura Conversations A Fundamental Misconception," in Offner, A. A. (ed) *America and the Origins of World War II, 1933-1941: New Perspectives in History.* Boston: Houghton Mifflin, 1971, P141.

more central as a stumbling block, and therefore as a potential trigger for war.

The US Navy wasn't the only agency urging caution at this point. Army Intelligence also had reasons for counseling a softer policy on China. Colonel H. A. Kroner, acting Assistant Chief of Staff of the Service, expressed his views in an important memo on October 2nd in which he cautioned that Konoe's cabinet "does not yet feel strong enough to enforce any order for withdrawal of Japanese troops from China, even though under pressure from the US it might be inclined to do so."[264]

He added that such a move would also be disastrous for American interests. Such a large movement of troops back to Japan would create enormous internal problems and would increase the threat to Siberia and the southwest Pacific. He concluded, "we must cease at once our attempts to bring about the withdrawal of Japanese armed forces from China." This is stunningly important intelligence from a very senior source. It seems inconceivable that both this and Ambassador Grew's positions could be disregarded or out-weighed by more militant voices.

On the same day, Hull delivered the oral statement that effectively killed the possibility of Konoe's pre-agreement for a meeting with Roosevelt, and therefore Konoe's hold on power.

The juxtaposition of these two events on the 2nd of October illustrates the powerful distinction between the two camps advising the President. The tough strategy with no compromise, typified by Hull and Hornbeck, and the counsel of caution and pragmatism from Military, Intelligence, and Ambassadorial sources.

Schroeder explained the transition:

> "As Japan began to retreat and as the United States grew steadily stronger the original problems lost their

---

[264] cited in Ibid P153

former urgency. Once the rift between Germany and Japan became plain and the American naval activities in the Atlantic went unnoticed in Japan, there was no longer any real need to worry about the Tripartite Pact. Objectionable it might still be, but hardly dangerous… Japan's repeated pledges not to extend her advance any farther south and to withdraw from Indochina upon reaching peace with China, backed up at the end by an offer of immediate evacuation of south Indochina, indicated that the southward drive was not an immutable part of Japanese policy."[265]

In 1940, America would not go to war for the sake of China. In 1941, it would. By continuing to insist on a complete withdrawal, the United States had slid into an offensive policy by default, since the Japanese could have overcome the other impediments to peace.

An extraordinary transition was complete. China was a moral cause, but it was also a tool in bogging down Japanese militarism and dissipating the threat to European interests. Without changing policy, America had used economic sanctions so successfully that they effectively raised the issue of China to the level of a choice between total capitulation and war. It is not clear how intentional this was. Some would argue that Hull used intransigence to buy time for American military preparation, not realizing that such a tactic would provoke the Japanese. Many observers certainly emphasize Hull's moderate disposition. It may be that Roosevelt indulged Hull in this to create that provocation.

To better our understanding of that, we will examine the personalities at work in setting policy.

---

[265] Schroeder. "Axis Alliance and Japanese-American Relations," in Offner, A. A. (ed) *America and the Origins of World War II, 1933-1941: New Perspectives in History.* Boston: Houghton Mifflin, 1971, P154.

Reconciling Conflicting Advice

The negotiations that attempted to find common ground between America and Japan in late 1941 were prejudiced not only by international difficulties but also by poor communication between the two countries and significant internal pressures within the Far East Division of the State Department.

These issues were made more significant, even dangerous, by the obvious chasm that existed between the advice being offered from the Embassy in Tokyo and the advice emanating from within the State Department.

To reiterate briefly, Cordell Hull was then the Secretary of State, and his political advisor for East Asian Affairs was Stanley Hornbeck. Hornbeck's two chief advisors on Asian affairs were Maxwell Hamilton, the Far Eastern Division's chief, and his assistant chief, Joseph Ballantine.

In the American Tokyo Embassy were Joseph Grew, the Ambassador, and Eugene Dooman.

How can we typify the two different paradigms? There was obvious trust and optimism displayed by Grew in Tokyo, with a starting premise that the relationship between the two countries was worth preserving by finding common ground. In contrast, distrust with uncompromising truculence in Hornbeck's memos portrayed a premise that Japan was not to be trusted and could only be negotiated with, upon complete acceptance of America's position.

We have seen that Hornbeck's early hard-line position in 1931 was ignored by the Administration of the time. He had a right perhaps to feel vindicated by the events that followed. Many observers would agree that a tougher line before Japan built up stocks of oil might have been more successful than the same policies applied later. However, Hornbeck's continued intransigence became destructive as the situation unfolded in the late 1930s.

Stanley Hornbeck had a background that predisposed him to sympathy with Chinese points of view, having lectured there for four years and having a good understanding of, and sympathy for, the instability there. He became Chief of the Far Eastern Division in the late 1920s and early 1930s, establishing an influence within the division, which outlasted his time there.

He earned a reputation for disregarding the observations and advice of the 'men in the field' and was often described as temperamentally argumentative, didactic, and intellectually rigid.[266]

President Roosevelt had his attention firmly fixed on Europe and was content to let Hull direct Asian policy without much guidance or interference until mid 1940. In turn, Hull was relieved to have the assistance and be guided by Hornbeck, and a close relationship developed between the two men.

Hull's position after the 1931 crisis was to urge caution and compromise with Japan, but he was reconsidering that caution as the decade unfolded. But even in 1937, he urged the use of the Neutrality Act.

Hornbeck's two assistants were seen to build balanced advice, one with extensive experience over a very long period in Japan, the other with experience of China. During the late 1930s, their advice amounted to a finely balanced policy, which favored neither side, nor appeased the Japanese toward the strategic goal of limiting communist penetration of northeastern Asia. It was felt that if Japan could gain a larger share of the Far Eastern and Chinese markets, communism could be neutralized in the region.

This thinking was in accord with Hull's position, which was that war and depression were fostered by economic

---

[266] Herring, H., cited in Libby, J. H. "Rendezvous with Disaster: There Never Was a Chance for Peace in American-Japanese Relations, 1941," in: *World Affairs*, Vol 158, Issue 3, 1996, P145.

nationalism and that both of these could be avoided if treaties could allow equitable access to materials and markets.[267] In short, he advocated free trade to stimulate prosperity and to reduce national competition.

It was Hamilton who alerted Hull to the need to understand Japan's apprehensions about communism, suggesting a buffer zone between Soviet and Chinese areas.

By 1937, Hornbeck and his team seemed to be in accord that "although neither China nor Japan could be allowed to succumb to communism…America had few interests in north-eastern Asia important enough to be defended at the risk of jeopardizing relations with Tokyo."[268]

At this point, there apparently was consensus between Hamilton, Hornbeck, Ballantine, and Hull in America, and Grew and Dooman in Japan. America should respond moderately to Japanese aggression in the belief that China was so big the Japanese would overextend their capacities resulting in a loss of face for the militarists. This would encourage a more moderate government.

In his "World Affairs" journal article, Justin Libby emphasizes the importance of Dooman's views and experience, pointing out that he had grown up in Japan and spent most of his life immersed in Japanese culture. But unlike Hornbeck, Dooman had made very few connections in US circles of power and, working from Japan, his influence did not match his experience.

Predictably, it was Hornbeck who in late 1937 broke with the moderate approach when he suggested the embargo to "squeeze the Japanese into better behavior."[269] Hornbeck argued that a timid West would only encourage the militarists.

---

[267] Hull, C. "The Memoirs of Cordell Hull," I, P96–97, cited in Ibid.

[268] Hornbeck to Sumner Welles, 10 Aug 1937 "Peace Proposals" folder, Box 334, cited in Ibid.

[269] McCarty, Stanley Hornbeck and The Far East, 1931–1941, cited in Ibid.

He was frustrated by what he perceived as Roosevelt's lack of leadership and the ineffectiveness of current strategy.

Hamilton took a very different view, and his concerns about the hardening policy against Japan were strongly supported within the Embassy in Tokyo. Dooman and Grew wrote many times about the danger of pressing Japan. Grew noted that sanctions could not be undertaken unless the United States was prepared to "resort to the ultimate measure of force."[270]

Grew's position can be summarized in three points. First, coercion would not halt aggression. Second, Japan was the nation's best customer in the Pacific, and third, sanctions might lead to war. Grew and Dooman had the advantage of being 'on the spot.' They could perceive in great detail the cultural textures, the effects of propaganda, and the mood of the people. However, Grew had a growing frustration that the embassy was not being heard and that their views were being overlooked and ignored in Washington.

In 1941, Dooman championed the idea of Konoe and Roosevelt meeting personally in the Pacific. In backing this idea, Grew argued that the meeting would be less dangerous to American security than were economic sanctions.

Konoe's career journey took him in pursuit of national self-sufficiency and the strength to stand up to the West. He was of a fascist frame of mind when his earlier cabinets were involved in the creation of a totalitarian state and the single party Imperial Rule Assistance Association in September 1940. He had inherited from his father the role of Patron of the Black Dragon Society, but he had also worked in the entourage at Versailles in 1919. In short, there were elements of liberal statesman as well as of dictator within him, but his purpose was to do whatever was necessary for the survival of his nation.

He grew up wanting Japan to flex its muscles against an unjust status quo, and now he was dealing with the

---

[270] Grew to Hull 7 January 1939, cited in Ibid.

consequences of his nation's flirtation with a movement of violent revisionism that was tearing Europe apart. But he was doing so with one hand tied behind his back.

At the September 6th Imperial Throne conference, the army and navy consented to Konoe arranging a summit, but in allowing this they set a strict time frame in which a rapprochement would have to be achieved. Failure of the civilians to deliver at the end of a month would see a military solution to relieve the economic squeeze that was choking the nation.

That same evening, Konoe met Grew and Dooman at a dinner party arranged to be far away from the prying eyes of officialdom and the secret police. At the end of the evening, Konoe discussed the idea of a Presidential meeting with the two Americans. Dooman must have greatly impressed Konoe, for he took Dooman's hand, clasped it, and shook it. "The gesture was highly significant to the counselor who, after a life-time of familiarity with Japanese customs, understood the symbolism attached to a Japanese handshake; it was more than a token of cordiality—it was a pledge of honor."[271]

Konoe also spoke privately with Dooman who recalled later that Konoe said:

> "Now I'm going to tell you something that I don't want you to report to Mr. Grew or in any way disclose. This is purely for your information so that you can advise the Ambassador with more intelligence as to what my thinking is. The fact is that as soon as I reach an agreement with the President I will report immediately to the Emperor and it will be the emperor who will command the army to suspend hostilities."[272]

---

[271] Dooman interview, cited in Ibid

[272] Ibid

Although diplomatic notes were exchanged, the meeting never took place.

Konoe was caught between the American expectation of a preliminary agreement and the Japanese military deadline. It was long held that the Americans were unaware of the time constraint under which Konoe was operating, so the pressure of the situation might have been perceived very differently in America. We now know that to be unlikely. The broken codes that allowed US access to Japanese diplomatic messages allowed the Americans to have a comprehensive understanding of the limited time available. We have to assume that the proposed meeting did not serve the American purposes.

Dooman blamed Hornbeck for the failure of the meeting to take place, but he was unaware of the confusion and miscommunication that was taking place in Washington over exactly what was being negotiated. For their part, Hamilton and Ballantine also had reservations about Konoe's sincerity.

The Embassy in Tokyo was very frustrated by their inability to convince Washington that, after a four-year bloodbath in China, Japan's leaders could not bring their soldiers home in apparent failure. Konoe needed to be able to present the returning soldiers in such a way as to suggest that the Emperor's purpose on the mainland had been accomplished and the Emperor was voluntarily withdrawing them from the area.

Expressed another way, the militarists could not see their forces returned through economic humiliation without the need for a face-saving strike on America. A more creative approach to American foreign policy over the war in China might have saved a great deal of further suffering.

Amateur Diplomacy

Kichisaburo Nomura had a distinguished career as an Admiral, Foreign Minister and, amongst other things, a naval attaché to the United States for two years from 1916. His work during the

1922 Washington Naval Conference allowed him to become acquainted with many officials in America, including Franklin Delano Roosevelt.

The appointment of an Admiral as Ambassador to the United States in preference to a career diplomat was unusual, as was the situation into which he was posted. He was reluctant to take the position but was encouraged by naval colleagues, in the apparent hope that his connections and his personal qualities might make an improved dialogue between the two countries possible.

His background gave him an authority that reflected the seriousness of his task, but it was a limitation in dealing with the complex negotiations that would have tested the capacities of a senior diplomat to the utmost degree.

The Hull-Nomura conversations that began in March 1941 came about as a result of the intercession of two missionaries who represented several prominent Japanese in seeking a peace agreement. They were both Catholic priests, Father James Drought and Bishop James E. Walsh. They were assisted and encouraged by Ikawa Tadao, a Japanese banker, and Col. Hideo Iwakuro, an army officer.

Before leaving for America, Nomura had traveled in Asia seeking opinions from army staff in Korea and Manchuria and, more generally, in coming to terms with the feelings of the key generals and other officers. When in Tokyo, he also conferred with the Chief of the Army General Staff and the Vice War Minister.

We have seen that the armed forces were not a unified body in the sense that Western armies might be understood. Regional, that is provincial competitiveness, historical rivalries, and factional differences served to make their representation as a single entity almost impossible. Similarly, it is important to remember that they were separate armies with unique experiences from different theaters of operation, uniquely endowed with the pride of their own individual achievements.

So it was not a newly forged 'national' army that Nomura was required both to represent and to control by negotiation. His thoroughness in preparation for this work in America is therefore particularly important and a measure of the seriousness which he brought to the task.

Nomura had requested that an army officer accompany him in his duties, reflecting his belief that the issue of China was a major stumbling block to peace. Colonel Iwakuro was described by Hull as a man that "had all the virtues and shortcomings of a Japanese army officer. He was a very fine type, honest, calmly poised, very sure of himself without being annoyingly self-confident. He could, of course, see only his army's viewpoint, not ours or the real interest of Japan."[273]

Father Drought was considered to be over enthusiastic and is recorded as having been energetic in re-writing speeches and memoranda that he hoped the Japanese Foreign Minister would use. It is even claimed that he 'corrected' translations of dispatches that Ambassador Nomura received from Tokyo to create a positive impression of Tokyo's position.

The private meetings he organized were designed to side step the hard-line State Department officials who were cynical in their outlook on the negotiations. Hornbeck referred to them as 'John Doe negotiators.' Drought was the prime motivator in the push for a summit between Konoe and Roosevelt.

The difficulties of negotiation referred to previously, which occurred in the Spring and Summer of 1941, arose from a draft proposal for peace that Hull thought was being submitted to him by the Japanese but that Tokyo thought was a proposal from Hull.

---

[273] Hull Memoirs, II, 1003, cited in Butow, R. J. C. "The Hull-Nomura Conversations A Fundamental Misconception," in Offner, A. A. (ed) *America and the Origins of World War II, 1933–1941: New Perspectives in History*. Boston: Houghton Mifflin, 1971, P130.

Far from being an official document, the draft had been written by father Drought and his three helpers in the hope that it represented a workable compromise. It is unlikely that they believed it would be acceptable to Matsuoka, the Japanese Foreign Minister, but they hoped that if the State Department accepted it, Matsuoka would have to accept it or lose face and resign.

They wanted to have something on the table to get past Hull's preconditions, in the belief that goodwill between Roosevelt and Konoe would enable the sorting out of the details.

For his part, Hull was very cautious. He would receive the draft but not accept it. He pointed out to Nomura that he was quite at liberty to submit the draft to Tokyo for their consideration, but not with any implication that there was any American commitment to it. Nomura cabled the draft proposal to Tokyo, recommending its full acceptance and implying that Hull had no objections.[274] Konoe was led to believe there was progress.

As often happens when the truth is twisted, the effects of this cable deepened the problem rather than solving it. Matsuoka reacted negatively and with some force, which was directed at Ambassador Grew. Presenting a more conciliatory tone, Nomura only deepened further Hull's suspicions about the duplicity and deviousness of the Japanese officials.

This was part of a crucial miscommunication. Backed by Hornbeck's negativity and Grew's optimism towards Japanese intentions, Hull was unaware that the same sort of polarity was happening in Tokyo. Konoe and Nomura were working towards an agreed objective of improving the relationship by whatever achievable means.

---

[274] Conroy, H. "The Strange Diplomacy of Admiral Nomura," in *Proceedings of the American Philosophical Society* 114, No 3, June 1970, Pp210–211.

Matsuoka was Konoe's Hornbeck.

The important difference was that Konoe acted to rid himself of Matsuoka's negativity by threatening to resign. A much more moderate Admiral Toyoda Teijiro replaced Matsuoka as Foreign Minister. Toyoda was in accord with Nomura in his desire for Japan to turn her back on the Axis alliance and in his desire for a rapprochement with the United States.[275]

This surely should have been read as a very strong signal of Japanese intent. In the context of the strategy discussions taking place in Japan at the time, Konoe's move to replace Matsuoka is sometimes portrayed as the only significant olive-branch offered by Japan at this time, and while the significance of it seems to have been largely overlooked in Washington, there is no reason to underestimate it in our retrospective view.

The men in the State Department remained rigid in their conviction that there was nothing trustworthy in the ambassadorial overtures that could tempt them to make a gesture. Nomura's association with the amateur negotiators was a well-intentioned but misguided attempt to create a productive conversation.

Hull's refusal to acknowledge the incremental shifts in the Japanese position away from the Axis appears to be a failure of intelligence, of advice, and of cultural sensitivity. There was no precedent that could lead them to believe that a cornered and hungry Japan would give up, back down, or lose face, and yet American policy demanded all three. We will see however that the issue of the Tripartite Pact became a significant sticking point and that good will on the part of the Japanese could not overcome the reality of their continued adherence to it.

According to John Emmerson, working in the Tokyo Embassy, when Secretary Hull asked Grew in May 1941 whether

---

[275] Ibid P211

the Japanese would observe an agreement if one could be reached with the United States:

"Grew recorded in his diary that his reply was 'perhaps the most important telegram' he had sent from Tokyo, drafted 'early in the morning after a night of most careful and prayerful thought.'"

His answer was in the affirmative, that a bilateral undertaking, sanctioned by the Army and Navy and approved by the Cabinet, the Privy Council, and the Emperor, would be carried out in good faith.[276]

---

[276] Emmerson, J. K. "Principles versus Realities: US Prewar Foreign Policy toward Japan," in Conroy, H., Wray, H. (eds) *Pearl Harbor re-examined: Prologue to the Pacific War.* Honolulu: Univ. of Hawaii Press, 1990, P40.

21

RECONSIDERING THE
NON-NEGOTIABLE, NOVEMBER 1941

T HE FINAL ATTEMPTS to reconcile the immutable with the intransigent began with a new Japanese cabinet on October the 17th. The task of Premier was handed to a man of the type you would wish to have on your side in an ugly situation in combat, a bull of a man who would never take a backward step in fear. The choice might have seemed an inevitable one to the Emperor, but the appointment would not have reassured those in the West who wished for peace.

Many observers in America must have had their view confirmed that control of Japan had passed into the hands of the militarists. In contrast, the Japanese Inner Court Circle felt a palpable relief in the achievement of extra time for negotiation because the September the 6th decisions that led to the October deadline could be put aside and re-examined. The psychology of the situation is quite interesting. It seems quite counter-intuitive that a career soldier possessed of strong loyalties to his own power-base could be the chosen instrument to re-evaluate the response to an international crisis. The scope of Konoe's negotiations had been undermined significantly by Tojo's insistence on the continued occupation of areas of China, which persisted to maintain the army's special place in the power structure in Japan.

The Emperor demanded something different, and Tojo found himself responsible for the interests of the nation rather than just for the army. This needed to involve a resolution of inter-service rivalry and the finding of a responsible path beyond the September 6th decisions, while working within the confines of the constitution. The task expanded the man. Whether we now regard his task as an achievable one depends on our view of the American purpose at this time.

Akira Iriye and several other historians emphasize the US desire to play for time and build capacity for war by keeping negotiations alive at this point. But we have seen that Roosevelt was surrounded by hard-liners who were bent on a confrontation before Japan seized alternative resources. Some American observers go as far as describing a 'war party' surrounding Roosevelt at the expense of the 'doves' who counseled for peace.[277] Roosevelt knew from intercepted diplomatic messages that all he had to do was negotiate without giving ground to make Japan attack first. He knew the Japanese were working within a time limit.

For his part, Tojo made some early decisions that read historically as being inclusive and far from militant. It was expected that he would recall Matsuoka as Foreign Minister, but instead he appointed a veteran who had been purged by Matsuoka in his radical reforms of the diplomatic service. It will be recalled that Togo Shigenori served in Berlin and Moscow as Ambassador, and his resurrection by Tojo represented a significant rebuff for the most radical elements within the army.

[277] Morgenstern, G. *Pearl Harbor: The Story of the Secret War.* New York: Devin-Adair, 1947, P102.

Another significant move was Tojo's keeping for himself the two roles of War Minister and Home Affairs Minister. The former role was kept to ensure the army's acceptance of any new ventures in foreign policy and the latter to prepare for any domestic emergency arising out of a future settlement with the United States. Iriye wrote that "such a settlement would, [Tojo] confided to his secretary, be likely to create a crisis like that of February 1936 which resulted in assassinations and an attempted army take-over of the government. To prepare for such an emergency, Tojo sought dictatorial powers by appointing himself concurrently war minister and home affairs minister."[278]

This concentration of power in one person appeared from the Western perspective to be an indicator of the aggressive position being adopted by Japan, but we can see that it might have been a decision born of fear for internal security. Japanese leaders had to contend with an internal enemy whose militancy grew in direct proportion to attempted accommodation of Western expectations. In the modern era, Western domination has created similar situations in several post-war struggles.

The chiefs of staff of the two services remained adamant that if war was inevitable it should happen as soon as possible. Their planning for a possible war with Britain, the United States, and the Netherlands proceeded to the point that they had outlined the multiple attacks by early November, pretty much as they would actually happen in December.

By the end of October, Tojo was clear in his mind that his nation had three choices, and he outlined them to his colleagues at a liaison conference on the 30th of October. They would have to choose one of these: 'perseverance and patience' without war; an immediate decision for war; or negotiation

---

[278] *Tojo naikaku kumitsu kiroku* (Secret records of the Tojo cabinet) Japanese Broadcasting Corporation (unpublished 1989) 1:39, 48–9, cited in Iriye P170.

during preparations for war.279 Discussion of these options was intense throughout meetings of marathon length, between November 1st–2nd.

Foreign Minister Togo clearly favored the first option of perseverance and patience. He pointed out the folly of going to war against the combined strength of the British, Americans, Dutch, and Chinese, a war that Japan could not possibly win. He believed that it was unlikely that Germany could defeat Britain, and Japan should therefore wait, observing the events in Europe. Admiral Nagano representing the navy argued that this kind of inaction would enable America to increase support to China and also the Soviet Union, while Japanese stocks of petroleum continued to become exhausted. The longer Japan waited, the more vulnerable it became on every front. While he agreed that the Japanese were unlikely to win a long war, fast early successes could gain sufficient resources to survive. General Sugiyama concurred, adding that the southern advance would also increase pressure on foreign intervention in China, increasing the possibility of Japanese success there. Tojo preferred the third alternative of building strength while negotiating, because, he noted, the emperor was opposed to the second alternative of immediate war.

The conclusions drawn from the liaison meeting favored the second alternative, which would satisfy the emperor that further attempts at negotiation would be carried out, but only until a new deadline that would be set. Initially, this was to have been the 13th of November, but after considerable pressure from Tojo it was extended to the 30th of November.

The armed forces could not reconcile themselves to the first alternative, because to do so was to submit to foreign domination (the embargo and perceived encirclement) without

279 The events of this meeting are discussed more fully by Iriye P173, sourced from Defense Agency, War History Division (ed) *Daihonei rikugunbu* (The Army Supreme Command; Tokyo 1968), 2:526–7.

a fight, and this would not be honorable. People from Western cultures should not underestimate the potency of the concept of honor in the Japanese military tradition. It was also agreed that the country could not exist in a state of uncertainty much longer.[280]

The question now remained as to what terms could be agreed upon in negotiations with the United States. After a great deal of debate, Tojo was able to shepherd into existence two related plans that could represent an initial negotiated position and, if necessary to avoid war, a second fallback position representing the limits of Japanese accommodation. This second plan proved to be impotent as it put aside the China issue temporarily in ways that would never be acceptable to Roosevelt.

Plan A resolved to withdraw most Japanese troops to certain specified places within two years of the establishment of an agreement with the United States. Withdrawal of troops from Indochina would occur after a peace had been achieved in China. With regard to trade, a non-discriminatory policy by Japan in China would be adopted if the same policy were adopted throughout the world. This was in response to one of Hull's "four principles" which, in the Japanese view, singled out Japanese dominance in China while overlooking similar American and British domination elsewhere.

With regard to the Axis Alliance, the Japanese position was that America would not be subject to Japan's participation in it unless America attacked Germany. This was explained in an intercepted secret message to the Japanese in Washington in the following terms on the 4th of November:

> "At the same time that you clarify to them that we intend no expansion of our sphere of self-defense, make clear

---

[280] Iriye, A. *The Origins of the Second World War in Asia and the Pacific*. London: Longman, 1987, P174.

as has been repeatedly explained in the past, that we desire to avoid the expansion of Europe's war into the Pacific."[281]

Later the same day, a further message indicates a measure of progress on the issue, adding further reassurance for the Americans.

"As for the question of the Three-Power Pact, your various messages lead me to believe that the United States is, in general, satisfied with our proposals, so if we make our position even more clear by saying that we will not randomly enlarge upon our interpretation of the right of self-defense, I feel sure that we will soon be mutually agreed on this point."[282]

It was recognized that the issue of the occupation of China would be a continued stumbling block to peace, but the intercepted messages reveal disbelief on the part of the Japanese that the Americans could fail to understand the difficulty of turning away from their sacrifices in China:

"Proposal A accepts completely America's demands on two of the three proposals mentioned in the other proposal, but when it comes to the last point concerning the stationing and evacuation of forces, we have already made our last possible concession. How hard, indeed have we fought in China for four years! What tremendous sacrifices we have made! They must know this, so their demands in this connection must have been only 'wishful thinking.' In any case, our internal situation also makes it impossible for us to make any further compromise in

---

[281] Intercepted Diplomatic Messages sent by the Japanese Government. US Army translation, 4/11/41. Referred to from here as Purple Intercepts. These are available at http://www.ibiblio.org/pha/timeline/411104b.html.

[282] Ibid

this connection. As best you may, please endeavor to have the United States understand this, and I earnestly hope and pray that you can quickly bring about an understanding."[283]

They certainly did know all of this, and breaking the Japanese diplomatic codes allowed American eyes to read first hand the very human messages passing between the capitals. No one can read these instructions to the Japanese Ambassador in Washington without feeling a very real sense of urgency and sincerity, even if it was to be couched in careful diplomatic vagueness. It is from these documents that the Americans would have accumulated an understanding of the limited time available to the negotiators and the pressure they were under:

"(of utmost secrecy)

"Because of various circumstances, it is absolutely necessary that all arrangements for the signing of this agreement be completed by the 25th of this month. I realize that this is a difficult order, but under the circumstances it is an unavoidable one. Please understand this thoroughly and tackle the problem of saving the Japanese-US relations from falling into a chaotic condition. Do so with great determination and with unstinted effort, I beg of you.

"This information is to be kept strictly to yourself only."[284]

The responses from Washington to Tokyo were sometimes less than encouraging. While the Japanese position was re-expressed and refined to fit Hull's perceived expectations, the response was often absolutely neutral:

"With regard to the matter of non-discrimination in trade, Hull showed indications of being satisfied. He did not indicate

[283] Purple Intercept Secret: Tokyo to Washington4/11/41.

[284] Ibid, 5/11/41

either approval or disapproval of the matters pertaining to the rights of self-defense and of withdrawal of our troops." [285]

By November the 10th, the sense of urgency had intensified in the communications from Nomura to Togo. In many histories, this dangerous period is referred to with passing reference to American indecision, or perhaps intransigence, but the details flow easily through a mechanical procession of discussions or policy decisions, without giving any sense of how it felt to be doing everything possible to prevent war while being met with indifference. The following intercepted message is very long but it is included almost in its entirety because it is the voice of Japanese frustration. This is a voice seldom quoted.

> "(Extremely Urgent)
> "My interview with the [American] President was held in a private room in the White House in order to avoid publicity. It is as follows:

"I said I have had no talks with the Secretary of State for about three weeks: ever since the resignation of the Konoe cabinet; and since the present situation between Japan and the United States is such that it could not be left as it is, I am very pleased to have this opportunity of speaking with you. The conversations on this question have lasted for more than six months. From their inception Japan has been wishing to arrive at a quick settlement. The people of Japan also looked forward to conversations with much hope; however, the conversations have dragged on and in the meantime the relations between the two countries have grown worse. It has become increasingly difficult for the people of my country to be patient. Now, the Government of Japan in the meantime has made many concessions, but the Government of the United States has held to its arguments and has shown no willingness to respond to

---

[285] Purple Intercept, Ibid, 7/11/41

our compromises. As a result some people in Japan have begun to doubt if the United States is really sincere in this matter. The Japanese people regard the freezing of funds as a kind of economic blockade, and there seem to be some who say that modern warfare is not limited to shooting alone. No country can exist without the supply of materials indispensable to its industry. From what reports I have received from Japan, the situation seems to be serious and threatening, and therefore the only way to keep peace is for Japan and the United States to come, without further delay, to some kind of a friendly and satisfactory agreement. It is for no other purpose than that of keeping peace in the Pacific that the Japanese Government is endeavoring so hard to arrive at a satisfactory agreement by continuing our conversations."[286]

> By their nature, these intercepts give only one side of the story, and it is considered necessary to include some, nonetheless, to redress the imbalance of information readily available since the war. The fact that Nomura mentioned his lack of opportunity to meet with Hull for three weeks in a short meeting with Roosevelt indicates the frustration he felt at the lack of progress, given that he had less than that much time in front of him to secure an agreement.

The urgency in the negotiations served to emphasize the encirclement of the Japanese, particularly when Secretary Hull insisted on further negotiation being inclusive of consultation with British, Dutch, and Australian representatives. The Americans wished to detach the Japanese from the alliance with Germany, while the Japanese were trying to weaken the growing alliance against them in the Pacific. The Japanese position was that the Axis would only become a problem if

---

[286] Purple Intercept, Ibid, 10/11/41

America attacked Germany, while the Americans could not accept a rapprochement with Japan while it was allied to the aggressor in Europe. The Japanese wished to keep the European crisis from spreading into the Pacific, while for Roosevelt this would provide automatic legitimacy to its de facto participation in support of Britain.

The awful truth was that war suited the American purpose, and for people in France, Holland, Poland, and Britain, for Jews and countless other victims of the Nazis, this was not only desirable it was desperately, frantically necessary. Japan needed to recognize that, just as America needed to recognize that Japan would implode if it were forced out of China. Both failed.

The Last Days of Peace in the Pacific

Hull had been working on what he called a 'draft *modus vivendi*,' a temporary proposal containing "mutual pledges of peaceful intent, a reciprocal undertaking not to make armed advancement in northeastern Asia and the northern Pacific area, southeast Asia and the southern Pacific area, and an undertaking by Japan to withdraw its forces from southern Indochina…"[287] The American Government would undertake a modification of the freezing of Japanese assets, fuel, and funds. This, expressed in a detailed and thorough draft, was communicated to Grew in Japan along with the decision that, after consultation with British, Dutch, Australian, and Chinese Governments, the draft would *not* be presented to the Japanese.

The American decision not to present the draft agreement to the Japanese Ambassador signaled a change in the nature of the proceedings. Grew had been informed by Hull about this on the 28th of November. This meant that Hull's re-statement

---

[287] Hull to Grew Nov 28 1941, Foreign Relations, 1941, Far East, Pp 683-684,

and elaboration of the Four Principles ('The Hull note'), which was delivered to Nomura on the 26th, was the final statement of the US position. While it was not a new position, it was taken by Japan to be an ultimatum, and it caused a very negative reaction after months of meetings and discussion. The negotiation process from this point was about language and posture but no longer about hope.

Grew continued to have Japanese representations made to him from all levels of Japanese society and was obviously frustrated by the signal implied in Hull's decision. He wrote to Hull saying in part:

"In all recent talks I have emphasized my personal view that the American draft conveys a broad-gauge objective proposal of the highest statesmanship, offering to Japan in effect the very desiderata for which she has been ostensibly fighting and a reasonable and peaceful way of achieving her constantly publicized needs. The Japanese Government is now in a position to mold public opinion to the justified conception that Japan can now achieve without force of arms the chief purposes for which she has hitherto allegedly been fighting."[288]

After noting his astonishment at the bellicose nature of a speech by Tojo at this critical juncture, he wrote that he realized "the difficulty of adjusting the respective positions of the two countries, [he was] nevertheless determined to continue the Washington conversations."

Having received the Hull note on the 27th, the leadership team in Japan immediately began the most fateful liaison conference of their careers. It was obvious to them that all attempts at negotiation had failed. They were bound by the

[288] Grew to Hull Dec 1 1941, Ibid p707

decisions made on November the 5th to make immediate preparation for war. On the 29th the inner cabinet, together with former prime ministers, met with the Emperor to brief him on the recent turn of events. He expressed his doubts about the wisdom of their decision, making particular enquiries as to the preparedness of the navy to execute a long war. The decision for war was made formally on December the 1st.

22

CONCLUSION: RESPONDING TO THE WHISTLE

OTH JAPAN AND America were possessed of a profound sense of destiny in the early 20th Century. Both cultures had reinvented themselves in an idealistic revolution, which fed and was fed by an intellectual journey that reflected a belief in their role as being unique, incomparable, and exceptional. In both cases, the national story became enmeshed in and confused with perceptions of their national *task*. Leaders of both nations have subsequently been surprised to find people of other nations resisting this singular vision in the playing out of their own stories.

Modern globalization has its roots in the Washington international system. An unfortunate worldview developed, combining paternalistic idealism with the pressing imperative and implied morality of economic growth. It was found that significant power could be achieved without recourse to conquest or empire and that markets could be manipulated with minimal interference from government if free market economics could be represented as an alternative to war. This worked well for those who were already wealthy, but world economic failure focused the impatience, which was festering within late developing industrial societies.

Internationalism as a framework had failed to provide Germany with just terms of peace in 1918, entrenching poverty, seething resentment, and state failure. This perpetuated a colossal imbalance of power in Europe. Together with the growing imbalance of wealth and the ravages of the Depression, it enabled revisionists in Germany to find enough support to challenge the system in the old-fashioned way, taking millions of innocent lives in the process. The Japanese fell under some of the same influences for some of the same reasons. The violent revisionists taught us in the brutality of their actions that change must be incremental, with goodness and decency as reference points. Extreme actions begin a perpetuating cycle of violent reactions.

The most profoundly heroic figures of the pre-war period are the failures, the people on both sides who persisted in their belief in peaceful co-existence and a creative public life, devoting their energies towards reconciling the angry with the greedy, the immutable with the intransigent, and the impatient with the indifferent. They did so, despite persistent evidence that self-interest is the default setting in the human mind. In this respect, their heroism overcame humanity, despite their failure.

Since World War I, many of us have wondered how the tens of thousands of troops who were ordered 'over the top' during trench warfare found it within themselves to propel their bodies forward when the whistle blew. They did so, knowing that they were unlikely to survive the sweeping fire or the barrage that would transform the ground under them. This response in the face of death can be found in soldiers from both sides, regardless of the merits or morality of their cause.

The same questions can be asked with regard to the Japanese decision to attack the outposts of several of the world's most powerful nations. When the plan to attack American, British, and Dutch outposts was about to be carried out, there was little doubt about the outcome. The line up against them would eventually number troops from China, Great Britain, The Soviet Union, the United States, Holland, and several dominions including Australia. Even the designer of the Japanese naval strategy believed it would fail and that he would probably die on his ship. They knew that they were unleashing an infamous wave of suffering. The Japanese knew that their compliant population would suffer willingly and extensively, and they knew that many thousands of enemy lives would also be taken.

In both examples, the engagement began well before the event: in the accumulation of small decisions that estimated the possibility of an engagement to be worth the risk of failure. When first considered, however, the possible failure was ambiguous and remote. For a soldier, joining the armed forces may have been motivated by having his first dependable income, or adventurism with a swagger of unproven manhood, or simply selfless national duty, but in any case, survival is always the most likely outcome in the optimistic perception of young men. Not so for the leaders of a nation. The risks for them are graver but less personal.

Standing on the brink of losing everything is a long way from the start of the journey, and the alternatives have converged over time into fewer and fewer possibilities. Each small step makes the subsequent one more inevitable, until the choices become reduced to two. The disciplined soldier, despite the odds, or the waste, or the futility, simply steps forward. The alternative would completely undermine the value and meaning of the journey.

Japan's journey to war began with the flexing of Western muscle in Asia. Arrival at the brink involved many examples of unfortunate circumstance, poor leadership, and bad judgment on both sides. By increasing the cost of peace, the Americans made war more palatable. Theirs was the superior position in the negotiations, and they bear significant responsibility for the way in which the talks played out. Japan was fundamentally wrong to go further. From the point of view of the Japanese leadership, however, the alternative would have seemed as it must have for the soldier as he leaned against the parapet waiting for the whistle. Going back would undermine the value and the meaning of the journey.

Despite the fact that security and economic power were always the goals, it was for want of meaning and value that the Japanese were ultimately unwilling to turn away from initiating the Pacific War. It should have been possible for them to find both of these things at the Paris Peace Conference in 1919.

AUTHOR'S NOTE

L IKE MANY AUSTRALIANS, I have inherited a certain pride in the Australian military traditions, particularly the slightly romantic notion of the free spirited volunteer who can face his mortality squarely in the belief that his mates will support him. We like to see ourselves as a nation that can dig deep for a good cause, but without being too serious about power, expansion, or conquest. We've even grown to believe that we are fair and decent, and by and large we are, but there are things we still have to face about our history before we can hold this belief in confidence and comfort.

I understand that for some people the conclusions drawn in this book will be challenging and uncomfortable. Some survivors of the Pacific War are still only able to live with the things they had to do by remembering, but scarcely mentioning, the brutality they faced in carrying out their task, or in simply surviving. Some of these fine men may think I have attempted to whitewash Japanese military brutality by skewing the story so much toward the Japanese perspective. I can assure such a reader that I have simply sought to put aside my own prejudices to understand better how it was that the war should come to pass as it did.

If I had been born in my parents' generation and had been brought up as they were, I would certainly have taken the same path as my father and my uncles by enlisting to defend the interests of the Empire. They were people of their time, as I am of mine. If I had joined up with my mother's two brothers, I would probably have died with them in the Japanese invasion of Rabaul. Most of their Battalion did. In the previous World War, I would have been proud to stand next to my father's brothers, one of whom was wounded at Gallipoli and the other in France. They didn't know, and I wouldn't have known then, the things we know now.

It is easy for me to make these claims, though, because I wasn't there, and I didn't have to face those tests. On the other hand, I can be more objective about the causes of these things for the very same reason.

SELECTED BIBLIOGRAPHY

Bailey, T. A. *The Man in the Street: The Impact of American Public Opinion on Foreign Policy.* New York: Macmillan, 1948.

Barnes, H. E. (ed) *Perpetual War For Perpetual Peace.* Caldwell, Idaho: Caxton Printers Ltd, 1953.

Beard, Charles A. *American Foreign Policy in the Making, 1932–1940.* New Haven: Yale University Press, 1946.

Beard, Charles A. *The Idea of the National Interest.* New York: Macmillan, 1934.

Beasley, W. G. *Japanese Imperialism, 1894–1945.* Oxford: Clarendon Press, 1987.

Berry, Prof. Mary Elizabeth. "Public Life in Authoritarian Japan," *Daedalus* Vol. 127. Issue 3 American Academy of Arts & Sciences, 1998.

Bix, H. P. "Re-Thinking Emperor-System Fascism: Ruptures and Continuities in Modern Japanese History" Bulletin of Concerned Asian Scholars Vol14:2 1982.

Bogart, Ernest Ludlow. *War Costs and Their Financing.* New York: Appleton & Co., 1921.

Borg, D. *American Policy and the Chinese Revolution, 1925–1928.* New York: American Institute of Public Relations, 1947.

Breslin, Thomas. A. "Mystifying the Past: Establishment Historians and the Origins of the Pacific War." Bulletin of Concerned Asian Scholars, Vol 8: 4, 1976 P18.

Breslin, Thomas A. Trouble Over Oil: America, Japan and the Oil Cartel 1934–1935." Bulletin of Concerned Asian Scholars. Vol 7 Issue 3 1975 P42.

Cohen, Carl. *Communism, Fascism and Democracy: The Theoretical Foundation.* New York: Random House, 1972.

Colegrove, K. W. *Militarism in Japan.* World Peace Foundation, 1936.

Conroy, H., Wray, H. (eds) *Pearl Harbor re-examined: Prologue to the Pacific War.* Honolulu: Univ. of Hawaii Press, 1990.

Ditterich Robert. *Two Lives; No Known Grave.* Rabaul 1942, Place of Mind, Geelong 2006.

Dower, John. *Is The U.S. Repeating the Mistakes of Japan in the 1930s?* first published in www.tomdispatch Nation Institute, 2003.

Duus, P. and Okimoto. D. I. "Fascism and the History of Pre-War Japan: The Failure of a Concept" in *JAS* 39:1 Nov 1979.

Feis, H. *The Road to Pearl Harbor.* Princeton, 1950.

Fullilove, Michael. *Men and Women of Australia! Our greatest modern speeches,* Random House Aust. 2005.

Harrison, Courtney T. *Ambon Island of Mist 2/21 Battalion AIF (Gull Force).* Harrison Geelong, *1988.*

Hewitt, Anthony. *Children of the Empire.* Kenthurst, NSW: Kangaroo Press, 1993.

Horne, Gerald. *Race War! White Supremacy and the Attack on the British Empire,* New York University, 2004.

Huffman, James L. *Creating a Public: People and Press in Meiji Japan*. Honolulu: University of Hawaii Press, 1997.

Iriye, Akira *The Origins of the Second World War in Asia and the Pacific*. UK: Longman, 1987.

Japan Press, Media, TV, Radio, Newspapers website wwwpressreference.com.

Kasza, Gregory. *The State and the Mass Media in Japan 1918–1945*. University of California Press, 1993.

Khan, Yoshimitsu. "Inoue Kowashi and the Dual Images of the Emperor of Japan." *Pacific Affairs,* Vol 71, issue 2, University of British Columbia. Gale Group, 1998.

Langer, W. L., and Gleason, S. *The Undeclared War 1940–41*. New York: Harper and Bros, 1953.

Lawrence, Carmen. *Fear and Politics*. Melbourne: Scribe, 2006.

Libby, J. H. "Rendezvous with Disaster: There Never Was a Chance for Peace in American-Japanese Relations, 1941," in *World Affairs*, Vol 158, Issue 3, 1996.

Lu, David J. *From Marco Polo Bridge to Pearl Harbor: Japan's Entry into World War II*. Washington: Public Affairs Press, 1961.

Maki, J. M. *Japanese Militarism: Its cause and Cure*. New York: Alfred Knopf, 1945.

Mamoru, Shigemitsu and White, O. (ed) *Japan and Her Destiny: My Struggle for Peace*. New York: Dutton, 1958.

Mayo, Marlene J. (ed.) *The Emergence of Imperial Japan*. Lexington: Heath, 1970.

McCormack, G. "Nineteen-thirties Japan: Fascism?" Bulletin of Concerned Asian Scholars, Vol 14; 2, 1982.

Mitchell, Richard H. *Political Bribery in Japan*. Honolulu: University of Hawaii Press, 1996.

Montuori, A. "How to Make Enemies and Influence People: Anatomy of the Anti-Pluralist, Totalitarian Mindset." *Futures*, Vol37: 1, 2005.

Moore, B. Jr. *Social Origins of Dictatorship and Democracy: Lord and Peasant in the Making of the Modern World.* Boston: Beacon, 1967.

Morgenstern, G. *Pearl Harbor: The Story of the Secret War.* New York: Devin-Adair, 1947.

Morton, Louis. *The Fall of The Philippines.* Washington: OCMH, 1953.

Myers, Ramon H. and Peattie, Mark M. (ed) *The Japanese Colonial Empire, 1895–1945.* Princeton, NJ: Princeton University Press, 1984.

Offner, A. A. (ed) *America and the Origins of World War II, 1933–1941: New Perspectives in History.* Boston: Houghton Mifflin, 1971.

Peattie, Mark R. *Nanyo: The Rise and Fall of the Japanese in Micronesia, 1885–1945.* Honolulu: University of Hawaii Press, 1988.

Reischauer, E. O., Firbank, J. K., Craig, A. *East Asia: The Modern Transformation.* Boston: Houghton Mifflin, 1965.

Sampson, E. E. *Dealing with Differences. An Introduction to the Social Psychology of Prejudice.* Fort Worth: Harcourt Brace, 1999.

Scalapino, Robert. A. *Democracy and the Party Movement in Pre-War Japan: The Failure of the First Attempt.* Berkeley: University of California Press, 1953.

Schieder, Wolfgang. *Fascism* in Kernig C D, (ed) *Marxism, Communism and Western Society: A Comparative Encyclopedia.*

Schroeder, P. *The Axis Alliance and Japanese-American Relations.* Ithaca: Cornell University Press, 1958.

Shimazu, Naoko. *Japan, Race and Equality: The Racial Equality Proposal of 1919.* London: Routledge, 1998.

Suganami, Hidemi. *On The Causes of War.* Oxford: Clarenden Press, 1996.

Takahara, Dr. Shusake. "Wilsonian Idealism and its Impact on Japan: The Case of Japan's Racial Equality Proposal." The Asiatic Society of Japan, lecture given 17/3/03.

The Economist. "Japan's Zaibatsu. Yes General." The Economist Newspaper Ltd 23 Dec. 1999.

Treffousse, H. L. (ed) What Happened at Pearl Harbor? Documents pertaining to the Japanese attack of December 7, 1941. New York: Twain, 1958.

Utley, G. Going to War with Japan 1937–1941. Knoxville: University of Tennessee Press, 1985.

Wigmore, Lionel. The Japanese Thrust. Canberra: AWM, 1957.

Willensky, Marcus. "Japanese Fascism Revisited," Stanford Journal of East Asian Affairs, vol 5 Number 1, Winter 2005.

Williams, David. Defending Japan's Pacific War: the Kyoto School Philosophers and Post-White Power. Curzon, NY: Routledge, 2004.

Williams, William A. The Tragedy of American Diplomacy. World Publishing Co., 1959.

Wilson, S. The Manchurian Crisis and Japanese Society, 1931–33. London: Routledge, 2002.

Young, Louise. Japan's Total Empire: Manchuria and the Culture of Wartime Imperialism. Los Angeles: University of California Press, 1998.

INDEX

1

H

I

147, 148, 156, 159, 161,
170, 191, 210, 217, 218,
219, 239, 243, 244, 250,
251, 284, 297, 312, 333,
339, 340, 341, 348, 351,
352, 353, 356, 364, 365,
368, 370, 371, 373, 374,
375, 376, 377, 378, 382,
385

Tosei-ha, 129, 141, 188, 191,
192, 207

totalitarian, 15, 41, 61, 107,
165, 261, 262, 264, 265,
267, 268, 273, 317, 371

Toyo Jiyuto, 40

trade, 2, 4, 16, 17, 21, 40, 85,
92, 93, 131, 132, 133, 141,
143, 146, 156, 157, 162,
163, 167, 170, 175, 176,
177, 179, 194, 201, 219,
221, 224, 225, 226, 247,
253, 263, 303, 305, 306,
307, 308, 309, 311, 329,
330, 331, 338, 370, 383,
385

Treaty Port system, 21, 25, 94,
131, 132

Treaty Ports, 5

Tripartite Pact, 232, 239, 279,
301, 303, 330, 332, 346,
348, 351, 352, 362, 367,
377

Tripartite Pact of Berlin, 301

Triple Intervention, 9, 18, 152

Truc, 20

U

Uesugi Shinkishi, 44

Ugaki, 122, 189, 207, 209–
211, 213–215

Ugaki Kazushige, 122, 209

ultra-nationalism, 38

ultranationalists, 40, 45, 282,
310

UNESCO, 11

universality, 284

US sanctions, 232

US Senate Nye Committee,
297

V

Versailles, 24, 152, 195, 230,
312, 327, 371

Vice Chief of Staff Tada, 205

Victor Wellesley, 25

Vietnam, 242, 296, 311, 331

von Ribbentrop, 214, 217,
233, 302

W

Wakatsuki, 123, 157

Wang Ching-wei, 224

War Minister Itagaki, 216,
218

War Minister Terauchi, 193

Waseda University, 42, 46

Washington, 26, 88, 92, 93,
95, 119, 134, 137, 138, 150,
153, 154, 155, 156, 159,

Made in the USA
Middletown, DE
04 August 2021